Academic E-Books
Publishers, Librarians, and Users

Academic E-Books
Publishers, Librarians, and Users

Edited by Suzanne M. Ward, Robert S. Freeman, and Judith M. Nixon

Charleston Insights in
Library, Archival, and Information Sciences

Purdue University Press
West Lafayette, Indiana

Cataloging-in-Publication data on file at the Library of Congress.

Contents

Foreword

Roger Schonfeld

One of the great scholarly publishing success stories of the past decades has been the systematic transition from print to electronic that major academic publishers and libraries alike have conducted for scholarly journals. We tend to focus on the limitations of this transition, such as bundled pricing models and challenges such as smaller publishers still clinging to print or richly illustrated titles that do not always display well in digital formats. At the same time, the overall transition has been remarkably orderly and responsible, yielding meaningful improvements in discovery and access. Compared with journals, the possibility of a format transition for books presents a different set of opportunities, and far greater complexity, for academic libraries and publishers alike.

In this book, contributors review some of the exciting initiatives that are being mounted in an effort to incorporate e-books into library acquisition, discovery, and access channels. As has been the case for e-journals, we are developing institutional licensing models, allowing for the creation of library "collections" of e-books often spread across a variety of platforms. Although publishers try to retain the revenues associated with heavily used materials, libraries seek to manage expenditures by maintaining sharing models and responding to community demand with greater sophistication. Even if e-books are growing unevenly, libraries and content providers can take much satisfaction in the progress that has been made to introduce this valuable new format for books.

Readers have another perspective.[1] For journals, their perspective initially was shaped largely by ecosystems created by scholarly publishers and libraries; for books, their perspective is shaped as much by Amazon and Google. Amazon's pervasive reading interfaces, robust cross-device syncing, seamless delivery from numerous publishers, and familiar discovery environment set high expectations for book discovery and delivery. Scholars, at least, regularly pay out of pocket to read e-books through the Kindle and similar ecosystems. In academic e-book environments, scholars and students have the fragmented experience of numerous platforms, the unavailability of many titles, discovery limitations, multiple confusing digital rights management (DRM) solutions, and poor device support. Since most academic readers have had at least some experience with both ecosystems, they have the ability to evaluate them comparatively. Even without out-of-pocket costs, the academic e-book ecosystem poses comparative barriers for readers.

Reading is not the only, and indeed perhaps not the most important, use for scholarly books. Search and browse functions, enabled in print books through tables of contents, illustrations, and indices, are vital to humanists who only sometimes read a book cover to cover. Although there is some evidence that scholars and students alike have continued to prefer reading in print, these other functions are eased tremendously by using e-books and online tools (Housewright, Schonfeld, & Wulfson, 2013; see especially the discussion around Figure 14 on pages 31–32). Notably, Google Books offers an outstanding discovery experience, not only in searching for books but perhaps even more importantly in searching for phrases and ideas within books, offering a powerful supplement, if not a substitute, for the traditional index. Google Books may not be widely used as a source for reading, but for many scholars it is an outstanding complementary resource that indicates another important way in which scholars and students use e-books (Rutner & Schonfeld, 2012; see especially pages 17–19 and 44). At this early stage in the development of scholarly e-books, there is every reason to believe that expectations for discovery, reading, and perhaps other uses are being set by one major ecosystem (Kindle) and a small set of other major initiatives (especially Google Books). If this is true, there may be other approaches that libraries and content platforms should consider. For example, they might determine that it makes more sense to find ways to work as a part of this consumer ecosystem, or they might create a more coherent user experience that offers an academic alternative to the consumer ecosystem.

Ultimately, librarians should bear in mind that user experience does not begin and end with a single content platform. Even when the experience is strong on a single content platform, readers experience the often-awkward transitions across platforms and challenges moving books seamlessly into reading-optimized interfaces. Libraries may find it helpful to consider these issues more systematically rather than as a part of a selection and procurement process. Indeed, these processes often show their limits in trying to manage a format transition no less fundamental than that from scroll to codex. Content platforms, too, may find that by interoperating more seamlessly and serving the reading experience more richly, they will attract more readers to digital formats.

The introduction of e-books offers some very exciting opportunities for the academic community. Recognizing the place of academic e-books in relation to a broader consumer e-book ecosystem may suggest opportunities to embrace this new format more fully.

NOTE

1. I use the term "reader" in this piece to indicate individuals whose objective is to read a book, in whatever format. Individuals who have other objectives with books, such as skimming the illustrations, consulting an index, or conducting text mining, are grouped generally as "users." Readers and users alike take many steps, and have many needs, in order to find and use one or more books.

REFERENCES

Housewright, R., Schonfeld, R. C., & Wulfson, K. (2013). *US faculty survey 2012*. New York, NY: Ithaka S+R. Retrieved from http://www.sr.ithaka.org/research-publications/us-faculty-survey-2012

Rutner, J., & Schonfeld, R. C. (2012). *Supporting the changing research practices of historians*. New York, NY: Ithaka S+R. Retrieved from http://www.sr.ithaka.org/research-publications/supporting-changing-research-practices-historians

Introduction to *Academic E-Books*

Suzanne M. Ward, Robert S. Freeman,
and Judith M. Nixon

Academic librarians have planned for, experimented with, and generally been waiting for the e-book revolution as a solution to many library challenges and for the advantages the e-book provides to users. Unlike its print counterpart, an e-book can never be lost, marked-up, or worn out. It does not take up any shelf space, and so saves the overhead on the building. It does not require a staff member (or self-check kiosk) to check it out or to check it back into the library. Student assistants are not needed to reshelve it or to make sure it is on the right shelf and in the right order. Just the savings in the staff time of scanning the bar codes for an inventory and reshelving the misshelved books make e-books very attractive to librarians. Another advantage is that librarians do not even need to buy e-books before users begin to check them out. Instead they can load the records into the online catalog and wait to see which books are borrowed, paying only after there has been demonstrated use. The e-book has great advantages for the users as well. In many cases, an e-book can be checked out by multiple users at the same time and is available wherever and whenever the user needs it. However, perhaps the most valuable advantage is that every single word and phrase in an e-book is searchable. Indexing systems, library online catalogs, and search engines like Google Books now help users find, or discover, the content inside e-books. The reader does not need to know which book has the information needed, instead he can use a search engine and go to the exact page and sentence with a few clicks.

With so many advantages, it seems logical that librarians would be eager to switch from purchasing books in print and embrace the electronic format. However, the transition to e-books in academic libraries has not been a smooth or quick one; the reasons are myriad and complicated. Aware that this is still a time of transition and that there are many issues surrounding the e-book, the editors set out to present the state of e-books in academic libraries today. They invited knowledgeable publishers and librarians to write about the current challenges, successes, and trends. In addition, there is a section that analyzes new data about user interaction with e-books and an essay written by a teaching faculty member who uses e-books and encourages her students to do so as well.

LITERATURE REVIEW

To set the stage, a literature review is in order to identify the challenges facing the e-book revolution. The major problems can be summed up in two statements: (1) lack of sufficient content and (2) users' stated preference for print books in many cases. Although time will eventually solve the problem of lack of content, librarians still face the issue that many users prefer print books. The reasons for this preference are complicated, but the literature suggests that the primary reason is that in-depth reading of an e-book is difficult, partly because of poor interfaces, but primarily because the e-book is not a print book.

Background on E-Books and E-Readers

Some writers trace the origins of the e-book back to the 1940s ("E-book," 2014, p. 10), but the current e-book, as we know it today, defined as a book-length publication in digital form that must be read on some computer device, can be traced to Project Gutenberg, founded in 1971 by Michael S. Hart and now a collection of nearly 50,000 books ("Project Gutenberg," 2014, p. 1). E-books did not become an option for library purchase until 1997 with ebrary and 1999 with NetLibrary. Safari, SpringerLink, and Ebook Library (EBL) appeared between 2001 and 2004. In late 2004, Google began digitizing books from the New York Public Library and several major academic libraries. This project, now known as Google Books, provides bibliographic information on copyrighted books and full views and downloads of books no longer protected by copyright laws. For a detailed discussion of this history, see the articles by Connaway and Wicht (2007) and Zeoli (2013).

During these early years, patrons read e-books on their personal computers, but the invention of e-readers sparked a major change. E-books became easier to read. An early but unsuccessful e-reader came on the market in 1998, the Rocket eBook, but the major turning point dates to the introduction of the Sony Librie and the Sony Reader in 2004–2006. The Sony e-readers were followed quickly in 2007 by Amazon's Kindle and in 2010 by Apple's iPad, a tablet computer that can be used as an e-reader. With the widespread availability of affordable e-readers and tablets, the sale of e-books, especially on the consumer market, took off. It is estimated that half of U.S. adults own an e-reader or a tablet (Zickurh & Rainie, 2014).

Complication #1: Lack of Content

Statistics on size of e-book collections in academic libraries indicate lack of content

Given the advantages of e-books and the high use of them that libraries report, it is not surprising that academic libraries are increasing the percentage of their budget allocated to e-books. (Over 65% of most academic library budgets are spent on journals, with about 25% spent on books.) The *Ithaka S + R Library Survey 2010* asked library directors about their anticipated changes in the book budget allocation: "Respondents predicted a steady shift towards digital materials over the next five years. They reported that 6% of their materials budgets will be shifted from print books to electronic books (bringing book expenditures in five years to 46% digital and 54% print)" (Long & Schonfeld, 2010, p. 28). Other studies show similar increases. The 2012 *Library Journal* survey found that 95% of the academic libraries surveyed carry e-books; this figure has been constant for three years, but the total number of e-books offered increased 41% between 2011 and 2012. In libraries that support graduate programs, this represented an increase from an average of 97,500 to 138,800 e-books per library. Academic spending on e-books increased from 7.5% of the total acquisition budget to 9.6%, and libraries anticipate that this percentage will continue to increase ("2012 Ebook Usage in US Academic Libraries," 2012, pp. 5–6). These statistics indicate that libraries, with a few rare exceptions,[1] are increasing digital monograph percentages and numbers, but the e-book is not replacing the print book completely.

The vast majority of academic libraries continue to buy both print and electronic books. The balance may be approaching half print and half electronic, but libraries have not yet transitioned to primarily electronic for books as they have for journals. Part of the explanation for slow adoption is because many publishers have been hesitant to produce and then sell libraries the majority of their listings as e-books, especially as unlimited use e-books. Many current titles are either not published in electronic format or the publisher delays the e-book format until the printed version achieves market saturation. Some publishers fear loss of revenue if the printed edition is not the exclusive format available at least for the first few critical months (Hodges, Preston, & Hamilton, 2010, p. 198). Another issue is that publishers are sometimes slow to offer their backlists in e-format. Since librarians cannot afford to buy many titles in both formats, they often feel that they must choose between buying the print version upon publication or making their patrons wait, often for months, before the e-book appears. For a detailed discussion of the issues see William H. Walters' (2013) article.

Just as library budget statistics show this print priority, so do market statistics. YBP handles 85% of English language books sold to academic libraries in the United States and Canada, and is in a position to compile statistics on book sales. In September 2013, Michael Zeoli (2013) of YBP reported that only 15% of YBP's book sales are for e-books, with 85% of the sales still of print books (p. 7). Comparing this statistic with the one in the *Library Journal* survey for the same year indicates that although many of the e-books in libraries come from large publisher or vendor packages and are thus not reflected in the YBP statistic, libraries still buy print books. On an encouraging note, YBP also has seen the simultaneous publication of print and electronic books move to 40%, or nearly 10,000 books per week (Zeoli, 2013, p. 9). Even with this change in the e-book market, Zeoli found that only 25% of the 1,400 publishers that YBP represents make over 10% of their content available in digital format (p. 10). Understanding the state of the e-book market compared to print books explains why libraries continue to buy print books, and why librarians often comment that there is not sufficient e-content available.

Users cite lack of content

In many studies users also identify the problem of lack of content. In the *US Faculty Survey 2012*, users placed the highest need on "access to a wider range of materials in digital format" (Housewright, Schonfeld, & Wulfson, 2013, p. 33). In a detailed study at Laurentian University over a nine-year period, Lamothe (2013) found a relationship between the size of the e-book collection and its use. He wrote that "The level of usage appeared to be directly proportional to the size of the collection" (p. 44). In other words, increasing the amount of content directly increases the use of the collection. During a study of the circulation of e-readers at the bookless satellite library for Applied Engineering and Technology at the University of Texas at San Antonio Library, the first problem that users cited was limited selection of content. Textbooks in particular were unavailable: "Of the 25 textbooks titles in use by more than 500 engineering students, none was available on an e-reader platform" (Kemp, Lutz, & Nurnberger, 2012, p. 194). The JISC National E-Book Observatory on the perspective of e-book users on e-books, the largest survey conducted with over 20,000 staff and students participating, asked users the advantages of e-books. Clearly these users found online access the most important advantage. However, very low on their list of advantages was wider choice, thereby identifying lack of content as an issue (Jamali, Nicholas, & Rowlands, 2009, p. 39).

Libraries have many ways to buy e-books,
but sufficient content is still a problem

Part of the problem is that purchasing e-books is complicated and time-consuming. Several e-book acquisition models have been tried and adapted over the past 10 or 15 years, yet the industry is still in a state of transition. Libraries have several options available and new methods become available frequently. One method is to buy directly from a publisher, or libraries can purchase through vendors such as YBP or Coutts. Usually the access to these e-books is limited to the students and staff at the institution, although some libraries have successfully acquired e-books available to members of a consortium.[2]

Whether a library buys from a publisher, aggregator, or vendor, it has options such as selecting title-by-title, setting up approval plans (automatic purchasing of whole subject categories), setting up delayed payment plans (patron-driven [PDA] or demand-driven acquisitions [DDA]), or buying bundles. A bundle, or package, of titles usually contains a substantial portion of the publisher's titles at an extremely advantageous price per title.

Examples of publishers that offer these bundles are Springer, Brill, Elsevier, and Wiley. Similar package options are available from aggregators like JSTOR and Project Muse, both of which offer e-books from many publishers. Other aggregators offer subscription models with thousands of titles from many publishers. The advantage of buying or subscribing to a large e-book package is that the library adds a large corpus of e-books. However, although the per-title price is usually attractive, the total cost of the package may be high, and often only a fairly small percentage of the titles receive significant use.

In addition to these choices, when librarians buy e-books they purchase only the access rights to the titles, and those rights vary by publisher or vendor and by the license that the library signs with the provider. Rights variables include the total number of simultaneous users and the amount of a title that can be downloaded or printed. The digital rights management (DRM) restrictions indicate whether or not a library can provide chapters to resource sharing partners. Until recently, the ability to lend the entire contents of an e-book was impossible.

Complication #2: Users Say They Prefer Print Books

A more complicated issue to solve is users' preference for print. Lack of sufficient content in electronic format is an issue that will be resolved in time as more publishers' attitude to e-books change and as more books are published in e-format, especially earlier in their life cycle. However, user preferences are more difficult to understand and study, and therefore to address and change. Librarians like e-books because they solve many of the library's long-term logistics problems (e.g., shelving, checking in and out, shelf-reading, and replacing lost or worn-out volumes). However, users like print books. This sentiment is clearly stated in Polanka's book *No Shelf Required* 2 (2012):

> Perhaps most important for this chapter, however, e-books suffer from simply not being print books. People like print books. They like the way they smell and feel, how they give libraries a sense of gravitas, and how they present a physical embodiment of scholarship and creativity. People rally around print books; it is difficult to imagine e-books inspiring the same level of loyalty. When Newport Beach library system in

California announced this March that they were looking into changing one of their branch libraries into a primarily digital space, there was an immediate uproar. (p. 5)

User reluctance to use e-books, but statistics show high use

Users are reluctant to adopt the e-book unilaterally, often telling librarians that they want a "real book." For example, a large international study done by ebrary and the United Kingdom National E-Books Observatory in 2008 found that one of the reasons for never using e-books was preference for print (ebrary, 2008). The librarians at the University of California conducted a study of Springer books, important in part because of its size. This study found that 49% of those surveyed preferred print books, while 34% preferred e-books, and 17% had no preference. Preference for the electronic book is highest among postdoctoral students, followed by graduate students, then undergraduates, with faculty being the least interested in e-books (Li, Poe, Potter, Quigley, & Wilson, 2011, pp. 4, 11). A recent annual study also confirms this user preference. The "2012 Ebook Usage in U.S. Academic Libraries" (2012) found that the statistic on preference for print was climbing, not declining. In 2010, 40% of those surveyed said they preferred print; in 2012, 50% stated preference for print.

Studies indicate an acceptance of e-books, despite the fact that users state a preference for the print book. Levine-Clark (2006) surveyed University of Denver users in 2005 and, even though more than 60% indicated a preference for print, more than 80% indicated some flexibility between the two formats (p. 292). In a study published in 2009, participants were asked to indicate what book format—electronic or print—they thought they would be using: "Eleven percent indicated that they would mostly be reading electronic books and 26% indicated mostly print; 56% indicated that they believed they would be reading a combination of formats" (Shelburne, 2009, p. 65). For other examples, see the literature review in Smyth's and Carlin's (2012) article, "Use and Perception of Ebooks in the University of Ulster: A Case Study."

Statistical studies indicate extremely high use of the electronic version even when a printed version is available. Examples include the Connaway (2002) study at the University of Pittsburgh using NetLibrary titles. This study showed that e-books were used 3.7 times compared to 1.7 circulations of the same title in print (p. 22). The Littman and Connaway (2004) study also confirmed heavier use of the e-book compared to its print equivalent; this study compared nearly 8,000 titles available in print and electronic format at Duke University. It found that e-books were used 11% more than the print versions (p. 260). Several other studies report similar findings.

It is difficult to understand users' stated preference for print in light of the statistics that indicate higher use of the electronic versions. Do users say one thing but do something else? Or are they using e-books in other ways? This difference can be partially explained because users like to browse through e-books and use the search feature to pinpoint the page or chapter they need. If the book looks useful, they might obtain a printed copy for in-depth reading. In some cases, if a small portion of the book is sufficient, the e-book may be all that is consulted. In a study of over 1,000 users at the University of Denver, Levine-Clark (2006) found that "56.5 percent read a chapter or article within a book, and 36.4 percent read a single entry or a few pages within a book, but *only 7.1 percent read the entire book*" (p. 292, italics added). One study that demonstrates this dichotomy looked at undergraduates' attitudes toward e-books and found that 66% preferred the print format, yet 89% said they would use an e-book if a printed copy was not available (Gregory, 2008, p. 269). Another important study at the University of Iowa compared use of the same titles in both print and electronic format; the authors concluded that users *demonstrated* a preference for the electronic. This result conflicts with what users state as their preference. This University of Iowa study analyzed 850 e-books purchased through a PDA program. During the study period, the authors realized that 166 of the e-book titles were duplicated in print. They compared the use of the print version with the electronic versions, found a preference for the online version, and concluded "it is very apparent that the circulation of the print copy drops dramatically once the electronic version is available" (Fischer, Wright, Clatanoff, Barton, & Shreeves, 2012, p. 480).

Research on use and reading of e-books

So how are e-books being used? Users are interested in the very features that make it an e-book. For example, Li and colleagues (2011) found that users placed highest value on the search capacities, both within an e-book and across e-books. The ability to download the entire book (something that can only be done with e-books) was also an important feature valued by these users (pp. 15–16). In the *Ithaka S + R Faculty Survey 2012*, "70% of the respondents reported using scholarly monographs in digital form 'often' or 'occasionally' during the previous six months" (Housewright et al., 2013, p. 31). Although this high percentage seems in conflict with the stated preference for print, the authors note that this is partially because there are many ways to use an e-book besides reading it: scanning the table of contents, reviewing the tables and figures, searching the citations. Those surveyed indicated a preference for print or electronic depending on the activity (Housewright et al., 2013, p. 32).

In another study, which used interviewing techniques with eight students at Fu-Jen Catholic University in Taiwan, college students used different strategies when reading academic material as compared to leisure reading. For example, they first evaluate what they need to learn and allot reading time accordingly. They also used more rereading and elaborating, and utilized the e-book features (ChanLin, 2013, p. 340). The author concluded that the presentation and features of a scholarly e-book may need to differ from those of a leisure e-book for the consumer market (p. 342).

Another study conducted in Australia also sheds some light on how users read e-books. This study used exploratory log analysis of e-book use in an academic library and found that "While strictly sequential reading in ebooks is hardly ever seen in this data set, the trend (with the exception of the large jumps back) is generally to begin near the beginning of a book and work forwards" (McKay, 2011, p. 207). Despite this trend, readers moved back and forth through a document when reading closely (p. 207). Corlett-Rivera and Hackman (2014) surveyed liberal arts users at the University of Maryland with the primary goal of understanding the gap between heavy use of e-books and users' preference for print. One of their major findings was that the majority (52%) indicated they do not download and nearly 75% said they never or rarely print portions of an e-book (Corlett-Rivera & Hackman, 2014, p. 267). Overall e-reader ownership (like the Kindle) had an important effect on preference, 46% compared to 32% (pp. 270–271). Their finding about rarely printing is one that needs more research.

The Shrimplin, Revelle, Hurst, and Messner (2011) study found that users approach books differently depending on personal preferences; these researchers categorized readers into four different groups: book lovers, who preferred print; technophiles, who preferred electronic formats; pragmatists, who use whatever format best suits their needs at the time; and printers, who print out electronic texts (pp. 185–186). Foasberg (2013) also studied when students prefer print or electronic. She used a diary methodology and found that e-readers and tablets were used for nonacademic reading, while paper printouts were nearly always used for academic reading; "60% of the participants' reading with a computer was not for class, while 66% of their reading with print books was" (Foasberg, 2013, p. 715).

In sum, readers search, scan, skip around, and reread, but generally they move forward. They are more likely to read an e-book if they have an e-reader or tablet, but they prefer print books for cover-to-cover reading and for academic reading.

What e-books to purchase? Early subject studies of e-books in academic libraries

Despite users' stated preference for print, they consult the e-books purchased by libraries. One of the advantages of e-books is that librarians can scrutinize use data that is far more detailed than circulation figures for print books. Librarians who were early adopters of e-books naturally investigated what subject areas received the most use with the goal of then increasing purchases in high-demand subjects. They anticipated that the answer would be computer science or the broader fields of science and technology, and some early studies confirmed this. Christianson (2005) examined NetLibrary use during the 2002–2003 school year for five academic institutions and found computers and specific sciences to be the most popular (p. 361). In a similar study, Littman and Connaway (2004) at Duke University found that their users favored e-books about computers, medicine, and psychology (p. 260). Dillon (2001) at the University of Texas, Austin conducted one early study of subject analysis of 20,000 titles from three e-book collections. Although he reported heavier use in some subjects (computer science, economics, and business), there was sufficient use of all subjects to continue e-book purchases across all areas (p. 119). Levine-Clark's (2007) study of humanists' use of e-books confirms this concept. He found that "humanists tend to use e-books at about the same rate as the rest of the campus community" (p. 12).

A question related to high-use subjects is whether librarians are selecting the books patrons want. One way to study this is to compare books purchased based on patron demand with those selected by librarians. In patron-demand e-book programs—DDA or PDA—librarians load catalog records for books in profiled subjects and delay buying them until patrons make sufficient use of specific titles to warrant a purchase. In these programs, books are "rented" until a predetermined number of uses triggers a purchase. Price and McDonald (2009) compared librarian-selected and patron-selected EBL e-books at five academic libraries from 2005 through 2009. The titles that the users selected were similar to those selected by librarians in four of the five libraries. However, the major finding of this early study of PDA was that the user-selected titles were used twice as often as librarian-selected titles (on average 8.6 times per year vs. 4.3 times per year.) This study was very influential in promoting PDA models (p. 6). Other studies have found similar results; the e-books patrons use repeatedly are those chosen by other users (Fischer & Diaz, 2013; Fischer et al., 2012).

STEPPING UP TO THE CHALLENGE

The editors believe that the library and scholarly publishing worlds stand at the crossroads for two major reasons: first, the increase in the size of e-book collections, and second, the widespread ownership of e-readers and tablets, devices that make online reading a better experience. More books than ever are being published simultaneously in print and electronic formats, and publishers and aggregators offer new bundles (or packages of thousands of titles) to libraries at advantageous per-title prices. Both of these events increase the availability of e-books. However, the major influence on the number of e-books available at any library is the PDA or DDA acquisitions model. Via PDA, librarians can offer an extremely large corpus of books, far more than they could with either title-by-title selection or bundling, and then only buy the titles that patrons use.

Students' and researchers' widespread use of e-readers and tablets may slowly change users' attitudes toward e-books; people who enjoy leisure reading on their devices will eventually make the transition to reading professional and scholarly works on them as well. In the past, there was little information or research on how scholars read. New research indicates that scholars scan, skim, skip around, and reread. In many cases, they do not read a book from cover to cover, but rather skim or skip to find relevant sections. E-readers and tablets are ideal for this kind of perusal. Recent research indicates that scholars do not print chapters as librarians had thought; they read on screen, more and more frequently on hand-held devices (Corlett-Rivera & Hackman, 2014). Finally, e-books, especially on e-readers or tablets, are very convenient; scholars and students may prefer print, but for convenience they use e-format.

So why this collection of essays about a product that, while no longer in its infancy, is clearly still some distance from maturity? In as few as five years the landscape may look very different. It is precisely for this reason that the editors gathered this collection of essays about e-books at this stage in their development. This book provides a snapshot of both the e-book reality and its promise in the mid-2010s. The editors specifically excluded consideration of e-textbooks since this particular topic introduces many specialized considerations beyond the scope of this book.

Further, the editors wanted to capture the viewpoints of all three major players for e-books in libraries: the producers and vendors, the libraries, and the users. Much of the library literature about e-books to date has focused on the topic as it affects librarians and their users, but seldom addresses the publishers' and vendors' perspective (except to complain about perceived shortcomings). The editors invited each of the chapter authors to write their essays, carefully balancing contributions between all three perspectives. For the case studies, the editors issued a call for papers and selected seven of the 20 resulting proposals to represent the wide range of interesting projects that librarians are undertaking amongst the burgeoning array of collection development opportunities that e-books offer.

ACKNOWLEDGMENT

The authors gratefully acknowledge Ashley Butler's work in converting a wide variety of tables and figures into graphics with a consistent overall look.

NOTES

1. However there are a few academic libraries that have switched fully (or almost fully) to digital only. The University of California Merced campus is the prime example. It opened in September of 2005 with only ten print journal subscriptions compared to 15,000 online journals and the *History E-Book Collection* (now the

Humanities E-Book Collection), ebrary, and NetLibrary. It started a PDA program with Ebook Library (EBL) and also added Coutts/MyiLibrary and several publisher packages. Overall 83% of their collection was electronic in 2007 (Dooley, 2007, p. 24). By 2010 the library had 800,000 records in the catalog, approximately 88% were electronic (Dooley, 2011, p. 118). Another bookless satellite library opened in 2010 at the University of Texas at San Antonio, the Applied Engineering and Technology Library (Kemp, Lutz, & Nurnberger, 2012).

2. One example is the Scholars Portal Books, the locally built platform for university libraries in Ontario, Canada (Horava, 2013). Other examples include California State University Library Consortia (Shepherd & Langston, 2013); Triangle Research Libraries Network, which includes Duke, North Carolina Central, North Carolina State and University of North Carolina (Lippincott et al., 2012); and Orbis Cascade Alliance, a consortium of thirty-six academic libraries in Oregon and Washington (Hinken & McElroy, 2011).

REFERENCES

2012 ebook usage in U.S. academic libraries: Third annual survey. (2012). Retrieved from http://www.thedigitalshift.com/research/ebook-usage-reports/academic/

ChanLin, L. J. (2013). Reading strategy and the need of e-book features. *Electronic Library, 31*(3), 329–344. http://dx.doi.org/10.1108/EL-08-2011-0127

Christianson, M. (2005). Patterns of use of electronic books. *Library Collections, Acquisitions, & Technical Services, 29*(4), 351–363. http://dx.doi.org/10.1016/j.lcats.2006.03.014

Connaway, L. S., & Wicht, H. (2007). What happened to the e-book revolution?: The gradual integration of e-books into academic libraries. *Journal of Electronic Publishing, 10*(3). http://dx.doi.org/10.3998/3336451.0010.302

Connaway, L. S. (2002). The integration and use of electronic books (e-books) in the digital library. In *Computers in Libraries 2002: Proceedings* (pp. 18–25). Medford, NJ: Information Today.

Corlett-Rivera, K., & Hackman, T. (2014). E-book use and attitudes in the humanities, social sciences, and education. *portal: Libraries and the Academy, 14*(2), 255–286. http://dx.doi.org/10.1353/pla.2014.0008

Dillon, D. (2001). E-books: The University of Texas experience, part 1. *Library Hi Tech, 19*(2), 113–125. http://dx.doi.org/10.1108/07378830110394826

Dooley, J. (2007). From print to electronic: The UC Merced experience. *Against the Grain, 19*(3), article 7. Retrieved from http://docs.lib.purdue.edu/atg/vol19/iss3/7

Dooley, J. (2011). E-books for higher education. In K. Price & V. Havergal (Eds.), *E-books in libraries: A practical guide* (pp. 117–138). London, United Kingdom: Facet Publishing.

E-book. (2014). Wikipedia. Retrieved from http://en.wikipedia.org/w/index.php ?title=E-book&oldid=629180335

ebrary. (2008). 2008 global student e-book survey. Retrieved from http://www .ebrary.com/corp/collateral/en/Survey/ebrary_student_survey_2008.pdf

Fischer, K. S., Wright, M., Clatanoff, K., Barton, H., & Shreeves, E. (2012). Give 'em what they want: A one-year study of unmediated patron-driven acquisition of e-books. *College & Research Libraries, 73*(5), 469–492. http://dx.doi .org/10.5860/crl-297

Fischer, K. S., & Diaz, C. (2013). Four years of unmediated demand-driven acquisition and 5,000 e-books later: We gave 'em what they wanted. In *Proceedings of the Charleston Library Conference.* http://dx.doi.org/10.5703/1288284315296

Foasberg, N.M. (2013). Student reading practices in print and electronic media. *College & Research Libraries, 75*(5), 705-723. http://dx.doi.org/10.5860 /crl.75.5.705

Gregory, C. L. (2008). But I want a real book: An investigation of undergraduates' usage and attitudes toward electronic books. *Reference & User Services Quarterly, 47*(3), 266–273. http://dx.doi.org/10.5860/rusq.47n3.266

Hinken, S., & McElroy, E. J. (2011). Chapter 2: Consortial purchasing of e-books. *Library Technology Reports, 47*(8), 8–13.

Hodges, D., Preston, C., & Hamilton, M. J. (2010). Resolving the challenge of e-books. *Collection Management, 35*(3–4), 196–200. http://dx.doi.org/10.1 080/01462679.2010.486964

Horava, T. (2013). Today and in perpetuity: A Canadian consortial strategy for owning and hosting ebooks. *The Journal of Academic Librarianship, 39*(5), 423–428. http://dx.doi.org/10.1016/j.acalib.2013.04.001

Housewright, R., Schonfeld, R. C., & Wulfson, K. (2013). *US faculty survey 2012.* New York, NY: Ithaka S + R.

Jamali, H. R., Nicholas, D., & Rowlands, I. (2009). Scholarly e-books: The views of 16,000 academics: Results from the JISC National E-Book Observatory. *Aslib Proceedings, 61*(1), pp. 33–47.

Kemp, J., Lutz, E., & Nurnberger, A. L. (2012). E-readers on trial: Qualitative results from an academic library pilot project. *Journal of Electronic Resources Librarianship, 24*(3), 189–203. http://dx.doi.org/10.1080/1941126X.2012.706110

Lamothe, A. R. (2013). Factors influencing the usage of an electronic book collection: Size of the e-book collection, the student population, and the faculty population. *College & Research Libraries 74*(1), 39–59. http://dx.doi.org/10.5860/crl-301

Levine-Clark, M. (2006). Electronic book usage: A survey at the University of Denver. *portal: Libraries and the Academy, 6*(3), 285–299. http://dx.doi.org/10.1353/pla.2006.0041

Levine-Clark, M. (2007). Electronic books and the humanities: A survey at the University of Denver. *Collection Building, 26*(1), 7–14. http://dx.doi.org/10.1108/01604950710721548

Li, C., Poe, F., Potter, M., Quigley, B., & Wilson, J. (2011). UC Libraries academic e-book usage survey. UC Office of the President: California Digital Library. Retrieved from: http://escholarship.org/uc/item/4vr6n902

Lippincott, S. K., Brooks, S., Harvey, A., Ruttenberg, J., Swindler, L., & Vickery, J. (2012). Librarian, publisher, and vendor perspectives on consortial e-book purchasing: The experience of the TRLN beyond print summit. *Serials Review, 38*(1), 3–11. http://dx.doi.org/10.1016/j.serrev.2011.12.003

Littman, J., & Connaway, L. S. (2004). A circulation analysis of print books and e-books in an academic research library. *Library Resources & Technical Services, 48*(4), 256–262.

Long, M. P., & Schonfeld, R. C. (2010). *Ithaka S + R library survey 2010: Insights from US academic library directors.* New York, NY: Ithaka S + R.

McKay, D. (2011, November 28–December 2). *A jump to the left (and then a step to the right): Reading practices within academic ebooks.* Paper presented at the OzCHI '11 Proceedings of the 23rd Australian Computer-Human Interaction Conference, Canberra, Australia. http://dx.doi.org/10.1145/2071536.2071569

Polanka, S. (2012). *No shelf required 2: Use and management of electronic books.* Chicago, IL: American Library Association.

Price, J. S., & McDonald, J. D. (2009). *Beguiled by bananas: A retrospective study of the usage and breadth of patron vs librarian acquired ebook collections.* Paper presented at the 29th Annual Charleston Conference Issues in Book and Serials Acquisition, Charleston, SC. Retrieved from http://scholarship.claremont.edu/library_staff/9

Project Gutenberg. (2014, September 7). *Wikipedia.* Retrieved from http://en.wikipedia.org/w/index.php?title=Project_Gutenberg&oldid=624536497

Shelburne, W. A. (2009). E-book usage in an academic library: User attitudes and behaviors. *Library Collections, Acquisitions, & Technical Services, 33*(2–3), 59–72. http://dx.doi.org/10.1016/j.lcats.2009.04.002

Shepherd, J., & Langston, M. (2013). Shared patron driven acquisition of e-books in the California State University Library Consortium. *Library Collections Acquisitions & Technical Services, 37*(1–2), 34–41. http://dx.doi.org/10.1016/j.lcats.2013.08.001

Shrimplin, A. K., Revelle, A., Hurst, S., & Messner, K. (2011). Contradictions and consensus—Clusters of opinions on e-books. *College & Research Libraries, 72*(2), 181–190. http://dx.doi.org/10.5860/crl-108rl

Smyth, S., & Carlin, A. P. (2012). Use and perception of ebooks in the University of Ulster: A case study. *New Review of Academic Librarianship, 18*(2), 176–205. http://dx.doi.org/10.1080/13614533.2012.719851

Walters, W. H. (2013). E-books in academic libraries: Challenges for acquisition and collection management. *portal: Libraries and the Academy, 13*(2), 187–211. http://dx.doi.org/10.1353/pla.2013.0012

Zeoli, M. (2013). Supplying and collecting books: An uneasy metamorphosis. *eContent Quarterly, 1*(1), 5–16.

Zickurh, K., & Rainie, L. (2014, January 16). Tablet and e-reader ownership. Retrieved from http://www.pewinternet.org/2014/01/16/tablet-and-e-reader-ownership/

Publishers' and Vendors'
Products and Services

1 | An Industry Perspective: Publishing in the Digital Age

Nadine Vassallo

ABSTRACT

The author reviews the state of book publishing in the United States and examines the impact of e-books on the market. Drawing on sources including *BookStats* from the Book Industry Study Group and the Association of American Publishers, she describes the size and shape of the industry overall as well as various segments (trade, education, scholarly publishing) and considers why some of these segments have been quicker to go digital. She examines the impact of e-books on pricing, marketing, and discoverability, and considers new opportunities and business models including e-book subscriptions and patron-driven acquisitions.

U.S. BOOK PUBLISHING TODAY

When asked to provide the industry perspective on the state of book publishing today, the first thing that comes to mind is just how difficult it has become to define the publishing industry because there are so many different publishing sectors.

Consumer publishing produces what are most traditionally thought of as books: fiction and nonfiction content packaged in various discrete forms—be they hardcover, softcover, e-books, or audiobooks—and sold to readers at specific prices via the book trade. Educational publishing blends the creation and distribution of educational content with tools to help students learn and instructors teach. Today, educational publishers employ a variety of business models and think of themselves as software manufacturers

19

nearly as much as book publishers. Scholarly publishers face an entirely different set of circumstances and challenges, many of which will be discussed in other chapters in this book.

When viewed in isolation, each of these facets of publishing can be almost unrecognizable from the others. Yet when viewed from afar, they are all publishing (L. Vlahos, personal communication, October 3, 2014). What unites them is the shared goal of delivering information, knowledge, and stories to their customers, and they face many of the same challenges in attempting to do so within today's complex media landscape.

This chapter presents a basic overview of the size and shape of book publishing in the United States, with a focus on digital books. It presents a context for understanding the publishing business overall, including many of its inherent contradictions and complications.

U.S. PUBLISHER SALES IN REVIEW

Given the diversity of businesses that make up the publishing industry, determining its exact size has always presented a challenge. From 2010 to 2014, the Association of American Publishers (AAP) and Book Industry Study Group (BISG) faced that challenge in a landmark joint study, *BookStats* (AAP/BISG, 2014). *BookStats* extrapolated the full size and scope of U.S. book publishing on an annual basis, providing a single baseline from which to consider industry trends, including the growth of the e-book. Over each of its annual volumes, *BookStats,* revealed a generally stable industry that managed to navigate the transition to digital media while avoiding some of the losses experienced by other traditionally print-based content industries (AAP/BISG, 2014). As shown in Figure 1, for each year that *BookStats* tracked, total net revenue for U.S. book publishers hovered around the $27.0 and $28.0 billion mark, reaching a peak of $27.9 billion in 2010 before dropping back to $27.0 billion in 2013. Nevertheless, this represented only a minor decline (0.4%) compared to the $27.1 billion in total sales reported in calendar year 2012.

Even the small drop in revenue from 2012 to 2013 is, in a way, good news for publishers. It suggests that, even in a year without a single runaway success story (like 2012's *Fifty Shades of Grey*, whose contribution of over $800 million in new romance sales, much of it from e-books, drove adult fiction revenue to historic heights), other titles can keep the industry

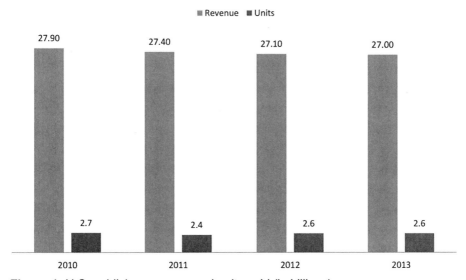

Figure 1. U.S. publisher revenue and units sold (in billions).

afloat. The results of book publishing as a whole rely on the entire long tail: a combination of blockbuster successes and backlist titles alike.

Shifting Sales Ratios

Between 2010 and 2013, digital formats (including e-books as well as apps sold by publishers, digital learning materials, and audiobook downloads) went from representing 14.8% of all U.S. publisher revenues to 20.5%. As of 2013, digital formats accounted for $5.4 billion in total sales, up from $5.1 billion in 2012. But the gains seen in 2013 came entirely from increases in revenue from digital course materials, downloadable audiobooks, and apps. What we think of as e-books showed virtually no growth at all between 2012 and 2013 (AAP/BISG, 2014). Of course, one could not expect the meteoric rise of the e-book to continue forever. However, compared with just a few years ago when the e-book growth rate was a startling 355%, the fact that it reached an apparent plateau and then stalled entirely cannot be ignored.

Meanwhile, physical books (hardcover, softcover, print textbooks, and mass market paperbacks, as well as physical audiobooks) continue to account for the vast majority of publisher revenues, representing 69.5% of all net earnings in 2013. The only print format to experience a major hit since the rise of digital reading was the mass market paperback. These low-cost, somewhat expendable books (the small-size paperbacks commonly seen on grocery and drug store shelves) were easily replaced with e-books, resulting in a 50% loss in revenue from their sales between 2010 and 2013. Meanwhile, hardcover and softcover books gave up less of their shares of the market, losing 6.9% and 12.5%, respectively, over the same time period (AAP/BISG, 2014). Hardcover and softcover formats continue to account for a large percentage of publisher sales; there is little reason to anticipate that a larger drop is coming for either of the formats in the near future.

What may be most surprising about the results of the *BookStats* project is just how predictable they became. Comparing 2012 and 2013 (see Figure 2), one is struck by how little the industry as a whole changed year over year, even in the midst of the so-called digital revolution. For a business whose tumult has been made much of in both the trade and general press, book publishing in general has not found its earnings particularly tumultuous, and the digital transformation has, for many industry sectors, not revealed itself in the end to be all that transformative.

Publishers' relationships with sales channels have changed dramatically over the past several years.[1] Since 2010, publisher earnings from online retailers (these include e-books sold online as well as print sales through the web components of brick-and-mortar retailers such as Barnes & Noble)

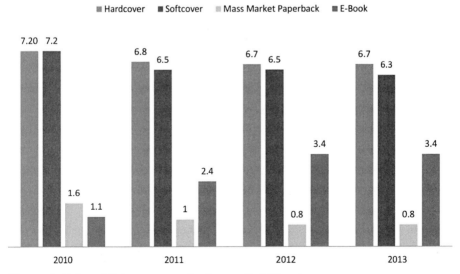

Figure 2. U.S. publisher revenue by format (in billions).

exploded. The online channel grew from $3.7 to $7.5 billion in four years, an increase of 102.7%. However, compared with 2012, when publishers earned $7.2 billion from online sales, the 2013 total represented a small growth rate of 4.2%, and e-book sales made online remained completely flat at $3.1 billion each year (AAP/BISG, 2014). As explained above, the online channel includes not just digital, but also physical sales made online. In 2013, physical books sold through online retailers still accounted for a sizeable portion (41.6%) of online revenue. The vast majority of these sales come from hardcover and softcover formats, while mass market paperbacks and physical audiobooks have virtually no presence online. The move to online retail has been particularly striking for the consumer publishing market, particularly adult fiction. Publishers now derive 47.4% of their fiction revenue from sales made online. Brick-and-mortar stores, on the other hand, account for only 16.4% of revenue from fiction titles, down from 29% in 2010.

This dwindling percentage is not meant to discount the value of physical bookstores. These retail outlets remain a vital part of the publishing landscape, and continue to occupy a unique position when it comes to keeping books relevant in our culture. Even as more consumers gravitate to online retail channels, they report bookstore staff as an important source of book recommendations (Zickuhr, Rainie, Purcell, Madden, & Brenner, 2012). This form of comparison shopping—when readers use physical stores as a key site for book discovery, then turn around and make the actual purchase online—creates a dilemma for bookstores and the publishers who traditionally rely on them (Norris, 2014, p. 16).

Pricing Issues

The general trend downward in publisher net revenues, accompanied with unit sales that have typically been flat, or up, year over year, suggests that readership is on the rise even as average book prices trend down. This is both good and bad news for publishers; while it may be encouraging to see books remain a vital part of the cultural conversation and to watch various blockbuster titles take off, it is unsettling to note that these factors do not necessarily lead to increased revenue for publishers. While publishers' best customers seem to be reading as much as they did before the move to digital began, they are reading in formats and shopping through channels where they have come to expect lower price points.

Publishers did receive some good news in terms of average net unit prices (ANUP) last year.[2] After falling from $11.42 to $10.35 between 2011 and 2012, ANUP rose slightly in 2013, coming in at $10.42, 0.7% above its 2012 value. Still, this figure represents a decrease of 8.6% compared with the higher mark in 2011. These shifts allowed unit sales to increase, as they did in 2012, or stay flat, as they did in 2013, even as publisher revenues fell (AAP/BISG, 2014).

Shifts in average net unit price are more dramatic still when considered in terms of individual formats. Since the dawn of the e-book, publishers watched the amount they could hope to earn from sales in that format drop dramatically. Between 2010 and 2013, ANUP for a single e-book fell from $8.26 to $6.52, a loss of over 20%. During that same time period, marked decreases in the amount readers said they were willing to spend on an e-book were also observed. About 2010, the "sweet spot" for an e-book price was within the $12 to $18 range (between what customers considered a good value and what they considered unreasonably high, or within the realm of what they were willing to spend), but by August 2013, it had fallen to a range of about $6 to $13. In fact, between 2010 and 2013, the price that e-book buyers had once considered "so inexpensive [they] would doubt its quality" became what they thought of as "a good value" (BISG, 2013).

At the same time, the average amount publishers earn from the sale of a print book has remained relatively stable. Average net unit prices for both hardcover and softcover books actually rose in 2013—from $10.96 in 2012 to $11.36 for hardcovers, and $6.34 to $6.43 for softcovers (AAP/BISG, 2014).[3] Again, there is little reason to expect that print is going away anytime soon; it continues to benefit publishers to distribute their titles in a variety of format types, including e-books and digital audio as well as hardcover and softcover formats.

E-Books and the Immersive Reading Experience

Despite what might be said about publishing in general, it is clear that major shifts have taken place within certain industry sectors, especially in terms of their expansion into the digital marketplace. Perhaps most clear among these is the split between "immersive" reading and "nonimmersive" forms, such as educational, professional, and other types of nonfiction content. In general, people who read e-books tend to have diverse tastes. When asked which genres they like to read, they will cite everything from romance and horror fiction to literary novels to cookbooks, biographies, and how-to guides. Yet when they indicate which genres they prefer to read in which formats, a very different picture appears (see Figure 3).

The divide seems to start at the split between immersive and non-immersive reading experiences. As industry expert Mike Shatzkin (2012) notes, the tendency of e-books to perform well in some genres and not well in others is directly related to this split and to publishers' ability to translate immersive reading experience seamlessly from page to screen. Mystery fans, for example, entangled in a gripping detective story, may not notice whether they turn the page of a physical book or flick a "page" on the screen of their tablet. Immersed in the story, they can ignore the format to focus instead on the pure quality of the content. In fact, these readers report that enhancements such as embedded audio/video, images and tables, and social media integration are of little value and, if anything, serve to detract from the reading experience (BISG, 2013).

On the other hand, consider the case of cookbooks, which have seen virtually no success in terms of e-book sales and yet remain, overall, the second highest selling nonfiction category (trailing only biography/

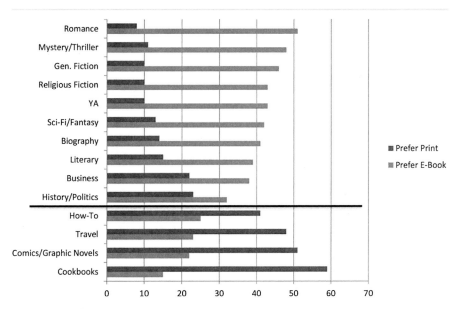

Figure 3. Preferred genres—e-books vs. print books.

autobiography, notably a form of immersive nonfiction). Readers inter- ested in cookbooks may enjoy looking at the beautiful, colorful photo- graphs of food contained therein, and may select a large, high-quality, hardcover cookbook for exactly that reason. They may also want to look up a single recipe for immediate use, in which case a website or app may be a far more logical digital alternative than that same cookbook converted into a static PDF form. The same is true of travel guides, for example, which can easily be replaced by some combination of note-taking and map software available on every smartphone. Consider the way users interact with these sorts of nonimmersive, nonfiction content, and it comes as little surprise that their book counterparts do not translate seamlessly onto the screens of e-reading devices. Instead, these categories are moving to the digital realm in other ways.

If the trends observed over the past few years continue, the industry may change to one in which some categories flourish in e-book format and some remain popular in print alone. So far, this line seems to be drawn between immersive and nonimmersive reading experiences.

Digital Course Materials in Higher Education

In contrast to other industry sectors, which have seen digital reading take off primarily for immersive narrative forms, higher education publishing sees its greatest opportunity in the increased interactivity facilitated by digital formats. Long struggling against a vibrant, low-cost used textbook market and faced with concerns about piracy, educational publishers, for the most part, welcome this news. Nearly all major higher education pub- lishers now offer some sort of integrated digital learning platform to their customers; many have made these new systems the core focus of their busi- ness, replacing the traditional hardcover print text. Over the past few years, students and faculty have indicated increased interest in, as well as comfort and familiarity with, digital learning materials. As of October 2014, 69.5% of students surveyed reported that they had used digital materials for a course within the past two years (BISG, 2014). Traditionally, college students have been somewhat conservative consumers, often resistant to changes to their habits and buying patterns—and for good reason. Knowing the importance of academic success on students' futures, one can hardly be surprised that they hesitate to try new materials which necessitate learning new behaviors and study habits to accompany them. But, as more students gain experience with digital materials (and most report satisfaction with their results), it seems this market is truly poised to hit a digital tipping point.

FOCUS ON: THE SIZE AND SHAPE OF SCHOLARLY PUBLISHING

There is perhaps no better example of book publishing's general stability than the scholarly sector (see Figure 4). While a nearly 10% decline in sales from 2012 to 2013 may sound like bad news for scholarly publishing, it is not necessarily cause for alarm. The U.S. scholarly book market experienced a six-year high at $201.3 million in sales in 2012; its decline back to $182.1 million in 2013 represents a return to a more normal, and indeed extremely stable, level. This, the smallest sector in the publishing industry, has seen its overall share (0.7%, in terms of publisher net revenues) remain unchanged for several years in a row (AAP/BISG, 2014).

In terms of net unit sales, scholarly publishing represents only 0.2% of the industry overall, pointing to relatively high average net unit prices in this sector. In 2013, scholarly presses reported an average net unit price of $29.19—more than two and a half times the average seen in the industry overall (AAP/BISG, 2014).

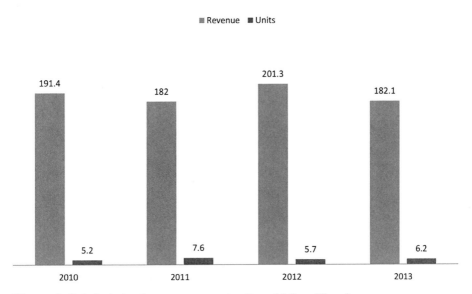

Figure 4. Scholarly books: revenue and units sold (in millions).

Given the dominance of electronic over print journals since the early 2000s and given scholars' increased willingness to rely on content in a variety of packages and forms, one might expect e-books to have caught on in this sector. To date, however, this has not been the case. Scholarly publishers continue to report that the vast majority of their sales derive from print formats. In 2013, e-books accounted for only 7.6% of scholarly publishing revenues, at $14 million in total sales. Other digital formats, such as apps and downloaded audiobooks, have no presence in this sector. Meanwhile, hardcover books, at $93 million, make up 50.9% of revenue for scholarly presses, and softcover books another 40.8% with $74 million in sales. Like higher education, scholarly publishing sees a relatively strong presence for bundled products, which combine some aspect of both physical and digital; these account for about $1 billion in scholarly publisher revenue (AAP/BISG, 2014).

The major market for scholarly books is academic libraries; purchases made directly by individual customers account for a smaller portion of revenue ($12 million in 2013, according to *BookStats*). Therefore, the relationship between scholarly publishers and libraries is a vital and defining feature of this market, and it is critical that libraries be prepared to accept e-books into their collections before publishers will begin to derive real revenue from their sales (Hill & Lara, 2014). In recent years, many libraries have expanded their digital book collections. Spending on e-books as a percentage of overall library book budgets increased from 6.6% in 2009 to 18.8% in 2013 (PCG, 2013). This increase suggests a potential for more digital sales of scholarly books in the future.

Conversations with publishers speak to the importance of libraries to this sector, but it remains difficult to account for the exact proportion of scholarly publisher sales that derive from the library channel.[4] As of 2013, scholarly publishers reported that sales to jobber and wholesalers accounted for 48.1% of their total revenues. Knowing that many libraries conduct business through wholesalers, one can assume that a large percentage of these books probably end up on academic library shelves (AAP/BISG, 2014).

While this sector relies on online retail more than it did a few years ago, that channel does not appear to be growing in any major way. Scholarly publisher revenue from online retail has been relatively stable, at $48 million in 2011, $56 million in 2012, and $52 million in 2013 (AAP/BISG, 2014). Still, for a sector of its small size, even these shifts can represent major percentage changes. Given what is known about digital books and falling average net unit prices, it may not be surprising to note that, while more scholarly publisher revenue continues to come from wholesalers, more units are now sold through online retailers, and by a fairly large margin. In 2013, 2.5 million scholarly books were sold online compared with 1.8 million sold to jobbers and wholesalers. Due in part to the lower price points at online retail, among other factors, these unit sales accounted for less in overall revenue for publishers. This is an issue for scholarly publishers to watch, especially if their sales continue to gravitate further toward digital channels and formats.

E-BOOK OPPORTUNITIES AND CHALLENGES

While e-books can help to make reading more instant and accessible than ever before, they also present new challenges to the book publishing industry and to the reading public. The following sections discuss a few of these issues.

Marketing, Discoverability, and Metadata

Perhaps the area of greatest difficulty—and of greatest opportunity—for today's book publishers lies in metadata and discoverability. As sales move further into online channels, it becomes increasingly critical to provide quality, well-formed, and complete metadata to facilitate readers' discovery of books. Publishers must ensure they are equipped to create and disseminate this metadata, and they must be able to rely on their downstream partners, including retailers, wholesalers, libraries, and data aggregators, to ensure it is effectively ingested and displayed. The link between accurate, complete metadata and book sales is well documented. A Nielsen Book study (Book Industry Communication, 2009)[5] concluded that titles meeting the BIC Basic standard see average sales 98% higher than those that do not and that the addition of a cover image to book metadata results in 268% higher sales on average compared to titles without an image. Improved metadata has a particularly strong effect on online sales, but it also can have a large impact on the ability of a book to sell offline (Breedt & Walter, 2012). Yet difficulties consistently arise when it comes to the production and dissemination of quality book metadata. This is an area where industry-wide collaboration and discussion is necessary to ensure success for all players in the publishing supply chain.

The Walled Garden Effect

One of the major issues that concern e-book buyers—and a factor that may prevent new readers from entering the e-book market—is the tendency of reading systems and devices to create "walled gardens" of book content. By its nature, ownership of an e-book must be different from ownership of a print book. When purchasing an e-book, one purchases a license to view a copy of that e-book file, often subject to rules and conditions set down by the store or reading system where that e-book was acquired. For example, a book purchased from Amazon's Kindle store cannot easily be opened on anything other than a Kindle application or device. There also may be restrictions in place on the redistribution or resale of that book to other readers (Vassallo & Maier, 2014, p. 28). E-book buyers report dissatisfaction with this state of affairs. Giving away, lending, and reselling books after they are finished with them are all behaviors that they developed while reading in print formats; they are not prepared to abandon these upon their switch to digital reading. They also frequently report a desire for easier management of their e-book library across or within their devices (BISG, 2013). While the ability to protect content and limit the used book market appeals, for clear reasons, to publishers, they also should bear in mind the affect these limitations may place on new customers' decision to enter the e-book market or how they might discourage current e-book buyers from buying more e-books.

Creating New E-Book Readers

Publishers may have succeeded in converting some of their most loyal print customers into equally loyal e-book readers. Where they continue to lag is in the conversion of nonreaders into e-book buyers. Even as more people become equipped for e-reading through the acquisition of e-book-ready devices such as smartphones and tablets, many of them fail to read as much as a single e-book. In fact, the stagnation of e-book sales may be directly linked with the influence of multifunction tablets like the iPad. When the first iPad was released, industry belief held that the e-book tide would rise because consumers had a new device with which to access e-books. However, as iPad sales increased in the subsequent years, the proportion of iPad owners who were also e-book users did not grow. By 2013, it was estimated that about half of all iPad owners were not e-book readers at all (Norris, 2014, p. 15).

The increased popularity of multifunction tablets at the expense of dedicated e-reading devices creates a new complication for publishers. They now find themselves competing not just with television, film, music, and other traditional forms of leisure entertainment, but also with a host of new entrants in the social media, gaming, and application space. As customers who had relied on dedicated e-readers like Amazon's basic Kindle abandon those devices in favor of multifunction tablets, publishers must figure out how to ensure that they do not lose them to new entertainment options (Vassallo & Maier, 2014, p. 26).

New Business Models: Getting E-Books Into Academic Libraries

A hot topic in the publishing industry today is the rise of new distribution models facilitated by the switch from print to e-books, especially the introduction of e-book subscription models, each vying to become the Netflix or Spotify of e-books. This issue plays a special role in the future of scholarly publishing. Given the importance of the scholarly publisher-academic library relationship, these new business models create additional opportunities to get digital scholarly materials onto library shelves, while also presenting their own set of new complications and challenges. A recent study revealed that, even as the market begins to go digital, academic librarians continue to prefer ownership of their content, ensuring it will be available for long-term access and preserved to meet the needs of future scholars. Yet new distribution models facilitated by the expansion of digital content—short-term loans, e-book subscription, and patron-driven acquisitions, among others—offer potential solutions to library budget problems, often reliant upon users being granted only access to (as opposed to ownership of) that content. Smaller and midsize academic libraries tend to look more favorably on these new subscription options than do their large research university counterparts, whose access to large budgets allows them to consider more outright purchases (Hill & Lara, 2014, p. 36). The study also found, however, that the transition to digital books can create additional library budget issues:

> In the past, most book acquisitions for a library meant a purchase of print books that would impact the library budget a single time. However, with the advent of e-books and, in turn, new acquisition models, libraries are required to adjust their purchasing strategies and consider potential new subscription lines in their annual budgets.

Some look to this new trend hesitantly, fearing a return to the "Big Deal" concept from the early rush to electronic journals. The Big Deal meant that publishers offered large packages of titles for a discounted price, often locking in libraries for a particular length of time to maintain the subscription. Over time, some libraries found the majority of their annual budgets tied up in these Big Deal packages, which limited their annual purchasing capability. Once burned, many librarians are taking a cautious approach to the new business models offered around digital book subscriptions. (Hill & Lara, 2014, p. 38)

Another option created by the digital transition is patron-driven acquisitions (PDA), a model that allows academic libraries to pay only for those titles actually used by their patrons. PDA raises a few concerns, however, as it cuts down on the librarian's direct role in collection development and may promote the purchase of works on popular subjects, leading to collections with decreased emphasis on less popular or newer areas of scholarship (Hill & Lara, 2014, p. 38). PDA still plays a minor role in most libraries, representing only 5% of the e-book budget of institutions surveyed (PCG, 2013).

WORKING TOGETHER TO PROMOTE READING AND SCHOLARSHIP

Although there is a digital future for scholarly books, the industry is waiting to see exactly how new business models will play out in this sector. Librarians also wait to see how digital reading changes users' habits; when they understand these changes, they will shift their approach to collection development and purchasing, in turn affecting publishers' plans for publication and distribution:

For librarians and administrators working to meet competing demands with limited resources, digital platforms promise an opportunity to view details about their patrons' usage habits that were simply not available in the print world. Armed with data about which resources are used most heavily, librarians hope they will be able to make better-informed, usage-based decisions about which resources to maintain. The common approach to collection development prior to the digital transition for journals and books was a "just in case" mentality. Large, broad collections of resources were required to ensure that the library would be able to respond to most inquiries and research needs. As more data becomes available to help collections developers pin down the needs of their users and identify the most cost-effective resources, some are shifting toward a "just in time" view of the supply of informational resources. (Hill & Lara, 2014, pp. 38–39)

Whatever becomes of the book publishing business, one thing that will not change is the fundamental human desire to share stories, information, and knowledge. Scholarly presses and academic libraries are uniquely positioned to help ensure that these assets remain available to the largest number of scholars in the most cost-effective, accessible, and beneficial manner. They can only benefit from each other's experience as they move, together, into the digital future.

NOTES

1. It is important to note, when considering the various sales channels via *BookStats* data, that *BookStats* is a publisher-side-only report. All values contained herein reflect that, and sales channel information refers only to publishers' relationships with any given channel, and not to the overall health of those channels. All prices, for example, reflect publisher average net unit prices—not prices paid by consumers at retail.

2. Average net unit price (ANUP) is the amount a publisher earns, on average, from the sale of a single book.

3. This also may be related to the genres of books that sold better in one year compared to the other. The romance and young adult genres, which traditionally have seen lower price points, even in print, exploded in 2012 with *Fifty Shades of Grey* and *The Hunger Games*, and could be expected to return to more normal levels the following year. In 2013, genres such as literary fiction—which tends to be priced higher in print formats—saw increased sales.

4. *BookStats*' tracking of sales channels does not include a specific breakout for libraries or for library-oriented wholesalers. What we are able to observe is dominance within this category for the single sales channel most likely to be associated with the library market: sales through jobbers and wholesalers. Unfortunately, as a publisher-side only report, *BookStats* does not track these sales further and cannot report with any specificity on where they end up downstream.

5. BIC Basic is a set of standards for bibliographic data provision developed and promoted by Book Industry Communication for the United Kingdom book industry, with the objective of improving the accuracy and timeliness of product information available to the book trade. It includes a statement of the basic metadata elements that publishers should be able to provide to retail booksellers and other supply chain intermediaries.

REFERENCES

AAP/BISG (Association of American Publishers and Book Industry Study Group, Inc.). (2014). *BookStats* [data file]. Retrieved from http://www.bookstats.org

Book Industry Communication. (2009). BIC basic. Retrieved from http://www.bic.org.uk/17/BIC-Basic/

BISG (Book Industry Study Group, Inc.). (2013). *Consumer attitudes toward e-book reading* [data file]. Retrieved from http://dp2.ztelligence.com/

BISG (Book Industry Study Group, Inc.). (2014). *Student attitudes toward content in higher education* [data file]. Retrieved from http://dp2.ztelligence.com/

Breedt, A., & Walter, D. (2012). The link between metadata and sales. Retrieved from http://www.nielsenbookscan.co.uk/uploads/3971_Nielsen_Metadata_white_paper_A4.pdf

Hill, T., & Lara, K. (2014). *Digital books and the new subscription economy.* New York, NY: Book Industry Study Group.

Norris, M. (2014). BookStats (Vol. 4) [PDF annual report]. New York, NY: Association of American Publishers and Book Industry Study Group.

PCG (Publishers Communication Group). (2013). Library budget predictions for 2014. Retrieved from http://www.pcgplus.com/wp-content/uploads/2013/03/Library-Budget-Predictions-2014.pdf

Shatzkin, M. (2012, January 4). The digital future still is a mystery if you don't publish "immersive reading." [blog post]. Retrieved from http://www.idealog.com/blog/the-digital-future-is-still-a-mystery-if-you-dont-publish-immersive-reading/

Vassallo, N., & Maier, R. C. (2014). The evolving e-book landscape: Two perspectives. In D. Bogart (Ed.), *Library and book trade almanac* (pp. 24–40). Medford, NJ: Information Today.

Zickuhr, K., Rainie, L., Purcell, K., Madden, M., & Brenner, J. (2012). Libraries, patrons, and e-books. Retrieved from http://libraries.pewinternet.org/2012/06/22/libraries-patrons-and-e-books/

2 | The Journey Beyond Print: Perspectives of a Commercial Publisher in the Academic Market

Rhonda Herman

ABSTRACT

Since 1979, commercial publisher McFarland has offered scholarly books to academic libraries. This paper covers early experimentation with e-books and more mature collaborations, as well as experiences with new acquisition models and a publisher perspective on patron-driven acquisitions. It explains the publisher perspective on the economics of publishing e-books, pricing considerations, and production. A discussion of e-book trends includes quotes from publishing industry publications.

EARLY E-BOOK HISTORY

McFarland first experimented with e-books about 1998. The investment group Willis Stein & Partners owned Baker & Taylor at that time, and their management intended to increase the value of their holding by leveraging a dominant market position in innovative ways. They invited McFarland to participate in a pilot e-book program for libraries. McFarland's toe-in-the-water commitment was roughly 125 titles that were two or more years old. That project did not work out in the way that Baker & Taylor anticipated. After about two years with no sales or apparent advertising activity, Baker & Taylor reached an agreement with NetLibrary for the latter to absorb their program. Founded in 1998, NetLibrary made a large splash when it entered the picture (Quint, 2000). NetLibrary sponsored lavish parties and a commanding booth presence at the American Library Association conferences, raising awareness about the potential of e-books and sparking the increasingly urgent dialogue that librarians, vendors, and publishers have been having ever since. The rising importance of library consortia grew NetLibrary's business; it became possible to negotiate larger contracts with a single organization representing many libraries.

McFarland's early involvement with NetLibrary was conservative, but this new relationship propelled needed adjustments, such as changing the publishing contracts offered to book authors to accommodate e-books. Permissions issues were one of the reasons the first experiments were small; it is a large time commitment to go through the file for a published book and read each permission document to determine the intent and legal implication. This labor could not be farmed out or delegated to a junior staff member without extensive training. The expected revenue was modest; in addition, the regular publishing program had to march on.

Publishers had many concerns about e-books. There was still a lot of fear in the industry about "cannibalization" of print, but it was apparent that there were many cases in which libraries, also in a period of experimentation, had budgeted funds to spend on e-books only. Publishers needed to confront their fears.

When e-books initially emerged, the first scenario in publishers' imaginations-run-wild was that existing consortia would grow larger and larger in scope until a few consortia would purchase access to one copy per state or one copy per sector (public, academic, etc.). There was even talk about how much it would cost for an umbrella entity to purchase permanent access rights for a single title for all public reading consumption. Then there was a fear that a work could never be protected from online theft or that a publisher could not reassure authors that the risk was worth taking. This fear was followed by the "cannibalization of print" fear. There might have been a brief period of hope when publishers thought they could maintain a healthy level of print sales while enjoying some e-book sales and increasing revenue overall.

It might be useful to note that consolidation began with the comparatively young companies that aggregate e-books; this consolidation continues today. OCLC bought NetLibrary soon after that company filed for Chapter 11 bankruptcy in 2001 (Jackson, 2004). In 2010, EBSCO purchased NetLibrary assets (EBSCO Publishing to acquire NetLibrary Division from OCLC, 2010). Also in 2011, ProQuest acquired ebrary and then added Australia's EBL in 2013 (Enis, 2014).

From the publisher perspective, e-book sales activity became less attractive during this period; McFarland turned down most of the deals that were offered. The comfort level of publishers like McFarland eventually improved when vendors began taking a more balanced approach. Ebrary set an early example of striking a balance between representing the interests of the publisher while reassuring librarians as well.

This is the history through a publisher's eyes related to the other players in the triumvirate of getting content to library users—acquisitions librarians—who made important changes to the way they acquired books from the 1990s onward. In addition to the consortial strategy to stretch budget dollars, the work of acquiring print books began to be privatized or outsourced to vendors. This change caused shifts in the library profession related to cataloging and other long-held traditions. As time went on, vendors used computers more and more to select books based on criteria obtained by library client interviews, surveys, and profiles. Early e-book acquisition activity seemed less uniform in process, presumably because the money came down through different budget areas in different libraries and because the individual consortial purchasing agreements dictated purchasing protocols.

As the e-book market began to grow, McFarland struggled to keep pace while dealing with multiple issues related to producing e-books. The labor-intensive process of clearing permissions and preparing files to the specs of an e-book vendor was a new activity that did not fit under anyone's job description. The amount of money received from the quarterly checks was not enough to spark interest. At first, McFarland limited its risk by contributing older books to vendor projects—for example, a directory with no illustrations. The company also restricted titles from becoming e-books if an illustration had to be blocked, partly because vendors seemed so reluctant and partly because the user experience would clearly be undermined in these cases. One of the things that slowed early participation was helping authors to understand what an e-book was and why they should obtain permissions in the manuscript stage that included electronic rights. Rights granters could be problematic; for example, getting the rights for an image from an historical society might raise concerns that the image would be downloaded. Later, when Kindle burst onto the scene, author relations improved dramatically because they now understood the concept and value of e-books.

By the 2010 Charleston Conference, it was clear that librarians were very interested in e-books and prepared to devote more of their budgets to acquiring them. It was time for McFarland to get serious. Staff held editorial meetings to discuss the goal of obtaining all permissions clearances for as many upcoming book projects as possible. Further, the company launched a massive project to obtain clearances on the backlist. McFarland built in-house expertise to conduct contract negotiations with a parade of new e-book vendors and developed processes for preparing and transmitting e-book files. In an effort to document these actions, McFarland developed a customized database just for e-books that integrated with data on print books; an exponentially more complex version of this database is still in use today with many more features and capabilities.

Today 98% of McFarland's titles are simultaneously published in electronic and print versions. There are still several issues that can prevent an e-book edition, the most common one being important photos or other elements for which releases related to electronic rights cannot be obtained. Then there is the issue of too many images. For example, a recent title had many, many gorgeous high-resolution color photos. The file size was huge. Even after making image resolution reductions, file handling was a problem; staff ultimately decided that the print format was simply more suitable and that the electronic format was not practical for this particular title. Simultaneous publishing does not literally mean on the precise same day. As soon as the master page layout file for the print book has been completely evaluated and final corrections executed and checked, staff export a PDF for web-ready preparation. This process could conceivably be completed before printing the physical book. As soon as the web-ready file is complete and checked, it is sent to four academic library vendors via FTP.

McFarland has occasionally been offered manuscripts that were worthy but were too large to be practical for print publication. The present e-book production process is built around the content's going through an editorial process that is interwoven with the page design and layout production process. There is no easy way to provide that activity outside the print production system. In the absence of a steady workflow of e-only content that would be profitable, experiments are not justifiable. So it is unlikely that McFarland will publish works in e-book but not print format in the near future, unless some element of the environment changes.

THAR BE A NEW SCALAWAG! ARRR!

The Internet era has presented a new problem for publishers—piracy. In the early Internet era, McFarland discovered one example of a television show fan website whose administrator provided all the text of one of our reference books, adding a section of episode guides. The website administrator posted a notice that she would add more material as she had time to enter it. She did not understand the implications of copyright law and removed the file immediately upon our notification of her illegal behavior. There was another more recent incident in which a very large and newly published McFarland reference work showed up on Scribd. It appears that someone had obtained a copy of a PDF and posted it. Scribd removed it immediately upon our request. The worst case of piracy involved McFarland's *Encyclopedia of Mind Enhancing Foods, Drugs and Nutritional Substances*. In this case, the physical book had been scanned and uploaded to a file sharing site. Once this happens, there is no reasonable rescue because it is replicated on thousands of sites. In 2011, a survey by Digital Entertainment revealed that "36% of tablet owners admit to illegal ebook downloads" (Bacon, 2013). About 2005, the representative of a major academic vendor pointed out that the level and sophistication of various vendors was far from uniform. With high-profile hacks being perpetrated against organizations with good or excellent safeguarding resources, it is not difficult to imagine a scenario in which a large number of publishers' files could be illegally obtained and instantly made available for free.

The cost of protecting digital content, dealing with cases of piracy, communicating with offenders and authors, investing in services to monitor for cases of piracy—these are real costs that did not exist when publishers were dealing only with print. The Hack Education website offers an element called Library Pirate that promotes civil disobedience to protest the costs of an education that should, they believe, be freely available; the site offers illegal downloads of academic textbooks (Watters, 2011). One hesitates to offer any mention of such sites in any public consumption venue for fear that *any* publicity whatsoever might tempt people to try them. So this information comes with this caveat: the research for this chapter did not include a visit to any of the sites mentioned because, in McFarland's experience, these websites are magnets for other kinds of nefarious virtual threats. One can expect exposure to viruses and other unpleasant outcomes. When McFarland investigates a possible incident of piracy, staff follow strict protocols to protect the company's network. It would seem to be the virtual counterpart of walking around a very bad neighborhood.

THE BUSINESS OF E-BOOKS

With print books, McFarland had a good communication system with vendors for orders on new books. In fact, these orders drive McFarland's production processes. That is, if there are a dozen projects ready to move into production, advance orders will drive the sequence in which the projects move. A book with a lot of orders will be expedited at every stage of production because these numbers are available to every decision maker in the production stream. This communication channel does not exist for e-books. A few years ago, there was talk of setting up a process for vendors to communicate with publishers about advance academic orders for e-books. If those data had become available, they would have been aggregated with the print advance orders and would have made an impact on the production process. Those e-book advance-order data never became a reality; perhaps the e-book acquisitions process is too abbreviated to bother alerting the publisher of advance orders.

Income From Retail Market vs. Academic Market

The McFarland income from e-books on the retail market trended faster as well as higher and is a more significant contributor to sales than income from the library market. Amazon has a 65% market share of total e-book sales in the United States (Bercovici, 2014). At McFarland, 59% percent of all e-book revenue came from Amazon in 2013. Library e-book vendors have so many complicated service considerations like proxy servers and library branding, and now the mind-boggling complexity of demand-driven acquisitions (DDA). The capital investments must be huge. While library vendors have been preoccupied with these matters, Amazon has been extending its global reach; McFarland receives checks from 10 various Amazon operations in countries around the world; the latest addition is Denmark (country number 11). It also is notable that in 2013, Amazon surpassed McFarland's largest library vendor and became the largest seller of our print books as well. This development is unsettling. Karen Christensen (2014) of Berkshire Publishing has blogged extensively about her experiences with what she called Amazon "bullying." In contrast, academic library vendors more and more have become true partners.

This chapter's tables illustrate the point that e-book revenue has been driven more by the retail than the library market. The e-book retail market requires a different type of file format called EPUB requiring a much greater time investment to produce. McFarland has many fewer EPUBs to offer vendors for this reason, although OverDrive, a leading public library e-book vendor, is a notable exception because it requests that publishers send both EPUB and PDF file formats. There are many more McFarland titles for sale on academic library vendor sites compared to retail vendors because of the format issue (see Figure 1).

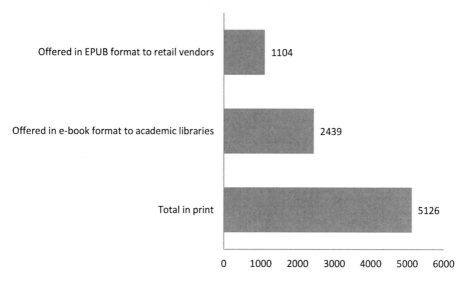

Figure 1. Summary of McFarland titles.

Tables 1 and 2 show year-over-year revenue. The numbers in Table 1 reflect all markets; Table 2 covers the academic market. In Table 2, the aggregated sales numbers for academic vendors (three vendors that merged during these periods) tell a different story. Note that 2014 saw a steep drop in e-book unit sales from library vendors. The reason for 2012's growth is because prior years' sales were modest. It is also notable that each year had at least 400 more titles for sale than the previous one.

Table 1. McFarland total e-book revenue, year over year.

Year	Percentage change over previous year
2012	Up 92%
2013	Up 21%
2014	Up 13% (estimated)

Table 2. McFarland academic e-book revenue, year over year.

Year	Percentage change over previous year
2012	Up 224%
2013	Up 11%
2014	Down 19%

Comparison of E-Books With Print Books

Considering a business analysis of e-books sales is not possible without also considering the matter of print sales. For print books, advance orders from academic libraries fell roughly 50% since 2010, presumably because budgets were tight and funds for print books were diverted to e-books. As a result, the economic proposition of printing a new book is now quite different. Cash flow is affected because transactions for print sales (and retail e-book sales) occur monthly with normal payment terms. E-book vendors in the academic market gather transactions for an entire quarter and pay after the quarter has ended. So the cash transfer to the publisher can be heavily delayed by as many as four or five months depending on the timing of the transaction within a quarter.

Figure 2 illustrates the split between print and electronic sales for one moderately successful title. The impact of the print sales is clear. Academic library sales probably will decline over time.

Pricing E-Books

Pricing models for academic e-books vary from publisher to publisher. McFarland's list prices are the same for print and electronic editions. For an e-book transaction, the publisher has no costs for order administration, production cost, and inventory. However, the wholesale discount to the vendor is much deeper for the e-book. Preparing a web-ready PDF file to go to an e-book vendor requires the same actions as producing a print book: acquisitions activity, peer review, editing, cover design, page layout,

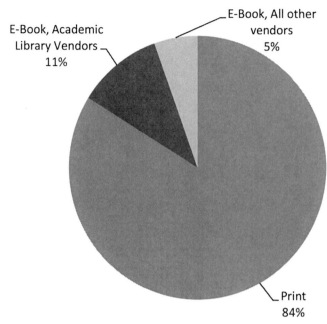

Figure 2. Sales split for one moderately successful McFarland academic title, lifetime sales, sold in two years.

marketing, sales, author relations, vendor relations, administrative activities like applying for CIP and copyright, royalty accounting, and payment. There also are additional costs associated with preparing the file for the e-book edition and distributing it to the various vendors. At McFarland, this is all done in-house, but one can imagine that outsourcing all of the activity associated with an e-book file, as often happens at smaller publishers and university presses, represents significant cash outlays.

Perhaps the question about why the e-book costs the same as the print edition still lingers. A certain amount of revenue from any source has to flow in or the project cannot break even. McFarland list prices are comparatively low, partly because some of our academic titles have popular appeal, so if the price is low enough to capture some sales contribution from the retail sector, then the work continues to be viable. In sum, McFarland settles the list price for each title that will yield a revenue mix from some combination of academic libraries, maybe public libraries, maybe retail. It is not an exact science or a mathematical exercise.

McFarland is comfortable with the idea that a portion of the revenue will come from e-books. However, there has been a drop in average per-title print sales from academic libraries, and the amount of revenue from e-books is not enough to make up for the drop in print revenue. The viability of a particular title then might depend on raising the list price to academic libraries, but in a McFarland proposition, this decision might mean that the contribution from the retail side will more or less disappear. From a business point of view, McFarland wants to maintain the viability of the unique kind of books for which the company is known. But the combination of DDA and the short-term loan (STL) has begun to undermine the equilibrium in the revenue of some titles.

Demand-Driven Acquisitions and Short-Term Loans

In Joseph Esposito's (2014) balanced article, "Revisiting Demand-Driven Acquisitions," he accomplishes quite a feat—presenting the big picture, the position of the academic library, and the perspective of the publisher all at the same time. He makes the point that "libraries do not exist for the benefit of publishers" and goes on to say that "DDA may be hurting publishers precisely because *librarians are doing their job*" of maximizing their budget resources and delivering content to their users at the most effective attainable cost (para. 3). He contends that publishers should and will raise prices. A more serious system problem, he points out, is the sampling of 10% of a book before a transaction takes place—too high and inappropriate for nonfiction. He proposes several models where the library becomes a sales outlet, benefiting both library and publisher (Esposito, 2014).

McFarland currently is revising DDA short-term loan rates. Many other publishers are considering or have already taken such an action. One vendor told us that some major publishers are electing to embargo frontlist titles out of the DDA option for at least a year, and some are choosing embargoes for as many as five years. Revenue has fallen too quickly so inaction is simply not an option. McFarland will make the necessary adjustments to maintain that equilibrium on a per-title basis whether tinkering with the list price, with the terms of the short-term e-book loan with vendors, or with some combination of revenue and cost strategies. It goes without saying that publishers have gone through the same changes as libraries in trimming expenses, from the attrition of staff vacancies to reducing travel budgets and constantly looking for new efficiencies.

Backlists and Other Ventures

In 2014, as part of a strategy to maximize revenue opportunity, McFarland pushed forward with a successful initiative to offer more backlist titles to academic libraries in e-book format. As an experiment, the company also reissued a modest number of books that had gone out of print. McFarland has experimented with offering a chapter-length work as a short work in the retail market. Such experimentation does not seem to make sense in the academic setting under the DDA model. There are also new and existing vendors who offer interesting new ways to serve the academic textbook market by providing parts of various titles in a student package. From the McFarland perspective, this approach makes a lot more sense than the old model of delivering a packet of photocopied pages from books.

Academic E-Books and University Presses

Visitors to the McFarland booth at an academic conference often remark how similar the titles appear to those of a university press. In an excellent article in *The Nation* titled "University Presses under Fire: How the Internet and Slashed Budgets Have Endangered One of Higher Education's Most Important Institutions," Scott Sherman (2014) gives an excellent short history, highlighting the case history of the shocking closure of the University of Missouri Press.

> The digital age complicates and threatens the mission of the country's approximately 100 university presses. Ellen Faran, who has an MBA from Harvard and is the director of MIT Press, recently told *Harvard Magazine*: "I like doing things that are impossible, and there's nothing more impossible than university-press publishing." (para. 5)

HOW MCFARLAND IS UNIQUE

This chapter's perspective might not be representative of any other commercial publisher. When the author negotiated with a vendor of publishing software, the vendor's representative repeated the comment several times that he had dealt with hundreds of publishers, and they were all quite different.

Here are some of the ways that McFarland may be different from other publishers: McFarland is located in a beautiful, rural Appalachian community 3,200 feet above sea level. Photos of the buildings on McFarland's

Facebook page show atypical headquarters—the main building (originally a house, but with several additions to create a unique commercial structure), a converted residence, a converted commercial building, and the warehouse/print shop built on four acres on a hillside. In fact, when a Baker & Taylor executive visited, he was so taken with the community that he resolved to sell Florida property and invest in vacation/retirement property in the area. McFarland has 55 employees who are passionate about publishing, and it is no exaggeration to say that the company is like a family. McFarland has never laid anyone off. All employees have a window in their offices. McFarland always favors in-sourcing over out-sourcing. The company is closely held[1] so there is no university umbrella or head office to smooth out a rough patch. We intend to be a viable company fifty years from now. We do not ever intend to merge or take the company public, and no principals are planning to cash out, now or later. McFarland believes that e-books are an important part of the future, and we intend to stay "all in" in every reasonable way to help figure it out with our library and vendor partners.

ONE VIEW OF THE TEA LEAVES

A daunting thought for all the partners in the scholarship stream—publisher, vendor, and library—is that the evolution of the e-book is just beginning. The moment that one phase of this process feels wrapped up at McFarland, there is a need to push forward on a new initiative because no matter what, one feels behind—a new format on the horizon, a new feature to consider for addition, a new vendor to add, a new wrinkle in the business model.

From the McFarland perspective of producing e-books for various library market segments as well as for various retail market segments, innovation seems more difficult for e-books in academic libraries. The chosen format for academic libraries is the PDF. Library vendors generally do not accept the other widely used format for e-books, which is EPUB. EPUB is the format that can flow text into a phone or iPad or onto a desktop, ignoring the page in the print edition (which arguably does not serve the academic audience). One might observe that the huge acquisition systems that librarians use are too large and complex by necessity to adapt quickly. When we recently asked a major library vendor if they accepted EPUB files, they asked which standard version we were using (which is EPUB2). They could not yet accept EPUB3. Keeping up with constantly changing standards is a challenge.

It is likely that upcoming innovations will happen on the device and software side in the near term. OverDrive, serving the public library market, is testing features allowed by EPUB3 that would offer a narrated book, using embedded and synced audio (Five digital publishing leaders weigh in on industry's future, 2014). Publishers and vendors of children's books have many incentives to explore such features. Google (not a library vendor, but an example of a company that develops features that can be adapted by academic vendors) has a new reading app offered through Google Play that allows the user more control over the table of contents along with bookmarking to facilitate highly customized navigation that changes depending how the user intends to use the book, even in a single session (Milliot, 2014). These are just a few examples of the stream of announcements about vendors experimenting with how their offerings can stand out in their market.

McFarland's offerings are primarily in the humanities, and one wonders whether the world looks quite different for publishers in the sciences, for example. At least one science publisher, AAAS/Science, does not seem to think so:

> The reality of digital publishing is proving to be quite different from the early promise. I say this as a member of the cohort that embraced it headlong in the mid-1990s and onward. The levels of complexity, the endless revision cycles, the uncertain commercial environment, the bilateral purchaser-seller costs which make transactions less frequent and more difficult, and the lingering misperception that all this can be made cheaper, faster, and easier with more technology—this is where we seem to be.—Kent Anderson, Publisher at AAAS/Science (Anderson, 2014, para. 11)

Publishers will see if any of the new features and capabilities offered by devices and vendors fit their publishing program. Publishing revenue will have to support development; the present revenue environment does not, without new waves of investment by university presses and independent publishers. This will continue to be a challenge. It may be that the coming evolution of information in the academic environment is not linear, but a tree-like fractal, in which the products between publishers become less and less similar, providing a rich environment of purchasing choices.

There has been some hand-wringing in the knowledge industry about e-books not fulfilling their promise. The premise that information seekers always need augmentations of video/audio and discovery paths is worth considering, but also should be questioned based on the type of need and material. Alison Flood (2014), in an article in *The Guardian,* explains that research in Europe is raising questions about whether users retain more or certain kinds of information better when reading print rather than electronic text.

At Charleston Conference sessions in about 2005, academic librarians told stories about students who stood in line to use library computers to access full-text journal articles rather than walking a few steps into the stacks to pull volumes off the shelf for immediate use. Statistics showed dismal out-of-the-library lending rates of print books with the presumption that the discovery model for books at that time was inconvenient. One of the greatest innovation potentials of this era in academic information service is to pool all academic e-books into one database and then offer that database to information seekers. Making this model economically sustainable for both the vendor and the publisher is one of the perplexing challenges of the partnership between academic libraries, their vendor partners, and their publisher partners.

NOTE

1. A closely held company is one that has only a limited number of shareholders; their corporation stock is publicly traded on occasion, but not on a regular basis.

REFERENCES

Anderson, K. (2014, November 20). Confounded complexity—Pondering the endless upgrade paths of digital publishing. *The Scholarly Kitchen.* Retrieved from http://scholarlykitchen.sspnet.org/20q4/11/20/confounded-complexity-pondering-the-endless-upgrade-paths-of-digital-publishing

Bacon, B. (2013, March 4). How to stop ebook pirates. *Digital Book World.* Retrieved from http://www.digitalbookworld.com/2013/how-to-stop-ebook-pirates/

Bercovici, J. (2014, February 10). Amazon vs. book publishers, by the numbers. *Forbes.* Retrieved from http://www.forbes.com/sites/jeffbercovici/2014/02/10/amazon-vs-book-publishers-by-the-numbers/

Christensen, K. (2014, June 4). How Amazon.com is hurting readers, authors and publishers. Retrieved from http://www.berkshirepublishing.com/blog/2014/06/04/how-amazon-com-is-hurting-readers-authors-and-publishers/

EBSCO Publishing to acquire NetLibrary Division from OCLC. (2010, March 17). *EBSCO.* Retrieved from http://www2.ebsco.com/EN-US/NEWSCENTER/Pages/ViewArticle.aspx?QSID=348

Enis, M. (2013). ProQuest acquires EBL, will merge with Ebrary. *Library Journal, 138*(3), 18.

Esposito, J. (2014, October 15). Revisiting demand-driven acquisitions. *The Scholarly Kitchen.* Retrieved from http://scholarlykitchen.sspnet.org/2014/10/15/revisiting-demand-driven-acquisitions/

Five digital publishing leaders weigh in on industry's future. (2014, November 20). *Digital Book World.* Retrieved from http://www.digitalbookworld.com/2014/five-digital-publishing-leadrs-weigh-in-on-industrys-future

Flood, A. (2014, August 19). Readers absorb less on Kindles than on paper, study finds. *The Guardian.* Retrieved from http://www.theguardian.com/books/2014/aug/19/readers-absorb-less-kindles-paper-study-plot-ereader-digitisation

Jackson, L. (2004). NetLibrary. *Journal of the Medical Library Association, 92*(2), 284–285.

Milliot, J. (2014, October 30). Google Play jazzes up e-book nonfiction. *Publisher's Weekly.* Retrieved from http://www.publishersweekly.com/pw/by-topic/digital/content-and-e-books/article/64564-google-play-jazzes-up-e-book-nonfiction.html

Quint, B. (2000). NetLibrary offers 1,500 e-book titles to 100 large public libraries in trial program. *Information Today, 17*(3), 18.

Sherman, S. (2014, May 6). University presses under fire: How the Internet and slashed budgets have endangered one of higher education's most important institutions. *The Nation.* Retrieved from http://www.thenation.com/article/179712/university-presses-under-fire

Watters, A. (2011, August 30). Free e-textbooks for students: Piracy, open education content, and the future of academic publishing. *Hack Education.* Retrieved from http://www.hackeducation.com/2011/08/30/free-e-textbooks-for-students-piracy-open-educational-content-and-the-future-of-academic-publishing/

3 | Production, Marketing, and Legal Challenges: The University Press Perspective on E-Books in Libraries

Tony Sanfilippo

ABSTRACT

A university press's mission is to disseminate scholarship, but the challenge is to fulfill that mission by issuing quality books at low cost, but with high impact. This paper explores topics such as the workflow for print books and e-books, the many options for including e-books on aggregator platforms, the challenges involved in digitizing backlist titles, a variety of legal issues, the reasons for pricing differences between print books and e-books, and placing titles where scholars and nonscholars alike will discover them.

INTRODUCTION

In preparation for writing this chapter, I asked my colleagues on the Association of American University Presses (AAUP) general listserv which university press first published an e-book and when that occurred. It would seem a simple enough question with a straightforward answer, but it wasn't. Nine different presses claimed to have published the first e-book, eventually causing many of them to dig into their archives to determine the actual release dates of their candidates. But the one factor that most of their books shared was that the customers for those first e-books probably weren't libraries. In fact, since all but two were published as floppy disks or CDs packaged in a sleeve attached to the back cover of the physical book, it's quite likely that most libraries that purchased the book actually removed those e-books and discarded them with the dust jackets.

From a university press's perspective, it's not a surprise that the first e-books were primarily add-ons to print books, or that the target audience wasn't actually the library market. Setting aside for now a couple of outliers, most university presses started experimenting with e-books in the mid to late 1990s, and almost always worked with outside partners, such as Voyager Expanded Books and Eastgate Systems, to create those early e-books. Although most print production at that time had moved to using digital tools, those tools were still producing files that were specific to print production. Complicating and frustrating the development of an e-book workflow in the 1990s was the lack of e-book standards and devices that could display e-books. Early software tools for print book creation, namely PageMaker and Quark, simply mimicked the page layout and composition work done by hand before digital tools were available. These processes were specific to fixed text and were only efficient at automating the parts of book production related to print products; features like automated header placement and page number placement, line and figure spacing, and note insertion were all features of those tools. Even today, the most widely used tool in page layout, Adobe's InDesign, contains only rudimentary tools that pertain strictly to e-book design, flowable text, and complex e-book file creation.

One of the likely reasons for the lag in university press e-book production is because of the realities of the current book marketplace. E-books are not the primary market for most books sold in the United States (Packer, 2014), nor are they for university presses, and they still aren't the primary market for most books sold to libraries. It also is difficult to say with certainty which format, print or digital, patrons prefer. Although use of electronic content seems to be growing rapidly, often outpacing circulation of the print versions, surveys of students and faculty seem to show a preference for print (Sacco, 2014). Defining use of digital material also can be difficult. Comparisons of digital access to print circulation are problematic because they are not measuring the same thing, and they do not include noncirculating/in-library print use, which, unlike digital access, is very difficult to measure. The initial triple-digit growth of the e-book market after the introduction of the Kindle has also slowed significantly, and the majority of that growth was and is concentrated in genre fiction, such as science fiction and mysteries, rather than in the humanities scholarship that university presses more typically publish. Even within the broader world of scholarship, compared to university presses, the for-profit STEM publishers seem to be reaching a larger proportion of their audience with their digital publications rather than with the print versions of the same content. The most likely reasons for this are the greater need in the STEM disciplines for fast delivery. The journal article typically is the preferred venue for scholarly communication in these fields, and the market and platforms for digital journals are more mature than those for digital books. According to AAUP's annual sales statistics, e-books make up less than 10% of sales for most university presses, with only one press's sales reaching 21%, and that was only for one year (American Association of University Presses, 2014). It also is worth noting that for that particular press, the majority of those books were sold on Amazon, which makes it highly unlikely that libraries used them. As of October 2013, Michael Zeoli (2013) of YBP, the largest U.S. academic library wholesaler, noted in a presentation at the annual Charleston Conference that e-books still only accounted for about 20% of the units his company sold. It also is worth recognizing that although the proportion varies from press to press, based on the composition of their lists, library sales do not typically make up the majority of monograph sales, although it is difficult to say this with great certainty as one can't be sure where books end up after being sold through certain wholesale distributors or online retailers (Esposito, 2014).

One of the reasons that market demand and file production workflows are important to understand when exploring how university presses allocate resources is that, so far, the expense of file creation for e-books remains an investment rather than a recoverable cost of a good sold. There's been a long running misunderstanding of the economics of book production, and specifically file production. Consumers who complain about the cost of e-books frequently point to the lack of a physical product at the end of the production line as justification for why e-books should have a significantly lower price when compared to the print price. But that rationalization often ignores how low the typical unit cost is on a print product. For a 300-page, 6 x 9-inch, all-text monograph, the paperback unit cost, including printing and binding, is about $5, or even less if the quantities printed are in the thousands rather than in the hundreds. The expense of the book is not so much in producing the physical object with its printing and binding, but rather in the book's editing, design, and marketing, and those expenses do not decrease when dealing with e-book editions. In fact, those expenses actually increase because very different files need to be created, and publishers incur very different marketing and distribution costs. If we include higher-end features in an e-book, such as robust tagging or embedded animation, those would add even more expenses to an electronic edition that will probably generate only a fifth of the demand compared with a typical university press title produced in print.

E-BOOK COSTS OUTSIDE THE PRINT WORKFLOW

So what are the added costs for the e-book workflow? The most obvious one is the creation of the digital files. There are three basic file types needed for submission to the largest e-book platforms a university press would want to use. These types would include a web PDF, with embedded fonts, downsampled image files, chapter and section bookmarking, and all print artifacts removed, such as crop marks. Most library-facing platforms could use that type of file. Next is the MOBI file format, a proprietary format used only by Amazon for the Kindle platform. And finally the EPUB file format, which is sold directly to consumers by some platforms and can be converted to PDF or MOBI for use by others. EPUB also typically is the most useful file type for a press to use for its archive as it offers the most flexibility in subsequent file conversion and modification. If a print book's page composition is outsourced, most commercial compositors also can create all three of those file formats for an additional cost of a few hundred dollars.

The next cost incurred is file submission. Although there is no cost for the actual submission to a given platform, there is a cost for the labor necessary to prepare and submit the files. This varies based on the number of platforms a press works with and whether or not any additional file manipulation is required before the file is submitted. Typically, modification is limited to changing the name of the file to meet the platform's specifications for naming conventions, but it can sometimes include removing third-party content to which the press does not have the digital rights. Although some platforms do not allow submissions without all of the content included in the print book, other platforms allow publishers to remove third-party content. File modification also might include changing references to the ISBN on the CIP page of a book or the removal of a barcode referencing a print edition from the back cover of the book's jacket file.

Beyond the labor involved in file modification and submission, there also is a significant amount of labor involved in the submission of the associated metadata for an e-book. Each platform has unique requirements for metadata submission, so each title requires a separate metadata submission, typically submitted in the form of an Excel spreadsheet. If the platform offers multiple sales and distribution models, metadata pertaining to each of the models also are required. These would include elements such as pricing, use restrictions or the lack of them, and regional restrictions or the lack of them.

To realize the greatest potential from e-book sales, the most important platforms a university press would want to be on would include the following: Amazon's Kindle, Apple's iBook, Google's Play, Barnes & Noble's Nook or Yuzu (Nook is for the retail consumer market, Yuzu is for the textbook market, and a publisher may only submit a title to one of the two Barnes & Noble platforms), ProQuest, EBSCO, JSTOR, and Project MUSE. These eight platforms make up about 90% of the market for a typical university press's e-books. My latest count found over 60 different e-book platforms taking submissions worldwide, but since 60 different file and metadata submissions per title typically are not economically feasible, limiting submissions to those eight would cover most of the audiences a university press would want to reach. If, however, a press wants to expand beyond those eight, it might consider a third-party digital asset distributor (DAD). A DAD handles file submission, including specific metadata submissions and submission using the multiple naming conventions. That choice, however, comes with a price. DADs charge by the number of files stored and/or distributed or by taking a cut of each e-book sold (or both), depending on the DAD and the agreement negotiated. For a press with over 500 e-book titles, that cost could easily pass $10,000 a year. If a press submits titles only to those eight core platforms and publishes about 50 e-book titles a year, the file and metadata submission could easily take up to 10% of a staff member's time, so using a DAD could pay for itself by both freeing up that staff member and increasing the market reach of a press's titles.

LEGACY TITLES, OR THE BACKLIST, AS E-BOOKS

Publishers generally divide the list of their publications into two categories: the frontlist, books published in the last year or two, and the backlist, books published prior to that. The reason for doing this is again economic. The frontlist represents the majority of costs a publisher is likely to incur in a given year, and the backlist represents costs already incurred. This makes the biggest difference when looking at cost versus revenue. In a given fiscal year, a typical university press publisher is likely to have about 10% of its frontlist titles earning back their costs. This leaves the other 90% of the annual title output in the red. The backlist, on the other hand, typically has a minimal cost after that first year, limited primarily to warehousing overhead and royalties, so the revenue it produces is essential to make up for the new titles published that had greater costs than revenue. In any given fiscal year, a mature publisher with a substantial backlist can expect half of all revenue to come from the frontlist and half from the backlist. New titles, of course, typically sell more copies immediately upon publication than the average title on the whole list, but the exponentially larger number of titles in the backlist, selling fewer copies of each title, can match or even surpass the amount of revenue the frontlist produces. For a midsize university press, this means that the thousand or so titles in the backlist are as important for their sustainability as the 20 to 50 new titles it will publish in a given year.

So it may seem odd that publishers do not always offer their full title list as e-books if the revenue potential seems equal to that of their new offerings, but there are very good reasons for this. Again, cost is one of the primary reasons. Digitizing the backlist is expensive, typically hundreds of dollars per title, depending on the complexity and length of the book, but cost isn't the only reason. The other reason is legal obstacles, among them third-party rights. Whenever a permission was sought and granted, the permission to use that material typically came with restrictions. University presses are in a unique position among book publishers in that as educational mission-based organizations, permissions almost always are granted and frequently without a permission fee, but the permissions frequently come with restrictions on the number of iterations, or on formats that did not or would not cover digital use. So a book with a photograph might have a cost-free permission for use in a university press book, but if the permission noted that it was for the hardcover edition of the title, that photograph would need to be repermissioned for use in a digitized version. For some titles that sell well year after year, it might make sense to spend the time to find the photograph's copyright owner and get it repermissioned for digital use, but for a backlist of a thousand titles, there isn't a simple way to do this on a large scale.

There is also the issue of the copyright infringement liability clause in author contracts and how the practice that developed around that clause has created a third-party permission documentation problem. A very typical infringement liability clause in a university press author's contract will put the onus of ensuring everything in a manuscript is either the work of the author or, where fair use might not apply, that the author has secured permission to use any third-party content. Typically it is the author who has secured the permission, not the publisher. This situation creates a problem if a publisher wishes to digitize an older title; the publisher needs to know who owns the third-party material and what permission parameters were first granted. Unless the publisher asked the author for a copy of all of that documentation when the book was initially published, and then kept those copies of that documentation, staff would need to start the permission process for a digital version from scratch. If the book is heavily illustrated, or if it includes poetry or song lyrics, the resources needed to do all that work would likely far exceed any revenue a digitized version of the book might be expected to earn, and thus the book simply doesn't get digitized.

Another possible legal obstacle is the author contract itself. Do older contracts with authors that include no specific wording about e-books still allow a publisher to release an e-book? Some author contracts might include language permitting the publisher the right to publish a manuscript "in all forms," and many publishers consider that wording sufficient to assume that it is permissible to issue the title as an e-book; however, further down the contract where royalty payments are enumerated, there would not be an e-book royalty listed, that is, no guidance on how the author should be paid. Many contracts might have an "all other uses" royalty clause that typically refers to subrights such as translations, serial rights, or film versions, but those often default to 50%. In the case of an e-book, if the publisher must incur the cost of repermissioning and digitizing, and then return half of all e-book proceeds to the author, does it still make sense to bring out that e-book version when it will compete with the print version on which the publisher is more likely to only be paying a 10% royalty and of which there are still likely to be plenty of print copies?

The approach to these challenges during my years at the Pennsylvania State University Press were twofold. First, we sent a letter to the authors of our backlist titles explaining these challenges and asking those who could afford it to sign an addendum to their original contract waiving royalties on e-books. The second thing we did was use our books database to identify titles that were very likely to have no third-party content. We also built a web portal in that database that used the Google Books Project API to allow us to inspect the CIP page of each title, where permissions are frequently mentioned, and sample a few pages looking for third-party content use. By filtering out illustrated books and examining the CIP page to sample each book's content for possible third-party material, we were able to identify low-hanging fruit and select a couple hundred titles where the risk of unauthorized use of third-party content seemed to have been minimized. In cases where we had author addenda, but the books didn't fall under the filtering criteria, we looked at each book to assess the level of difficulty that repermissioning would entail, and we assessed the market demand of the print version. Again, those titles that seemed to have enough revenue potential to cover the cost of repermissioning and digitizing were included in the digitizing effort. To my knowledge, no plans have been made for the rest of the backlist where there was significant repermissioning needed or where royalties would need to be paid at 50%. As of this writing, fewer than one-third of the titles in Pennsylvania State University Press's active backlist have been, or are scheduled to be, digitized.

THE FRONTLIST AS E-BOOKS

With new titles, the cost of digitizing doesn't exist since the press creates the books using a digital workflow. For most university presses, digital files of some kind exist for books published after 2000, so, other than nominal file conversion costs, most of those titles can be added to e-book platforms. It's useful to note, however, that although post-2000 contracts often expressly include e-book rights and a sustainable royalty, the third-party rights issue continues to impede the inclusion of some books. Some rightsholders have been reluctant to allow the use of their work, especially illustrations, in digital form. They have also sometimes set parameters that simply wouldn't be feasible in a digital context, like limiting the number of "views" or even iterations, which cannot always be measured. Other third-party rightsholders might impose a time limit, like five years, after which the image must be removed. Many rightsholders see the ease of duplication in a digital medium as a threat to the control of their content and thus charge a premium for digital rights. These kinds of restrictions may sometimes mean that only a print edition will be published, or that a particular title can't be included on a particular platform, because that platform's model might not limit the use of the content sufficiently. An example of this would be Project MUSE, where book chapters are allowed infinite downloads, which would conflict with both an iteration limit and a time limit.

For the most part, publishers would prefer to include as many titles as possible on as many platforms as possible, so the default tends to be inclusion, unless a legal issue prevents it. But it also is becoming evident that certain models are becoming rather problematic for publishers, so inclusion on all platforms may not be in a book's or a publisher's best interest. Demand-driven (or patron-driven) acquisitions and the typically accompanying short-term loan option, in which rentals or purchases only occur when certain use thresholds are reached, is one example. Although there may not yet be enough evidence to conclude that this model always will produce significantly lower revenues for university presses, one thing is immediately clear: this model is guaranteed to delay the majority of a title's revenue until one year after publication. Frontlist e-book titles put in platforms using this model are less likely to earn the same amount of revenue that their print counterparts do or—perhaps the past tense is more appropriate—did. Not only is the revenue deferred but, with its growing popularity among academic libraries, this model is also significantly cannibalizing print sales. This leads to inevitable price increases and then complaints from librarians about those higher prices (Stearns & Unsworth, 2014).

Another problematic model for publishers are those of Project MUSE and JSTOR, whose platforms allow a library to purchase a title at or close to the single copy price, thus impacting the textbook market for a title. Books that have textbook potential have had up to ten times more downloads at institutions where the books are used in courses. The only recourse that a publisher might have to this situation is to raise the price well beyond that of a single copy. If a title will be downloaded ten times more than all other titles published in a given year, is a tenfold increase in price even enough considering the course is likely to be taught year after year? Not only does a model allowing this practice hurt frontlist textbook revenue, but it will continue to hurt that title's revenue even in the backlist.

CONCLUSION

Raising prices on books isn't something that university presses want to do. The word *revenue* has come up often enough in this chapter that it is worth addressing why this is an overarching theme in how university presses think about libraries and e-books. Most university presses have the core mission of knowledge dissemination; cost recovery is an ancillary goal, so one might think that putting a book in a library where it can get ten times the average use at the same price as any other book would mark the pinnacle of success for that mission. In reality, the parent institution may not support its press's mission to that extent. Instead, as universities embrace the trend to be more like businesses, they look at their university presses as places with low costs and high impact. They tend to see university presses less as educational instruments and more as revenue centers, not unlike how many universities see their online course programs. In thinking about scholarly communication in the digital age, it would seem that the cost of that dissemination should be going down, trending toward zero, and the system should be embracing open access; but that's not happening. There are a couple of reasons for that, beyond administrators who are not currently interested in replacing a revenue center with a cost center. One has to do with the nature of what university presses do. As noted earlier, it is not the production of the physical book that creates the bulk of the cost, it is the need for very smart people to edit, design, and market the book. Although technology has aided significantly in reducing the costs associated with book production, algorithms are not yet sophisticated enough to do what editors or designers do.

The other reason that a shift to an entirely open program may not be the best idea is something that is not easy to see or admit, and that is that markets can often be significantly more efficient at informing people about a piece of scholarship, and about getting it to them quickly, than the open web. I am astonished at the number of scholars I know who prefer to look up a book on Amazon than on either Google Scholar or their own institution's online public access catalog. They also can have that book delivered right to their office in a couple of days or, in some places, on the same day. Although open access publications do a great service for scholars and scholarship, it is also important that they be in places where scholars look, and that means being in markets. The other benefit of engaging in markets is to reach nonscholars, or those who might never know about scholars' work were it not included in Amazon's catalog, and, unfortunately, to be in that catalog, the content needs a price.

Getting back to those first university press e-books, knowing which two were not bundled as disks packaged with physical books enlightens where we have been and where we may be going. The very first university press e-book actually turns out to have been two books, both from Oxford University Press: *The Oxford Dictionary of Quotations* and *The Oxford Shakespeare: The Complete Works*. Both of these came as freeware bundled into every NeXT computer that went on the market in October 1988; Steve Jobs negotiated a 74 cents-per-copy royalty (Isaacson, 2011). But the other early e-book that was not bundled with a print copy was the University Press of Virginia's *Afro-American Sources in Virginia: A Guide to Manuscripts* ("First book," 1994). The most notable fact about that e-book might just be its price—it was free. It also was produced in a collaboration between University of Virginia's press and its library. Perhaps the place where university press e-books are going is the exact same place where they first started.

REFERENCES

Association of American University Presses. (2014). *Digital book publishing in the AAUP community: Survey report: Spring 2014*. Retrieved from http://www .aaupnet.org/images/stories/data/2014digitalsurveyreport.pdf

Esposito, J. (2014, March 24). A survey of university presses. *The Scholarly Kitchen*. Retrieved from http://scholarlykitchen.sspnet.org/2014/03/24/a-survey-of -university-presses/

First book to be published on Internet by a university press will focus on Virginia's extensive African-American history records. (1994, January 25). Retrieved from http://www.upress.virginia.edu/plunkett/mfp-release.html

Isaacson, W. (2011). NeXT: Prometheus unbound. In *Steve Jobs* (pp. 224–225). New York, NY: Simon & Schuster.

Packer, G. (2014, February 17). Cheap words: Amazon is good for customers. But is it good for books? *New Yorker*. Retrieved from http://www.newyorker.com /magazine/2014/02/17/cheap-words

Sacco, K. L. (2014). Results of the 2013-2014 student & faculty ebook survey. Retrieved from http://www.fredonia.edu/library/about/EBook%20survey %20results%2020140730.pdf

Stearns, S., & Unsworth, J. (2014, May 27). Ebook pricing hikes amount to price-gouging. *The Chronicle of Higher Education.* Retrieved from http://chronicle.com/blogs/letters/ebook-pricing-hikes-amount-to-price-gouging/

Zeoli, M. (2013, November 8). Searching for sustainability: Strategies and choice in the ebook supply chain. Paper presented at the Charleston Conference, Charleston, SC.

4 | Delivering American Society for Microbiology E-Books to Libraries

Christine B. Charlip

ABSTRACT

The American Society for Microbiology's (ASM) publishing unit annually produces six to twelve new titles, a combination of college textbooks and practitioners' manuals. The ASM Press has three primary markets for its books: content resellers, institutions, and individuals. Distributing e-content directly to institutions is a relatively new endeavor and required developing a customized publishing portal, converting backlist titles to e-books, writing chapter abstracts, offering different purchase models to libraries, deciding how to price e-books, providing use statistics to institutional customers, and developing strategies for enhancing visibility for ASM titles in library discovery layers. The author concludes by considering the challenges and future directions for small scholarly publishers.

AMERICAN SOCIETY FOR MICROBIOLOGY AND THE ASM PRESS OVERVIEW

The field of microbiology has a large footprint within the life sciences and addresses our understanding of the roles of microbes—archaea, bacteria, fungi, parasites, and viruses—on our planet and their application to research and practice in improving global health and the environment. The ASM aspires to define the future of and lead the microbiological sciences; this mission is reflected in many activities, including publishing. The ASM is a niche publisher well-known to libraries for high-quality journals, reference works, textbooks, and monographs. Hundreds of books and

16 journals present a variety of work in microbial pathogens, food safety, molecular genetics, public health, ecology and diversity, clinical diagnostics, science education, and biotechnology; microbiology also informs much of the work being done in chemistry, medicine, and engineering. ASM is a credible source of vetted, peer-reviewed content in microbiology, making it a natural partner to libraries around the world.

The ASM Press, the book imprint of ASM, publishes six to twelve new titles per year, including the leading textbooks used to educate upper-level undergraduates and graduates: *Principles of Virology* by Flint, Enquist, Racaniello, and Skalka; *Molecular Genetics of Bacteria* by Snyder, Peters, Henkin, and Champness; *Bacterial Pathogenesis* by Wilson, Salyers, Whitt, and Winkler; and *Molecular Biotechnology* by Glick, Pasternak, and Patten. The *Manual of Clinical Microbiology* (11th edition, 2012) is the principal reference work in the field and is used in hospital and research laboratories around the world.

Print is far from obsolete and brings in most of the revenue (see Table 1). Customers often tell staff that they use e-resources for searching and discovery; then they often choose to read the print version. Also, because the ASM Press titles are sold internationally, print is required in the many places where Internet access is limited or absent. The ASM Press issues almost all titles both in print and as e-books.

Table 1. The ASM Press annual print and electronic revenue split.

Year	Electronic revenue*	Print revenue
2011	12%	88%
2012	14%	86%
2013	22%	78%
2014	30%	70%

*Electronic revenue includes journal subscriptions and e-book sales.

The ASM Press has three primary markets for its titles: content resellers, institutions, and individuals. Content resellers provide the largest source of revenue and include international print distributors, university bookstores, and e-book aggregators, but like other publishers, the highest volume of annual print sales in recent years has been with Amazon. Amazon's vast catalog of offerings, highly competitive pricing, and low-cost shipping are so attractive to individuals that it is difficult for publishers to sell directly to customers. The smallest revenue stream is sales to individuals; these are fueled by discounts offered to members on the association website and at bookstores during large ASM meetings.

In 2011, ASM made a strategic decision to distribute e-books directly to institutions, in part to meet these customers' needs better and in part to gain greater insight into how the content is used. Until then, the ASM Press made very few sales directly to institutions because libraries bought ASM titles primarily from book wholesalers or e-book aggregators. The opportunity presented by e-books changed that.

EVOLUTION OF ASM E-BOOKS

The ASM Press first experimented with electronic book publishing in 2006, using Ingram's Vitalsource service to trial several e-textbooks. Since then, the ASM Press has supplied PDF files to many e-book aggregators who then offer the content to institutions for a variety of licensed uses. For a small society publisher, it is advantageous to work with an e-book aggregator because that company is the one that builds and maintains the digital delivery platform and controls the digital rights management (DRM) of the e-book files. Before deciding which titles to supply to which vendors, it is important to become familiar with each aggregator's audience and business model (e.g., licensed access as part of a collection, multiple- and single-user perpetual licenses, nonlinear lending with user cap, short-term loan periods, patron-driven acquisition triggers, or microtransactions). Table 2 provides a basic overview of several e-book aggregators with which the ASM Press works.

The ASM Press supplies some but not all e-books for resale to the e-book aggregators. There is not much interest in the backlist, other than textbooks. Textbooks are the biggest sellers through ebrary, EBL, and R2; reference manuals and monographs also sell well on specialty platforms such as Stat!Ref (medical) and Knovel (engineering). Vitalsource has been able to offer institution-authenticated access for oral microbiology titles to entire incoming classes in certain dental schools. However, it is common knowledge that library patrons often complain about the use limits imposed by the aggregators' DRM. In addition, publishers receive no information about the

Table 2. Popular e-book aggregators.

E-book platform	Business owner	Customers	Subject matter	Business models/offerings
ebrary	ProQuest	Institutions, corporations	Variety	• Perpetual access sale: single user, three users, or unlimited users; users can download titles for specified lending period • Perpetual sale, nonlinear lending: multiple concurrent uses with use cap per year; when use exceeded, second e-book copy is purchased • Subscription to specified collection • Short-term loan: time-limited access at prorated price; single user only • Patron-driven acquisition with use-triggered perpetual access sale
EBL	ProQuest	Academic and research libraries	Variety	• Perpetual sale, nonlinear lending: multiple concurrent uses with use cap per year; when use exceeded, second e-book copy is purchased • Demand-driven acquisition: load catalog, set purchase trigger based on browse period • Short-term pay-per-use

Vendor	Provider	Customer	Subject	Details
MyiLibrary	Ingram	Public, academic, and research libraries	Variety	• Perpetual sale by title or by collection: users can download titles for specified lending period • Subscription by title or collection • Patron-drive acquisition
R² Digital Library	Rittenhouse	Hospital, academic, and institutional libraries	Medicine, nursing, allied health, dental, pharmacy, veterinary	• Purchase multiple concurrent access to titles for life of edition • Patron-driven acquisition
Stat!Ref Online	Teton Data Systems	Medical institutions, individuals	Medicine, nursing, dental, pharmacy	• Annual subscriptions to core collections or pick-and-choose collection • Concurrent user limits
Knovel	Elsevier	Corporations, research libraries, institutions, societies, government	Engineering	• Annual subscriptions • Customized plans that offer users unlimited access
Vitalsource	Ingram	Students	Variety	• Individual access to textbooks • Perpetual sale or one-year or half-year rental

use of their content from resellers. Not knowing the customers' consumption habits, it is difficult to know how to adjust content to meet users' needs.

To take advantage of the opportunities offered by digital publishing and distribution, the ASM Press adjusted its book publishing strategy in several ways to increase distribution to and understanding of institutional and individual markets. These goals guided several important decisions.

- The ASM Press made a commitment to publish titles in both print and e-book format simultaneously, assigning both print ISBNs and e-book ISBNs. An exception can occur at the author's request. Authors of a few titles will not permit them to be published as e-books, fearing either digital piracy or improper display of important color subtleties (e.g., laboratory test results) by monitors and other screens.

- The ASM Press has one list price for each book, regardless of format, so that a print book and an e-book cost the same when ownership is perpetual. ASM members enjoy discounts, which helps the association compete with the often deep discounts offered by resellers. Other than e-book rentals via aggregators, the ASM Press does not offer any discounts on textbooks, instead choosing to price them as reasonably as possible.

- The ASM Press realized the importance of preparing, preserving, and distributing accurate, robust book metadata to our business partners. In the case of libraries, this means creating and maintaining accurate, up-to-date MARC records and KBART files.

DIGITAL DISTRIBUTION BY ASM

The ASM Press embarked on an enterprise effort to present our content—books and journals—on one customized publishing portal, ASMscience (www.ASMscience.org), which launched in October 2013. In preparation for loading onto the ASMscience digital platform, the ASM Press active titles were converted from print-ready PDFs into XML (NLM DTD 2.3) files beginning in 2011. This effort is ongoing, and the DTD is being updated to the Book Interchange Tag Suite (BITS). For discovery purposes, abstracts were written for every chapter of every book (> 5,000 abstracts). This information also supports sales of individual chapters.

ASM structured ASMscience so that it allows both IP validation for institutional users to access their purchased e-books or journal subscriptions and password authentication for individual access. When accessed by authenticated institutional users, books are presented in a manner similar to how users are accustomed to reading electronic journals, with an HTML-driven full text for online reading and chapters presented individually as PDF files. Icons and text make it clear to patrons which e-books on ASMscience are owned and available for use.

Perhaps the most important feature of ASMscience is that it is free from DRM, allowing unlimited concurrent access that permits reading, saving, and downloading by chapter.

Individuals (not authenticated through institutional access) can browse ASMscience and find books or chapters of interest and purchase and download an entire e-book as either PDF or EPUB file or a chapter as a PDF file. The ASM Press has not included newer textbooks in our "all you can use" presentation to institutions because of the degradation it would cause to textbook sales. E-textbooks are sold on other platforms (e.g., Vitalsource, RedShelf) that limit the use of that textbook to the purchaser via DRM. However, the ASM Press has sold textbook files directly to a library for it to host securely for its patrons.

By fall 2015, ASMscience presented more than 215 full-text e-books. A few of these titles were published in the 1990s; because the field of microbiology is vast and microbiological concepts do not change rapidly, these older books still are being purchased in print, so ASM converted them into e-books. In the coming years, ASM will be able to determine the level of the interest in those titles based on the number of views and downloads of the e-books. The hypothesis is that presenting the entire list of titles, with chapter abstracts, will increase the discoverability of the backlist content. The long-term goal is for all ASM Press-generated content, including books, journals, reports, guidelines, webinars, and so forth, to be included in ASMscience and be cross-searchable. ASM believes that this approach will provide important synergy and opportunities for interested readers to learn as they search, browse, and discover this curated collection of vetted microbiology content.

DEVELOPING PRODUCTS THAT APPEAL TO LIBRARIES

When ASMscience launched in October 2013, the ASM Press finally had a direct distribution channel to institutional customers, presenting an opportunity to reach institutions that were familiar with the ASM Press e-journals but whose consumption of the ASM Press books previously had been hidden by the intermediaries in the supply chain. Major decisions included what products to offer, how those offers would be structured (purchase models), and pricing.

Products

Libraries already could buy single titles through the e-book aggregators, so the ASM Press chose to offer e-books in collections. Although this decision limited the potential customer pool to research-focused institutions and larger universities with life sciences programs, staff believed that the ability to buy e-books "in bulk" would be appealing. Those institutions not interested in collections could continue to buy e-books individually from aggregators. However, the user's experience with a title on ASMscience is enhanced compared to what is offered by the e-book aggregators. When using the ASM platform, library patrons are assured of access because there is no limit on the number of users reading the e-book at the same time. The user can search or read through the full text or, having found a chapter of interest, can print or save the chapter PDF to read later. Patrons can establish customized accounts on ASMscience that will allow them to highlight sections, create favorites, and bookmark pages. Patrons can save or print as much of a book as they want. They also can save books to their personal laptops, smartphones, and tablets.

ASM's first products were two e-book collections: a three-year frontlist collection (2010–2012 titles by copyright date) and a backlist collection (1993–2009). Since then, all of these titles have moved into the backlist and the frontlist consists of the most recent two years' imprints. The frontlist and backlist collections combined total 215 e-books. In response to librarians' requests, ASM also offers smaller collections of e-book titles: a basic microbiology collection (35 titles), an applied and environmental collection (45), and an infectious diseases collection (40).

The most popular collection is the complete collection. Librarians not only like the ability to buy the whole collection at once, but they also like the lower per-title cost with this option. Librarians who bought the complete collection typically continue to buy each new frontlist to keep their collection growing. Although ASM announced a recent frontlist in June, staff hope to make future annual announcements earlier. However, despite updated production processes with compressed timelines, publishers still cannot wrest manuscripts from authors and editors on demand. Writing, peer review, and editing all take time.

One large society journal publisher, the Institute of Physics (IOP), recently began a new e-books publishing program. This press successfully delivered a collection of about 30 e-books within a year or two by paying individual authors to write relatively short (about 100-page) e-books on current topics in their field. These e-books are available only within collections sold to IOP's international base of journal customers. This approach takes advantage of IOP's sophisticated proprietary digital platform to deliver e-books that go beyond PDFs; they include dynamic media elements and cross-linking. At the heart of this program is a library advisory board that helped shape the nature of the e-book publishing program and its offerings, and will continue to provide ideas and feedback.

Purchase Models

The ASM Press gives libraries a choice between perpetual access purchase and annual subscription. Overwhelmingly, 95% of libraries want to own the content. The business model offers pricing by tiers and negotiates pricing for multisite and other institutions having more users than the largest tier. The ASM Press tiers are based on the number of life science users who are graduate students, postdoctoral fellows, faculty, and researchers in one geographic location. The tier sizes are 1–200 (tier A), 201–1,500 (tier B), and 1,501–3,500 (tier C). Custom pricing is applied when there are more than 3,500 life science users and/or multiple sites.

The ASM Press preserves the electronic content on ASMscience in the CLOCKSS archive. This backup plan ensures that institutions that have purchased content will have continued use of it should the digital platform become unavailable.

Pricing

Deciding how to price the collections was difficult. How much should e-books with unlimited users and no DRM cost? The association followed the practice of using multipliers of the list price related to tier size, modified by the age of the book (see Table 3). Some librarians understand that having the e-book in their collections without DRM is in essence buying as many copies of the book as users need with just one purchase. Others do not seem to understand the need to pay more than list price for a title regardless of the unlimited access and use.

Table 3. Sample list price multiplier for collection pricing (ASM Press).

Age of book (years)	Annual subscription			Perpetual purchase		
	Tier A	Tier B	Tier C	Tier A	Tier B	Tier C
0–5	.375	.72	1.05	1.5	2.10	3.0
6–9	.300	.63	0.90	1.2	1.75	2.5
10–13	.200	.42	0.60	0.8	1.20	1.8
> 13	.100	.21	0.30	0.4	0.60	0.9

Publishers struggle with this dilemma; they may earn less on each published title compared with the print-only era, but there are many potential benefits of wider exposure of their content in a digital environment. As libraries push to spend less when acquiring content, publishers earn less by delivering it. Publishers find themselves in a transitional period, first experimenting and then "waiting and seeing." It is easy for end users to forget the costs involved in producing and delivering e-books; these costs often increase book prices because of the expense of the technology involved. The typical book represents an investment by the ASM Press of at least $25,000; the expenses are often double or triple that for a book with hundreds of chapters and thousands of pages.

USE

Publishers want to be able to demonstrate the value of their content. At present, the meaningful and most accepted measure of this is use. ASMscience provides COUNTER-compliant reports on ASMscience for librarians to review. Because the ASM Press books primarily are used by the chapter, customers tell us that the section report (BR2) is the most useful. Industry-wide anecdotal evidence says that only 20% of any collection shows use, and of that 20%, only 20% will be highly used and the rest lightly used. The goal is to analyze the use trends to inform future publishing decisions.

But low use is not necessarily a reflection of how much users value the content. Use is strictly dependent on seekers being able to find the content. Getting content to surface depends on getting it properly cataloged and included in libraries' e-holdings, and listed in the link resolvers and knowledge bases of the library discovery services. ASMscience offers free downloadable MARC records by e-book collection to help librarians get the titles they have purchased into their catalogs. But MARC records are of limited usefulness unless patrons can link to the full-text content in their digital holdings. It has been extremely challenging getting the ASM Press e-books added to the institutional link resolvers and the knowledge bases of the larger discovery services. Smaller publishers seem to be far down the list for this work.

Fine-tuning or customizing the "link resolver experience" is in the librarians' hands; they set the algorithms for what results are returned and in what order. For example, some librarians may prefer that patrons' search results display a particular publisher's platform or collection first. Other librarians set search results to display only one record, from what may be many aggregators holding a particular title, to avoid "confusing" users with multiple choices for the same item. JSTOR provides guides for how to do this (http://about.jstor.org/content/quick-reference-guides) for each of the major discovery services. Fine-tuning the library's search and display features are critical to ensure that patrons are able to find everything that has been acquired for them.

Does adding and integrating a new collection to the catalog mean that users will find it? Librarians should promote their digital acquisitions to faculty and students. To assist librarians in this marketing effort, larger publishers sometimes visit campuses to make presentations to librarians and faculty in an effort to increase awareness of new and subject collections; they also provide content for e-mail announcements, newsletters, and other communications that librarians send to faculty on a regular basis. These activities can result in higher use for the titles being promoted. Publishers with smaller promotional budgets also can provide materials, such as posters and e-mail messages, announcing e-book collections and highlighting content that can potentially be used in courses.

In addition to unlimited concurrent use, the license for the ASM Press collections grants liberal use of the content to the institution, including the right to incorporate the content into e-reserves or coursepacks, interlibrary loan of individual chapters to noncommercial libraries, scholarly sharing, and text and data mining. In particular, it is advantageous for instructors to review the library's e-book collections for resources that can potentially serve as course materials; since the library already has acquired unlimited access to these titles, they will be free to the students. Librarians seem to appreciate both ASM Press's license terms with the emphasis on sharing resources and the ease with which ASMscience enables this; the author hopes that librarians consider these features, along with statistics about downloads and views, when considering the value of the content to support purchasing decisions.

CHALLENGES AND FUTURE DIRECTIONS

There are significant challenges for small scholarly publishers in delivering e-books to libraries. The author has identified three major ones. First, because the cost of journal subscriptions has been rising at a significant annual rate for many years, it has been hard to compete for the relatively small budgets that libraries allocate to nonperiodical purchases. It also is hard to know exactly when in the year institutions around the world are likely to have funds available for one-time purchases. Next, few librarians have been willing to provide feedback on how e-book collections are being received and used by students and faculty; surveying patrons about the results of purchasing decisions appears to be a low priority. Librarians may also prefer platforms with a patron-driven acquisition feature rather than outright collection purchases. Finally, small presses like ASM take their role as the publishers of high-quality content very seriously. They have made significant investments in acquisition and production processes and in digital delivery systems. The financial sustainability of selling long-form books for scholars is under pressure from librarians who want each book to cost less and less.

Without a doubt, the business of book publishing has changed faster than ever before during the last 10 years, and book publishers are being asked to deliver more content, with more features, to more places for readers and researchers to find. It is a struggle to fulfill ASM's mission of supporting and communicating the science of microbiology, as well as intelligently incorporating efforts such as open access and open educational resources, while covering expenses. At its core, "free" is not a sustainable business model. Regardless, society publishers must continue to experiment with delivery systems, business models, and supply chains that will enable their content to find readers. Librarians play a valuable role in this ecosystem by choosing what content to collect for their scholars. Like many society publishers, the ASM Press struggles to get its peer-reviewed products to rise to the top of the list at buying time. The future lies in listening to each other and collaborating. Together, libraries and society publishers can help to support education and to ensure the future of scholarly communication.

ACKNOWLEDGMENTS

The author thanks Martha Whittaker, senior manager of marketing strategy at the American Society for Microbiology, for her review and astute edits that helped tailor this chapter for the librarian audience. As an ASM colleague, Martha has been inventive and supportive in working with the author on ASMscience.

5 | Platform Diving: A Day in the Life of an Academic E-Book Aggregator

Bob Nardini

ABSTRACT

The author takes a close look at the e-books opened and used on a single day, September 24, 2013, on one academic e-book platform: MyiLibrary. Library users from 584 libraries in 39 countries across every continent began 15,954 sessions on the platform that day. The chapter is not a deep statistical study; it relies less on data and more on the detail of reader sessions to form impressions, make observations, raise questions, and present e-book reading. This brief glance at the activity on this aggregator's platform sheds light on how, when, and even a hint at why users are opening e-books. The glance also looks at the day's statistics on the numbers of books that were only opened and those that were used more heavily.

THE DAY BEGINS

At 7 p.m. Greenwich Mean Time on September 24, 2013, a library reader from Northumbria University, Newcastle upon Tyne, England, opened an e-book about film entitled *Documentary*. It took this user under a minute to look at eight pages before moving out of the book. At that same time, at 2 p.m. in the Canadian afternoon, a reader associated with the Université du Québec à Montréal opened *Dictionary of Architectural and Building Technology*, viewed 16 pages over seven minutes, and left. At that very same time, users were viewing titles at Western University in London-Ontario, at Rutgers University, and at Vancouver Island University. At the University of Utah, *Nonparametric Statistics with Applications to*

Science and Engineering hosted a session lasting one minute just before lunch in Salt Lake City.

These six users all opened their e-books within the first minute of a 24-hour period. This is the subject of this chapter: a single day for one academic e-book platform, MyiLibrary. We do not know why these users chose these titles, do not know if they found what they were looking for, and do not know what projects had engaged them in the first place. We do know that by opening e-books, these users—all members of their local academic communities, joined another community of sorts, a temporary one comprised of e-book users from 584 libraries in 39 countries across every continent where there are libraries—converged to begin 15,954 sessions on the platform that day.

Of course, this was no real community, in that users were unaware of one another and likely had no idea that anyone had done anything to enable their e-book use. On September 24 and 25, MyiLibrary staff went about their work as always, preparing the platform to host users for many days into the future, as they have done day in and day out since MyiLibrary's launch in 2004, writing computer code, handling invoices, negotiating with publishers, and many other duties. Few staff members would have been directly aware that users from Newcastle upon Tyne to Salt Lake City were engaged with them at all. As thousands of their e-books were opened, publishers were more distant still from the day's users, who, as has usually been true across the history of books, would remain unknown to them. Onsite users were most likely to have engaged with the librarians and other local staff who no doubt fixed printers, provided e-book instruction, helped recover lost network credentials, answered questions, and solved other problems, while perhaps authorizing more orders to follow the thousands of orders that had built up local MyiLibrary collections for use on this day.

We do, however, refer regularly to the "academic community," and all these groups contributed to a shared experience that was a particle in the galaxy of higher learning spinning across those 24 hours. Today academic e-book use is well-established, widespread, and growing. Five, and certainly 10 years ago, it would have been stretching the truth to say that academic e-book use was "well-established." Today it might be another stretch to refer, quite yet, to academic e-book use as "routine." This chapter will be something like a one-way mirror on those users who visited the MyiLibrary e-book platform that day in 2013. It will attempt to piece together stories from this representative day, one that ended at 6:59 p.m. Greenwich Mean Time on September 25, when a user from Arizona State University spent 33 midday minutes with *Understanding Religion and Popular Culture.*

The chapter does not aspire to statistical significance, nor attempt to prove anything, and does not closely engage with past studies of e-book use, not even the 2009 *JISC National E-Books Observatory Project,* a "deep log analysis of MyiLibrary" (JISC National E-Books Observatory Project, 2009). This study relies less on data and more on the detail of reader sessions in order to form impressions, make observations, raise questions, and present e-book reading in a less disembodied way than studies sometimes do.

It is difficult not to be struck by how broad—geographically, topically, and temporally—use of the platform was. To take a few of what seemed limitless examples of that breadth: at 9:41 in the evening a reader from the University of the Highlands and Islands in Scotland opened *Mountain Geography* to begin the first of four sessions for the e-book at the university that night. At 5:53 the next morning, a different member of this community opened *Debating the Highland Clearances,* the first of as many as 14 users who consulted that e-book into the afternoon, before another Highlands and Islands-based reader spent 32 minutes in *International Business Economics: A European Perspective,* to close the day's MyiLibrary activity at that archipelago of 13 colleges in the Scottish north.

Meanwhile, a hemisphere away but within the same minute as *Mountain Geography* was first opened, a user in Armidale, New South Wales, at Australia's University of New England opened *Cardiac Arrhythmia Recognition,* the first of 18 sessions at that university, while 1,328 kilometers south, in Melbourne, a La Trobe University patron spent five minutes with five pages of *Cancer Supportive Care: Advances in Therapeutic Strategies.* In an age of technological miracles, nothing here qualifies as one of them. To step back for a moment, though, it seems remarkable that users so far flung can briefly share online space to pursue interests as varied as these.

In other ways, though, the view is different, and use seems less broad. Users opened 6,412 e-books on the platform, just over 1% of some half-million titles available on the platform. However, over 40% of the time, users left their e-books within a minute. With nearly 7,000 sessions as short as that, how broadly could users have engaged with these e-books?

DOWNLOADING TEXTBOOKS

While many users must simply have closed unhelpful sessions, other users did engage with their one-minute e-books—if not at that moment, then later. These were users who either downloaded or printed pages. Downloading, which took place in 315 of these brief sessions, was by far the more common route to this form of "engage later" behavior.

Most download sessions involved textbooks, structured reading expressly assigned to students. A textbook assigned at the University of Bath is a typical story. *Integrated Marketing Communications* hosted 16 sessions there, 10 of them one-minute sessions where most of the day's 11 downloads took place, with most of these for an identical 80 pages. Nobody printed anything.

It is not hard to see why users would dip into their textbook, download, and leave. Having pertinent course readings from a variety of sources conveniently closer at hand than their printed textbooks would be one reason, but another is surely that these students did not own these textbooks and were relying on downloads to make their coursework possible at all. While United Kingdom academic libraries have been more accustomed than North American ones to providing textbooks (print and electronic) to students, there are limits to what any library can do. In recent years the high cost of textbooks has become an issue on both sides of the Atlantic. Rather than bear the expense of buying a textbook, students turn to their library.

Faced with lost sales, publishers counter with strategies such as raised prices, so more students look for alternatives, and prices go even higher. Another publisher strategy is to limit concurrent use of an e-book on aggregator platforms. This way, an entire class cannot rely on the library's online textbook unless students wait their turn, or the library buys more licenses for multiple simultaneous use, which then becomes a budget question. Publishers, too, sometimes withhold textbooks from aggregator platforms, eliminating this free (for students) option. Aggregators receive frequent requests from libraries, who ask on behalf of their students, to add a given title to a platform. More often than not, these titles are widely assigned textbooks that the publishers have specifically withheld from the aggregators.

However, this is not always the case. A Pearson textbook sometimes referred to as Giavazzi and Blanchard provides an example. Olivier Blanchard first wrote *Macroeconomics* in 1977. Working with a number of coauthors over the years, he collaborated with Francesco Giavazzi, of MIT and Italy's

Bocconi University, in 2010 to bring out an edition subtitled *A European Perspective*. It was assigned at two universities this day: the University of Exeter, where there were 43 user sessions, and the University of Sussex, where there were eight. During the Exeter sessions, 12 users downloaded pages. Nine of these users downloaded exactly 61 pages, one downloaded 60 pages, and another 59. Exeter's license permitted three simultaneous users in the e-book, and we can see in the use log how students laid their strategies to get access.

Remarkably, 16 of the Exeter sessions took place between 2 a.m. and 6 a.m. on September 25, with sessions beginning at 3:07, 3:28, 3:38, 3:39, 3:44, and 3:57, to take examples from just one of those late hours. Another nine sessions, by early risers, took place between 6 a.m. and 8 a.m. These students must have known, probably from hard experience, than trying to get into the e-book during normal daylight hours would be difficult. Exeter also owned the book in print (or did at least on November 12, 2014, according to an online public access catalog [OPAC] search), but the chances of gaining access to the print book were possibly even more difficult (Exeter's two print copies were both checked out, according to the OPAC). Some students no doubt bought the book, but the image of weary students who had not bought it, opening their economics e-textbook at 3 a.m., is a most concrete way to suggest ideas about the nature of academic aggregator platforms. MyiLibrary was, of course, a lifeline to those students, for whom it was a way to save some money and pass a course. But surely these students would rather not have had to arise at 3 a.m. or stay awake till that hour. Professors assigning the e-book would prefer to prepare reading lists and not have to think about matters like this. Libraries would prefer to serve students with whatever was needed at all times. Of course, Giavazzi and Blanchard, not to mention Pearson Publishing, would naturally wish that that every student would just buy the book in print or e-format instead of using the library's electronic copy.

TURNAWAYS

Things could have been worse at Exeter. There was only one "turnaway" for the e-book (meaning, only one user attempting to open the e-book was turned away because all licenses were in use at that moment). The library had purchased a multiuser license, and students' late nights and other strategies were enough to limit concurrent use to three in all but that one instance. This was not always the case across the platform that day, since many titles at many libraries had turnaways. At Central Michigan University (CMU), patrons were turned away 43 times from *Theories of Delinquency: An Examination of Explanations of Delinquent Behavior*, no doubt another assigned reading. CMU's license for the e-book, permitting one reader at a time, was on the other hand sufficient to enable 36 successful sessions, likely sometimes on the part of persistent students who had been turned away earlier. In contrast to Exeter, few students opened the e-book in the middle of the night (only one did so at CMU), and none downloaded or printed pages to read later.

Need on the part of CMU students seemed somewhat less acute than at Exeter. That may have been because students in the United States have come to expect relatively low support for textbooks from libraries, and so they turn elsewhere more quickly than would students in the United Kingdom ("Library Attitudes Are Changing, However: Charles Lyons, Library Roles with Textbook Affordability," 2014). The MyiLibrary use log for the day, in fact, showed heavy online textbook use at United Kingdom academic libraries, when compared to the United States, Canada, and most other parts of the world. This is possibly due to a difference in teaching styles, to a difference in library textbook policies, or, in some measure, to both. E-book reading in the United Kingdom focuses on assigned readings more than seems to be the case elsewhere.

Nobody likes turnaways. Locked-out students and their professors complain to librarians, who complain to aggregator representatives, who bring complaints to publishers, who weigh the economic impact of license terms proposed to alleviate the distant—at that point—frustrations of users. The economics are expressed on aggregator platforms by the various license types offered to libraries. They go by different names on different platforms, and not all platforms offer all types. Typical options include single-user, multiuser (usually three), unlimited use, fixed number of annual sessions, and short-term loans.

SHORT-TERM LOANS

Publishers and aggregators go through cycles of negotiation and renegotiation over the conditions under which academic e-books may be read, causing periodic turbulence. Short-term loans, a recent example, are a pay-per-use license designed to reduce turnaways while expanding title breadth and saving libraries money. While MyiLibrary has not offered this license type, other platforms have developed and promoted the model. In 2014, based on the model's impact on sales over a number of years, a succession of publishers changed pricing terms or withdrew altogether, alarming librarians who had built their local e-book strategy around short-term loan licensing (Wolfman-Arent, 2014). How many users in an e-book at a time? One reader, as the laws of physics dictates for print books or, since those laws are suspended online, as many as need a particular title at the same time? It is all a matter of economics. Should libraries pay for user access to e-books just in case they are needed or when needed? As the terrain of online academic reading is being mapped out, these are significant boundary disputes.

LONG READING

Beyond the business relationships, aggregators act as advisors to both libraries and publishers: as ombudsmen to publishers on behalf of libraries and as enforcement agencies toward libraries on behalf of publishers. This role of policing use so that license limits are observed is most evident with textbooks. Monographs, on the other hand, or books that might only occasionally be assigned as course reading, have less need of being policed since simultaneous use is less frequent. The unlucky University of Bath reader, who tried to open *Market Place: Food Quarters, Design and Urban Renewal in London* but was turned away, was the exception, not the rule, for an e-book that invites sustained reader attention and did support six successful sessions. More typical was the Canadian user at MacEwan University in Edmonton who turned 16 pages of *Aristocratic Vice: A History*, or the German user from Leuphana University of Lüneburg who looked at 28 pages of *The Entropy of Capitalism*. Neither one was turned away. In fact, they were those e-books' only users.

More than 60% of the day's e-books were only used once. Slightly over half of these sessions were very brief visits of a minute or less. Many of those e-books, when opened, must have seemed of no use. The other half of these single-visit e-books, however, was used more intensively. Among these e-books used once, nearly 14%, over 500, hosted sessions of 10 minutes or more. This contrasts with e-books used more than once, where ten-minute sessions took place not quite 6% of the time.

It is easy to imagine that a user in Mexico from the Universidad de Colima was as grateful to be able to spend over an hour with *No Word for Welcome: The Mexican Village Faces the Global Economy* as the scholar at Concordia University in Montréal who read *Democracy and National Identity in Thailand* for more than two hours, or a reader at the University of Cambridge whose session with the *Routledge Philosophy Guide-Book to Kant and the Critique of Pure Reason* lasted for over three hours. Although these three long sessions suggest the kind of deeper reading for which print is probably the best format, these three users would likely say that title breadth is a valuable platform quality. That almost 90% of the 6,411 titles opened that day were used at only one library suggests the same thing.

TOPICAL INTRODUCTIONS

The day's MyiLibrary use suggests that there is a different type of reading for which e-books might be the ideal form. This is when a user needs a brief view of a large topic: an authoritative "introduction." That is, the word chosen by Oxford University Press for its *Very Short Introduction* series, whose use on this day was difficult to miss. More than 30 different titles in the series were opened at more than 30 institutions, from Canada's Athabasca University to Nizhny Novgorod State Technical University in Russia. Books from the *Very Short Introduction* series were opened 73 times on the platform, and sessions lasted over six minutes on average, which suggests that users found the introductions helpful. Sessions included one lasting 28 minutes with *Feminism: A Very Short Introduction* at the University of East Anglia, and sessions across the world with *Advertising* and *Geopolitics, Marx,* and *Psychiatry.* These sessions were only the most noticeable among those where gaining hold of a topic seemed the goal, such as for a user at the University of Johannesburg who spent three minutes with *Introducing Architectural Theory,* or at Nottingham Trent University where a user spent two minutes with *Geology: The Key Ideas.* More accessible than print, more focused and authoritative than the web, and easy enough to skim or browse, these e-books must often have fulfilled their purpose.

SUBJECT USE DATA

Business and Economics

Studies of e-book use often present data by subject (for example, Christian-son, 2005). Since library budgets usually are organized this way and work assignments frequently are, this makes institutional sense. It may not tell the entire story, however. Two of the most heavily used subject areas this day were in Library of Congress Classification subclass HD (industry, land use, labor), which had 1,096 sessions, and HF (commerce), which had 832. Both would be the territory of academic work in business or economics, whose students were clearly busy. Many of these sessions were assigned readings: textbooks such as *Theories of Development*, for example, had 51 sessions at Rhodes University in South Africa.

Literature

By contrast, use was low in the subclasses PR (English literature), with 178 ses-sions, and PS (American literature), with only 50; both high book-publishing areas, even considering that only part of that output is nonfiction. Although interest in e-books may well be lower among literature students than business students, is their interest truly that much lower? Textbook-based reading, so common in other fields, is largely absent in literary studies, which accounts for a sizable part of the difference in use. Looking at use by subject, then, and not by the different types of reading experience, might be too narrow a view. Use might have been higher had there been more opportunities for topical introduction, such as two titles: *Shakespeare: The Basics*, read for 20 min-utes at Ryerson University in Toronto, and *Edith Wharton in Context,* also opened for 20 minutes at the University of Melbourne. Instead, carrying the textbook-use handicap, it is conceivable that e-book use in literature is mis-understood, and so possibly underfunded. Perhaps close reading sessions such as one for over two hours at Florida State University with *The Indistinct Human in Renaissance Literature* would be more common if more e-books were available, instead of reinforcing by their absence a pattern of lower use.

THE BUSINESS OF SELLING E-BOOKS

Like literature, the sciences saw relatively low use, for example subclass QC (physics) only 163 sessions and QH (natural history, biology) just 161, neither close to the total of GN (anthropology), which hosted 233. Does that mean that interest in online book reading is stronger in anthropology than in physics or biology? That is not likely the case. A more plausible explanation is the success publishers in the sciences have had in drawing libraries to their own platforms, instead of to aggregators. By withholding or delaying titles, by pricing and licensing policies, by imposing digital rights management (DRM) limitations, and by other means, large publishers who are able to build their own platforms have defined boundaries for aggregators.

Of course these publishers, in moving users in their own direction, have every right to act as a business would. Aggregators, also businesses, provide their value in maintaining relationships with buyers and sellers who could do business otherwise only with greater difficulty. Publishers are in a constant state of discussion with aggregators, who offer access to library sales across a wider base than the publisher might achieve on its own. Here publishers face a fundamental question: How much autonomy in controlling their titles can be ceded profitably to aggregators? If a patron at the University of Nottingham was able to open *Understanding the Steiner Waldorf Approach* and print 14 pages, but users at the University of Plymouth were turned away four times, that was because of the terms Taylor & Francis and MyiLibrary had agreed to offer libraries and the differing arrangements these libraries chose to make within those terms.

Although e-books from more than 400 publishers were opened this day, 11 publishers' e-books accounted for nearly 70% of all sessions, about 11,000 of some 16,000 sessions. If publishers withheld or restricted some e-books, enough were available for MyiLibrary to fulfill its part of the bargain by delivering large numbers of e-books to users whose libraries paid the bills. Of course, the day's reading on the MyiLibrary platform occurred alongside reading sessions on other aggregator platforms, on publisher platforms, on personal devices whose owners had bought e-books, and in printed books. So if MyiLibrary reading was low in the sciences and lacked any e-books from leading trade publishers who had barely begun to explore the academic library market, and if e-books even from some well-known university presses, such as Harvard, were not on the platform, it does not mean those books went unread. It does illustrate, however, that for publishers the role of academic aggregators can be seen as a marketing role, which individual publishers choose to use extensively, selectively, or not at all.

Patron-Driven Acquisitions

Today the plainest illustration of this marketing role is the prevalence of patron-driven acquisitions (PDA) or demand-driven acquisitions (DDA) programs, whereby aggregators in effect advertise availability of titles via MARC records loaded into libraries' online catalogs, and no purchase takes place unless a certain use threshold is reached. Although large publishers usually do not have the capability on their own platforms to track use against a trigger threshold and aggregator platforms generally do, PDA activity is largely aggregator-based. Some publishers permit their e-books to be offered this way, while others, troubled by free, prethreshold PDA use arrangements, do not.

Free use, that is, prepurchase use, was relatively uncommon on MyiLibrary, on this day at least, since only 103 prepurchase sessions occurred. Thirty-four libraries accounted for those sessions, so a small number of libraries, those most invested in PDA, accounted for the lion's share of use. They were led by Arizona State University, where 21 prethreshold sessions took place for titles as varied as *Leisure Programming for Baby Boomers* and *Data Analysis in High Energy Physics*. The day's 1,692 post-PDA purchase sessions (meaning, for e-books already acquired this way) far outnumbered the prepurchase sessions and, in fact, amounted to over 10% of all sessions. These took place in 96 libraries in 11 countries, showing how widespread PDA has become.

Platforms

Companies like MyiLibrary aggregate e-books, of course, but it is equally the case, and just as important, that they aggregate users. In doing that, MyiLibrary aggregated the needs of library patrons across the world who, for all their varied purposes, accessed the platform around the clock, or tried to, for short sessions and long sessions, with e-books assigned and unassigned, in many subject areas.

Every academic aggregator would probably tell a day's story that would be in some ways different, but in many ways the same; different, in that each company has its own strengths that would probably be reflected in the experience of users. When it comes to their challenges, whether looking at emerging customer interests like analytics or interlibrary loan, or at unfamiliar languages or even alphabets in newer world markets, aggregators would likely tell the same story: one of constant change and even volatility. There is no need for them to tell it, since the public record provides a chronology of the start-ups, mergers, acquisitions, partnerships, successes, and failures that have shaped the industry ("Academic E-Publishing: Some Key Players," 2001; "Baker & Taylor's 'ED' Resurfaces," 2002; "Baker & Taylor Announces E-Book Partnerships," 2000; "Coutts Library Services Kicks Off E-Book Initiatives," 2006; "eBooks Corp. and Blackwell Book Services Have Extended the Scope of Their Collaboration Into the U.K. and Europe," 2007; "ebrary Snags Key Investors for Pay-Per-Use Service," 2000; "Alliances & Deals," 2010; Hane, 1999; "JSTOR Is Expected to Release Books at JSTOR in November," 2012; "Project Muse Editions (PME) and the University Press E-Book Consortium (UPCC) Merged to Create the University Press Content Consortium (UPCC) Set to Launch Jan. 1, 2012," 2011; "ProQuest Puts Ebrary on Its Books," 2011; "ProQuest Recently Acquired Ebook Library (EBL)," 2013; "Re: Coutts Bought by Ingram," 2006; "Strategic Partnership Announced Between Ebooks Corporation and Dawsonbooks," 2004; Young, 2001; 2002).

If users need a broad and always available base of academic titles, there is one usually unstated factor that librarians need from aggregators: stability. For that, "platform" might be the perfect word to convey stability with substance, activity, and purpose. Google`s Ngram Viewer shows that use of the phrase "computer platform" began to take off in the mid-1980s. Its earliest uses, though, were literal, in reference to the massive machines of the time, for example, a 1961 advertisement for "ELAFLOR . . . a solid, noiseless floor, free of vibration . . . a completely flexible computer platform, easily modified and suitable for end-of-room, wall-to-wall, or island installation without significant engineering changes" ("Advertisement," 1961, p. 62). Or in 1975, when a scholar of ancient astronomy described the "excitement of the hour when I stood one night on the computer platform of the Hayden Planetarium" (Pomerance, 1976, p. 18). Today e-book users around the academic world stand on platforms whose stability depends on the interwoven interests of libraries, users, publishers, and aggregators, all aiming to secure their place within the future of online reading.

ACKNOWLEDGMENTS

Special thanks are due to colleagues Aaron Wood and Whitney Murphy for providing the activity log this chapter is based upon, and for answering all of my questions.

REFERENCES

Academic e-publishing: Some key players. (2001). *The Chronicle of Higher Education, 47*(36), A37.

Advertisement. (1961). *Datamation, 7*(6), 62.

Alliances & deals: EBSCO publishing has acquired the NetLibrary division of OCLC. (2010). *Online 34*(3), 9.

Baker & Taylor announces e-book partnerships. (2000). *Information Today, 17*(10), 51.

Baker & Taylor's "ED" resurfaces. (2002). *Librarian's eBook Newsletter, 2*(3). Retrieved from www.lib.rochester.edu/main/newsletter2-3/ed.htm

Christianson, M. (2005). Patterns of use of electronic books. *Library Collections, Acquisitions, & Technical Services, 29*, 357–360. http://dx.doi.org/10.1016/j.lcats.2006.03.014

Coutts Library Services kicks off e-book initiatives. (2006). *Information Today, 23*(5), 25.

eBooks Corp. and Blackwell Book Services have extended the scope of their collaboration into the U.K. and Europe. (2007). *Online*, 12.

ebrary snags key investors for pay-per-use service. (2000). *Information Today, 17*(11), 41–42.

Hane, P. H. (1999). E-book vendor debuts. *American Libraries, 30*(4), 90.

JISC National E-Books Observatory Project. (2009). *Scholarly e-book usage and information seeking behaviour: A deep log analysis of MyiLibrary, CIBER, Final Report, November 2009.* Retrieved from http://observatory.jiscebooks.org/reports/scholarly-e-books-usage-and-information-seeking-behaviour-a-deep-log-analysis-of-myilibrary/

JSTOR is expected to release Books at JSTOR in November. (2012). *Information Today, 29*(8), 29.

Library attitudes are changing, however: Charles Lyons, library roles with textbook affordability. (2014). *Against the Grain, 26*(5), 1, 12.

Pomerance, L. (1976). *The Phaistos Disc: An interpretation of astronomical symbols.* Göteborg, Sweden: Paul Åströms Förlag.

Project Muse Editions (PME) and the University Press E-Book Consortium (UPCC) merged to create the University Press Content Consortium (UPCC) set to launch Jan. 1, 2012. (2011). *Online, 35*(3), 8.

ProQuest puts ebrary on its books. (2011). *Online, 35*(2), 6.

ProQuest recently acquired Ebook Library (EBL). (2013). *Information Today 30*(3), 14.

Re: Coutts bought by Ingram. (2006). *Liblicense*. Retrieved from http://liblicense .crl.edu/ListArchives/0612/msg00076.html

Strategic partnership announced between eBooks Corporation and Dawson-books. (2004). *Liblicense*. Retrieved from http://liblicense.crl.edu/List Archives/0404/msg00075.html

Wolfman-Arent, A. (2014, June 16). College libraries push back as publishers raise some e-book prices. *The Chronicle of Higher Education*. Retrieved from http://chronicle.com/article/College-Libraries-Push-Back-as/147085/

Young, J. R. (2001). NetLibrary files for bankruptcy protection. *The Chronicle of Higher Education, 48*(14), A31.

Young, J. R. (2002, June 14). New owners of NetLibrary try to make e-book offerings more appealing. *The Chronicle of Higher Education, 48*(40), A32.

Librarians' Challenges

6 University of California, Merced: Primarily an Electronic Library

Jim Dooley

ABSTRACT

The University of California, Merced (UC Merced) opened September 5, 2005, as the tenth campus in the University of California system and the first American research university of the 21st century. Collections planning began in 2003. While the intention has never been to create an all-electronic library, the current collection is over 90% electronic. Almost all serials are electronic. Librarians use demand-driven acquisitions (DDA) plans extensively to provide access to e-books. There are no traditional librarian bibliographers or selectors. This chapter describes the decisions made at the beginning, evaluates the results after 10 years of operation, and looks forward to developments in the next 10 years.

INTRODUCTION

The transition from print to electronic format for information resources has been underway for some time and at varying speeds, depending on individual library environments. Even with extensive print collections developed over many years, research university libraries often have been leaders in this transition. Factors such as pressure to reuse space, changes in scholarly communication, the increasing importance of born-digital resources, the documented decline in the use of print materials, and growing preferences (albeit varying by discipline) of faculty and students for information in electronic form have all combined to cause research libraries increasingly to favor the acquisition of information resources in electronic format. Along with changes in collection development practices, many research university library services to faculty and students. One question is how far can a research university library go in this direction? By itself, the history of the University of California, Merced Library does not answer this question, but it may point to an answer.

CREATION OF THE UNIVERSITY OF CALIFORNIA, MERCED

The University of California (UC) is the public research university of California, distinct from the California State University system that focuses on undergraduate instruction. Currently, the university consists of nine general campuses enrolling both undergraduate and graduate students and one campus, the University of California, San Francisco (UCSF), which enrolls only graduate and professional students in medicine and health sciences.

The University of California, Merced (UC Merced) opened on September 5, 2005, as the tenth campus in the University of California system and the first American research university to open in the 21st century. As of August 2014, UC Merced has almost 6,400 students, of whom nearly 400 are graduate students. The current plan is that by 2020 there will be 10,000 students, including 1,000 graduate students. For a detailed account of the founding of UC Merced, consult Merritt and Lawrence's (2007) book, *From Rangeland to Research University: The Birth of the University of California, Merced.*

INITIAL COLLECTION PLANNING

Planning the library's collection began in 2003, two years before the campus opened. At this time, the university librarian and the head of collection services developed some basic collection development principles that have remained intact during the past decade. Library collection management policies favored a just-in-time approach to collection building rather than the traditional just-in-case approach. Materials would primarily be acquired to meet a specific information need rather than to build a collection for future use. Every effort would be made to leverage the collections and services available through the University of California libraries. In this context, access would be much more important than ownership. Books and journals would be acquired prospectively; interlibrary loan (ILL) would be relied upon for access to retrospective materials. Librarians would buy some older books in response to high levels of local use. The librarians believed that the number and scope of information resources available in electronic form would continue to increase over time. While the library would attempt to acquire a needed resource in any appropriate format, information resources in electronic form would be preferred. Although not directly related to these policies, librarians also decided not to acquire microforms, although they purchased microform reader/printers in case microforms were received through ILL. Additionally, the library would not collect textbooks; students would be expected to buy their own copies of required textbooks.

Although not directly related to collections, two additional policy decisions were made very early in planning for the operation of the library. First, librarians would not sit at a public reference desk. The library services desk would be staffed by students who would refer users to a librarian for individual reference consultation. Second, and related to the policy not to acquire textbooks, the library would not maintain a reserve operation. Librarians would assist faculty in placing links to electronic resources in the course management system, and, at faculty request, designate specific print books as "Library Use Only" for a semester.

The librarians needed to make some intelligent guesses about what the academic programs would look like in the next two to five years. The initial academic vision, which has remained largely intact to the present time, was that research and teaching would be highly interdisciplinary. To foster interdisciplinary work, the primary academic organizational units would be schools, rather than traditional discipline-based departments. Initially, there were three schools: Engineering; Natural Sciences; and Social Sciences, Humanities and Arts; plus a Graduate Division. While the original intention was that all three schools would develop at the same pace, it became apparent during 2003 and 2004 that the Engineering School and Natural Sciences School were developing at a faster pace than Social Sciences, Humanities and Arts. As a result, the library needed to plan for an initial collection to support primarily engineering, life sciences, and physical sciences. Given the realities of scholarly communication in these disciplines, librarians would therefore need to focus on the acquisition of electronic resources, which at UC Merced largely meant gaining access to appropriate electronic resources already available through the University of California.

UNIVERSITY OF CALIFORNIA LIBRARIES

To understand collection development policies at UC Merced, it is first necessary to understand the position of the UC Merced Library within the University of California system of libraries. Considered as a whole, the UC libraries constitute the largest research university library in the world with over 39 million print volumes and 3.7 million digitized volumes. In 2013–2014, the 100 libraries that make up the UC system had a total budget of $237,000,000. The California Digital Library (CDL), which despite its name is an office of the University of California, provides a variety of central services to the campus libraries. These include negotiating and licensing electronic resources, managing the union catalog (Melvyl) using the OCLC WorldCat Local platform, managing an internal ILL system and courier service that exchanged 102,000 items between UC campuses in 2012–2013, and developing and managing a variety of data management and digital library services. The CDL also manages the UC Shared Cataloging Program (SCP) located at UC San Diego, which provides MARC records to the campus libraries for centrally licensed electronic information resources as well as acquisitions services for centrally licensed resources.

Given all of these available resources and services, the central planning question was which collections and services could be accessed by the UC Merced Library simply by virtue of its being a UC library, and which collections and services needed to be developed locally?

ACQUISITION OF RESOURCES

This section describes UC Merced Library's collection planning and acquisition in four areas: journals, e-books, U.S. government publications, and print books. While each of these information resource types is addressed sequentially, it should be understood that they were acquired simultaneously.

Journals

In 2003, the UC Merced librarians believed that there was no reason for a new research library to acquire journals in print. Accordingly, the first formal collection development policy was that the library would acquire journals in electronic format only unless a desired journal was only available in print. If it subsequently became available electronically, the print subscription would be cancelled. If a publisher bundled print and electronic versions together, the print version would neither be shelved nor cataloged.

Access to very large numbers of electronic-only journals required UC Merced librarians to select those packages already licensed by the University of California that supported UC Merced research and teaching, and that the library could afford. The UC libraries operate on a coinvestment model for system-wide licensing of electronic resources: negotiation and licensing are conducted centrally by the CDL, but each campus is responsible for paying its proportional cost. Once the librarians selected the desired resources and returned the spreadsheet to the CDL, staff at the CDL worked to add UC Merced to the existing licenses and to arrange for payment.

E-Books

The librarians recognized that the transition from print to electronic format was much farther along for journals than for monographs. In fact, in 2004 it could fairly be said that the monograph transition had barely begun. Both libraries and publishers were beginning to develop mutually acceptable business models and licensing terms, but consensus was still far from being realized. Various vendors had appeared, but it was unclear which ones would still be in business in a few years. The basic question had not been resolved: were books so fundamentally different from journals that a transition to electronic format would not, and indeed should not, happen? Despite the underdeveloped marketplace, the UC Merced librarians believed that e-books would become an important format, and that the level of acceptance by faculty and students needed to be determined. It seemed appropriate for a new research university library to ask this question and to try to answer it.

It was in this environment that the UC Merced Library began its initial, cautious experiments with e-books. The first acquisition was a subscription to ebrary Academic Complete, which provided access to a growing collection, now over 115,000 titles, of scholarly e-books in many disciplines. The cost per title is extremely low, but the library does not receive perpetual access to any of the titles. If the library stopped paying the subscription fee, all access would cease. At the same time, librarians wanted to purchase some titles and acquire perpetual access to them. Approximately 8,500 titles were purchased from NetLibrary, now part of EBSCO. Librarians did not continue to purchase titles from NetLibrary, however, because of dissatisfaction with the one-user-at-a-time use model that mimicked checking out a print book. This model appeared to be an artifact of print book publication and did not reflect the possibilities, such as unlimited simultaneous access, possible with electronic publication.

In 2004, the author attended a presentation at the American Library Association Annual Conference on patron-driven acquisition (PDA). Presenters included Andrew Pace, then at North Carolina State University and now at OCLC, and a representative from Ebook Library (EBL). Inspired by this presentation, the UC Merced Library began a PDA or, as EBL calls it, demand-driven acquisitions (DDA) plan with EBL in 2005 employing the short-term loan model. For the past seven years, the library also has maintained a DDA plan with MyiLibrary, now part of Ingram. This is a much smaller plan than the one with EBL and focuses exclusively on academic science and engineering titles. Its primary purpose is to provide coverage of certain publishers not available through EBL. It does not employ short-term loans; titles are purchased on the second access.

U.S. Government Publications

As a research university library, the UC Merced Library needed to provide access to U.S. government publications. When the library was being planned in 2004, there was one Federal Depository Library within the congressional district that included Merced, even though each district could have two such libraries. This depository library was over an hour's drive from Merced. Under the circumstances it seemed reasonable for UC Merced to apply to become a depository library. The main question was whether it was appropriate to try to build a depository library by acquiring physical items when federal government publications were becoming increasingly electronic. A practical problem was that the library simply did not have the staff to perform all of the inventorying and accounting activities required by federal regulations to track physical depository items. One possible solution was to become an all-electronic depository library, even though there were no such libraries at the time. The library already maintained a subscription to the Marcive Documents Without Shelves service, which provides MARC records for over 55,000 titles published by the Government Printing Office (GPO). After negotiation with the GPO, the UC Merced Library was approved as a Federal Depository Library based on the availability of Documents Without Shelves. The library also has access through ILL to the extensive physical document collections of other UC libraries.

Printed Books

When the library was being planned, librarians understood without question that they would acquire print books, regardless of what they may have believed the future to be. At the same time the librarians, if not all of the faculty, realized that a long-range goal of building a one- or two-million-volume book collection on campus was completely unrealistic. The university was being planned as a general UC campus, so the library was expected to support a range of disciplines, including many in the social sciences and particularly the humanities, which were heavily dependent on print books. The rapid transition to electronic content did not change this reality.

Librarians began the process of book acquisition by contracting with YBP Library Services for an "opening day" collection of approximately 13,000 volumes published in 2003 and 2004. These were delivered to an off-site facility, shelved in call number order, and moved to the campus by a professional book moving company for the September 2005 opening. Along with the "opening day" collection, the library established two approval plans with YBP: one in social sciences and humanities and the other in science and technology.

It is somewhat a misnomer to speak of approval plans since all books received from YBP come completely shelf-ready. The only tasks for technical services staff are to check the books against the packing lists and to load the files of bibliographic records that also contain item and invoice data. Normally new books are shelved and available for use within 24 hours of receipt.

As stated earlier, the librarians decided at the beginning of planning that the library would not retrospectively acquire print monographs except in response to high levels of local use or faculty requests for specific titles. At the same time, the library would be open to supplementing the purchased book collection with strategic gifts. The library continues to decline offers of print journals and back runs of *National Geographic,* but accepts gifts of academic books in areas of collection focus. The personal libraries of retiring UC faculty members continue to be an important source for acquiring older print titles, particularly in history, Spanish literature, and ecology.

STAFFING

In 2003, the decision was made to focus additional librarian recruitment on instruction and reference positions with minimal, if any, responsibilities for collection development or academic liaison activities. This decision recognized that funding for new librarian positions would be difficult to obtain, so the library should focus on its core needs. The founding librarians also believed that the traditional subject specialist/bibliographer/academic department liaison model was ill-suited to a new research university library such as UC Merced. The traditional model did not align well with the academic focus on interdisciplinary research and the academic organization of the campus into schools rather than discipline-specific departments. At what level would the liaison activities occur? If at the school level, what type of subject knowledge would be necessary or useful for such an assignment? As mentioned above, collection development at UC Merced largely occurs at scale (e.g., online packages, approval plans, and e-book DDA) rather than at the individual title level. The traditional selector model did not seem to be a good fit in this environment. Within UC, subject selectors/bibliographers are organized into discipline-specific groups. One of the important functions of these groups is to recommend system-wide acquisition of new electronic resources. While the UC Merced Library would not have assigned selectors, the librarians could participate in these groups as appropriate to convey UC Merced's interest in specific new resources, to get assistance in answering highly specialized reference questions, or for other purposes. Finally, the traditional model carries with it significant overhead in the managing of discipline-specific funds. Such a fund accounting structure also seemed poorly aligned with the way UC Merced handled collection development. Librarians wanted to keep collections budgeting as simple as possible through the use of a small number of broad categories; fine-grained subject level accounting was not considered useful. As a result of all of these factors, the head of collection services was the only librarian with any responsibility for collection development and management.

A DECADE OF OPERATIONS

UC Merced welcomed its tenth freshman class in August 2014. This date provides a suitable vantage point to look back at 10 years of operations. The UC Merced Library has demonstrated that it is possible to establish a real, effective research university library with a small staff by relying on central services and vendor services. Central UC services include the Shared Cataloging Program, CDL acquisitions, SFX link resolver management, management of Melvyl, the UC union catalog, a central institutional repository and digital publishing platform, and extensive support for digital library services and technologies. Vendor services include the approval plan and firm order book services, Documents Without Shelves, and serials subscription management. It is also possible to evaluate the results in the four areas of collection management discussed earlier: journals, e-books, U.S. government documents, and print books; and in staffing as related to collection management. While there was never any intention to create an all-electronic library, the reality today is that the UC Merced Library is certainly a primarily electronic library. As of July 1, 2014, the collection included 1,357,538 volumes of which only 118,071 (8.7%) were print. Including electronic journals and databases, as well as all physical formats such as DVDs and CD-ROMs, the total collection is 92% electronic. For fiscal year 2013–2014, 85% of the total collections budget was devoted to the acquisition of electronic resources.

In 2014, UC Merced has access to 68,940 electronic serials licensed through the CDL, as well as to 43,254 freely available electronic serials cataloged by the SCP. These totals are equivalent to the numbers of centrally licensed electronic journals available at other UC campuses, even the larger ones. At faculty request, the library currently subscribes to 141 locally licensed electronic journals not available through UC agreements and to 20 print journals not available electronically. After 10 years of operation, the library has not received faculty or student complaints regarding the policy of acquiring journals exclusively in electronic form whenever possible. Articles from older print journals held by other UC libraries are scanned and delivered online through ILL. In fiscal year 2013–2014, almost 1,500 articles were provided in this manner.

During the past decade, the acceptance of e-books by faculty and students at UC Merced has significantly increased as evidenced by use data and focus groups. At the same time, print books have not become obsolete or unwanted; a significant number of faculty and students, primarily in the humanities and social sciences, still prefer print books. Some of this preference is related to difficulties in using e-books, primarily digital rights management (DRM) limits that control how the content can be used, and problems with using various interfaces. Probably the most important barrier to more widespread use of e-books in academic libraries is the sheer number of available publisher and aggregator platforms, each with its own rules, which must be navigated by users. Some of the preference for print books also is related to the belief that the reading experience is better with a print book and that print books provide superior image quality (particularly for scholars in some disciplines in which images are very important). Another issue for research libraries is that many important works continue to be available only in print, or else the availability of the online version is significantly delayed.

Despite these barriers to acceptance, in 2014 approximately 10 times more e-books are available to UC Merced Library patrons than are available in the local print collection. DDA remains the primary means of locally acquiring e-books rather than package or single-title purchases. Over 300,000 titles currently are available through the EBL DDA plan. After three short-term loans (STLs) that may be for either one or seven days at the patron's choice, the title is purchased on the fourth access. STLs and purchases are completely unmediated. While many libraries limit titles in their DDA pool by subject or publisher, UC Merced had made almost the entire EBL catalog available; the only exception had been titles with a list price over $300. The large increases in STL costs suddenly announced by certain publishers in the summer of 2014 forced librarians to remove content from about a dozen publishers and to institute a price cap on STLs to contain costs. Despite these increases in STL rates, DDA remains the primary means of acquiring locally licensed e-books.

In addition to the EBL plan, the library has maintained its non-STL DDA plan with MyiLibrary. The library also maintains its subscription to ebrary Academic Complete. When UC Merced began acquiring e-books in 2004, there were very few titles available through UC system-wide agreements. This situation has changed significantly in the past decade. Now large e-book packages are available from publishers such as Springer, Wiley, and Elsevier, either linked to their journal packages or as smaller stand-alone packages. Currently, there are approximately the same number of e-books available through system-wide packages as through local acquisition. Of course, there is always the possibility that a system-wide e-book package linked to a journal package may be cancelled in the future due to issues with the negotiating of journal package renewals.

To provide additional support for the social sciences and humanities, the UC libraries currently are conducting a system-wide e-book DDA pilot with 65 university presses and ebrary focused on social science and humanities titles. The pilot began in January 2014 when the first set of MARC records was distributed to the libraries by the SCP; the pilot will continue through December 2015. It works similarly to other DDA plans: a title is purchased on the fourth access after three STLs. Prior to the pilot, the libraries examined their print acquisitions from the participating publishers. Based on this data, a multiplier of three times or, in a few cases, four times list price provides perpetual access to all campuses. As of August 2014, there were 2,733 titles available; there have been 843 STLs and 65 titles have been purchased system-wide.

The library remains a Federal Depository Library relying exclusively on the Marcive Documents Without Shelves service to provide access to federal documents. Currently, approximately 160,000 federal documents are available electronically. This number will significantly increase as a result of projects to digitize physical federal documents being undertaken by several library consortia, including the University of California.

The library has the space to house 200,000 physical items. With a print collection of 118,000 volumes and 2,300 DVDs and CD-ROMs, the library is currently 59% full. At the current rate of acquisition, it will be at least 16 years before physical items will need to be withdrawn or sent to off-site storage. The library continues to purchase print books through approval plans and some firm orders with YBP. In response to faculty requests, individual titles also are acquired through used-book dealers and Amazon. When the approval plans were initiated, both the humanities and social sciences plan and the science plan had relatively wide coverage since academic planning was so fluid. As the campus has matured, librarians have focused both plans on existing programs. Approval plan coverage also was narrowed in response to the increasing acceptance of e-books accompanied by increasing pressure on the collections budget. In early 2014, the science plan was completely shut down as a result of decreasing circulation and budget cuts.

In spite of the decreasing rate of acquisition of print books, circulation remains robust for a research library. In fiscal year 2013–2014, users checked out 28,994 items (24% of the collection); undergraduates checked out 18,575 (64%) of these items. Undergraduate circulation as a percentage of total circulation has remained constant over several years, indicating that the print collection primarily supports undergraduate instruction.

Staffing for collections has remained constant with one librarian responsible for the management of collection development and technical services. Librarian hiring continues to focus on instruction and reference as well as on digital assets. The lack of librarians with specific liaison responsibilities has so far not proven to be a significant disadvantage since all of the librarians conduct outreach activities to the faculty as appropriate. At the same time, the diffuse academic organizational structure has made it difficult for librarians to communicate with groups of faculty at the same time. The real staffing question is whether the library will be able to hire or develop librarians with the necessary skill sets to support new initiatives such as data curation and digital humanities.

The way collection development and management have been carried out, as well as the availability of central services from the UC libraries and outsourced services, have had implications for technical services staffing. The library began with one staff person and one full-time equivalent student employee responsible for cataloging, acquisitions, and stacks maintenance. These staffing levels have worked for 10 years because most of the cataloging and acquisitions work involves importing and exporting large files of records rather than cataloging or ordering individual titles. There is clearly some work with individual items, but this is a small fraction of overall activity. Because of the emphasis on large-scale acquisition of information resources, and also because of extensive outsourcing, one librarian and one staff member have been able to assemble a research library collection in 10 years. In 2013, the library received approval to recruit for a new staff position to handle electronic resources with the existing staff position repurposed to handle physical materials, stacks maintenance, and database maintenance.

The library continues to employ its triage model for providing reference services. For the past several years, the library has also participated in 24x7 chat reference using OCLC's QuestionPoint. For fiscal year 2013–2014, the library reported 2,500 reference transactions with 1,550 of these being virtual. Many of the virtual transactions involved UC Merced students when the library was closed. The library still does not have a reserve operation and still does not collect textbooks. While some humanities faculty have advocated for a reserve operation and some faculty and students want the library to acquire course textbooks, the consensus remains that these activities are not a good use of the library's resources.

THE NEXT 10 YEARS

As with all libraries, future developments will be constrained by the availability of funding for staff (including librarians), collections, and operations. Within that context, it is possible to make some predictions with a reasonable degree of certainty. The transition from print to electronic formats will continue; print as a percentage of the collection will continue to decline at UC Merced. In 10 years it is likely that 95% of the collection will be electronic and that at least 90% of the collection budget will be spent on electronic resources. The same trends will be manifest at most research university libraries for prospective acquisitions. An increasing number of research university libraries will adopt just-in-time collection development policies, and a decreasing number will be staffed and funded to continue to build collections according to the traditional model. At UC there will be an even greater emphasis on system-wide acquisition of electronic resources with a concomitant increase in the proportion of the collections budget at UC Merced going to the CDL for such resources. This is but one example of the increasing importance of working at the network level for academic library systems and consortia. Other examples are HathiTrust, the Western Regional Storage Trust (a distributed retrospective print journal repository program serving libraries and library consortia in the western region of the United States) and similar large-scale print archiving programs, the adoption of a single integrated library system (ILS), and the increasing provision of central services in cataloging, acquisitions, licensing, reference, and instruction. E-books will become more accepted, even by humanities and arts faculty, as a result of improvements in usability and image quality. There will be greater clarity in the marketplace regarding business and licensing terms for e-books. Digital library services writ large—digitization of physical materials, development of online research portals and digital exhibits, data curation, electronic publishing, curation of born-digital materials, development of open access educational resources, administration of faculty open access mandates—will become increasingly important with significant impacts on hiring and professional development.

Many decisions made by UC Merced librarians at the beginning were novel and even controversial at the time, but have become less so during the past decade. The UC Merced Library will continue to follow the statement on its webpage: "Not what other research libraries are, what they will be."

REFERENCE

Merritt, K., & Lawrence, J. F. (2007). *From rangeland to research university: The birth of the University of California, Merced.* San Francisco, CA: Jossey-Bass.

7 | Patron-Driven Acquisitions: Assessing and Sustaining a Long-Term PDA E-Book Program

Karen S. Fischer

ABSTRACT

The author describes the e-book patron-driven acquisitions (PDA) program at the University of Iowa Libraries. By analyzing almost five years of data about e-books purchased as a direct result of patron use, librarians made decisions about refining the PDA profile and learned which subjects and publishers attracted the most use. Understanding the collection of profiled PDA titles, or risk pool, helps librarians control and manage program costs. The data reveal the high quality of the books purchased through the program, as well as the high rate of subsequent use, the reasonable per-book cost, the breadth of subject coverage, and the cost-control results of using the short-term loan option. The author also mentions the desirability of removing unused older titles periodically.

INTRODUCTION TO PATRON-DRIVEN ACQUISITIONS

Academic libraries have always been responsive to their patrons' needs. They usually buy patrons' suggestions for purchases if the resources support research or curricular purposes. Interlibrary lending between libraries also has been a standard service for over 100 years. Both services were developed to supply books at the point of need when they were not available for patrons locally (Goldner & Birch, 2012). Today, combining these two services, many libraries buy (instead of borrow) books that meet certain criteria when patrons request them through interlibrary loan (ILL); early adopters of this service have been doing this for nearly 25 years (Hodges,

Preston, & Hamilton, 2010). Before the terms *patron-driven acquisitions* (PDA) or *demand-driven acquisitions* (DDA) were coined in the late 2000s, librarians were setting up and administering successful programs to buy books requested through interlibrary loan (now referred to as print PDA programs), formalizing the concept of building collections based on expressed user needs. ILL staff buy books that meet preestablished criteria, such as price, publisher, and publication date; upon receipt, patrons check out the books and then return them to be added to the local library collection (Nixon, Freeman, & Ward, 2010). The success of print-based PDA programs, as documented by studies that analyze titles purchased through such programs, eventually led to the development of PDA for e-books (Anderson et al., 2010; Bracke, 2010; Hodges et al., 2010; Nixon & Saunders, 2010; Nixon, Ward, & Freeman, 2014; Tyler, Falci, Melvin, Epp, & Kreps, 2013). Swords (2011a) states that "PDA is the product of technology and very specifically of the coming of the age of e-books" (p. 2). Writing about PDA as a "disruptive technology," Rick Lugg (2011) suggests that "libraries have begun to adopt a new role: curating a discovery environment for digital materials," which allows librarians to stop "buy[ing] speculatively" (p. 11).

E-book PDA programs look considerably different than their print counterparts. Librarians develop a subject profile with the vendor who then sends a weekly batch of matching bibliographic records; librarians load these into their catalog. The librarians also decide whether significant patron use of a PDA e-book (such as printing a chapter or reading online for more than a certain number of minutes) will trigger an immediate purchase or whether it will trigger a short-term loan (STL). An STL is essentially a rental fee of a publisher-set percentage of the list price. If librarians choose the STL model, they also decide the threshold after which the next use triggers the purchase. In an e-book PDA plan, when patrons discover and use these titles there is usually little or no mediation (such as a librarian or staff member approving the order), thus allowing instant access to content at the patron's point of need. The patrons are never aware that their use of these e-books triggers loan fees or purchases that their library pays.

Although many academic libraries have implemented unmediated PDA e-book programs, many do not embark on large-scale, long-term programs due to fears about uncontrolled spending. The University of Iowa Libraries' experience can inform other libraries about how to manage the ongoing costs while still offering patrons a large universe of titles with fairly liberal limits on price and other parameters. Iowa's PDA e-book program is large-scale for the size of the institution; however, in relation to a year's worth of monographic purchases, one can see that although it is a significant collection development tool, e-book PDA is certainly not the primary method for acquiring monographs. In fiscal year 2013, Iowa bought more than 30,500 print and electronic books for a cost of nearly $2.07 million. The PDA e-book purchases during the same fiscal year accounted for 2,023 (6.6%) of those titles for a cost of almost $200,000, or about 9.6% of the monographic book expenditures.

This chapter presents findings from examining Iowa's PDA e-book data for 5,904 titles purchased over nearly five years and includes analyses of subject areas, prices, publishers, and other relevant metrics. It suggests ways to monitor a PDA plan so that costs stay within budget, includes outcomes from implementing short-term loans, and assesses the unpurchased collection for weeding.

UNIVERSITY OF IOWA'S PDA PROGRAM FOR E-BOOKS

In summer 2009, the University of Iowa Libraries began to explore ways to acquire e-book content outside of bundled frontlist or subscription e-book packages. Intrigued by hearing Dennis Dillon's (2009) presentation about the University of Texas Libraries' robust PDA e-book program and desiring title-by-title acquisition of e-books, Iowa librarians explored options and vendors. Following a one-month pilot with ebrary during which PDA e-books showed unprecedented use, Iowa embarked on a large-scale e-book patron-driven acquisition program in October 2009. Librarians committed to the program for a year and initially allocated $50,000 for it. During that year, instead of pausing or stopping the program when challenges arose or funds depleted faster than expected, librarians worked with vendor partners (ebrary and YBP) to modify and refine the program, allocating additional funds as needed (Fischer, Wright, Clatanoff, Barton, & Shreeves, 2011). Staff at ebrary indicated that Iowa's PDA program is comparatively midsized in the spectrum of academic library PDA e-book programs. The analysis of four years and ten months of data (October 2009–July 2014) presented in this chapter offers insights into how best to manage a PDA program, illustrates that data can greatly assist in decision making and refinement of a PDA program, and proves the value of PDA.

The Profile and Parameters

Developing the PDA e-book profile that manages the subject and nonsubject parameters that align with Iowa's standard YBP approval profile was a critical element of the program's success. Because Iowa was one of the first libraries to explore modifying an approval profile with YPB to accommodate PDA e-books, the program's first six months saw many modifications, big and small. Setting up a successful and sustainable PDA program involves considerable engagement between the library, the e-book vendor, and the book distributor. Key elements of Iowa's current PDA profile are:

- Price cap of $225.
- Single-user license option.
- No limits on publication date; e-books often have variable publication dates with their print counterparts, so limiting the publication date would result in excluding some seminal works reissued as e-books.
- Exclusion of selected publishers based on previous frontlist package purchases or publisher quality.
- Exclusion of titles that are duplicated in ebrary's subscription product (Academic Complete).
- Exclusions of juvenile, popular, and travel guides, and K subclasses (Iowa's Law Library operates independently).
- Exclusion of duplicate e-books and titles held in print.
- No exclusions based on language.

The approval profile drives the automatic selection of ebrary titles that are made available for discovery in the catalog. At the end of 2014, the set of unpurchased books totaled about 20,000 titles, forming what Dillon (2011) called the "risk pool" (p. 163). Each year, the Iowa risk pool grows by about 5,000 titles.

E-book vendors and publishers with demand-driven options for buying titles make different decisions to set activities that "trigger" an e-book purchase. ebrary's trigger parameters are generous: 10 pages viewed in a single browser session, 10 minutes of viewing in a single browser session, one print of any page, or one download of any page. YBP's GOBI interface added a "manual DDA" option in March 2012, which lets librarians select individual nonprofile titles to add to the risk pool. By July 2014, Iowa librarians had added 2,715 titles using this method. Additionally, in October 2013, Iowa implemented the one-day short-term loan option, meaning that instead of buying each title outright as a result of the first trigger event, every book in the risk pool now triggers as a one-day loan after the first significant patron use; the second trigger event buys the title. The author discusses below why these options were employed and what their impact has been.

USING DATA ABOUT PDA PURCHASED E-BOOKS

Examining PDA program data informs the process of refining a PDA profile and increases the librarians' understanding of patrons' need for and use of e-books. Knowing information such as pricing trends, which disciplines benefit best, and which publishers' books are purchased the most can all assist in managing the future refinements and costs of a PDA program.

The following analysis is based on four years and ten months of data (October 2009–July 2014); it is especially useful when compared with the first year of data because it illustrates that even one year of data from a well-planned PDA program can indicate future purchasing and spending trends (Fischer et al., 2011). Analyzing the tables suggests ways that librarians can use PDA data to support better decision making by understanding the intricacies of what is purchased. To gather the most comprehensive data, the author asked ebrary staff to run a special report that showed cumulative use, rather than the yearly use provided by the standard COUNTER Book Report 1 (BR1). Cumulative data better reflect individual titles' use over time. The most important fields in the customized report included: title, ISBN, publisher, call number, publication date, price, license type, trigger and purchase dates, first and last use dates, and cumulative use (for all elements of use, including printing, viewing, copying, chapter downloads, and user sessions).

Costs

Between October 2009 and December 2014, Iowa patrons' use of PDA titles triggered 5,904 e-books purchases, totaling $588,765 and averaging of $99.72 per e-book (see Table 1). Notes for Table 1 include refining the profile between 2009 and 2010 and the steady growth in buying between 2011 through 2012, followed by a significant drop in purchases (and therefore in costs) in 2013 when Iowa implemented the one-day short-term loan option.

Table 1. PDA expenditures at the University of Iowa Libraries (October 2009–December 2014).

Year	# of purchased titles	DDA cost	# of one-day short-term loans (STL)	STL cost	Total cost
2009	397	$41,875	n/a	n/a	$41,875
2010	713	$69,698	n/a	n/a	$69,698
2011	996	$103,110	n/a	n/a	$103,110
2012	1986	$196,862	n/a	n/a	$196,862
2013*	1482	$144,250	447	$5,563	$149,813
2014	699	$69,525	1432	$27,500	$97,025
TOTAL	6273	$625,320	1879	$33,063	$658,383

*One-day short-term option implemented October 2013.

Table 1 illustrates several aspects of managing a PDA plan, such as the steady growth of purchases as the risk pool grows, the ability to curb spending with profile refinement, and the results of implementing short-term loans. These will be discussed in more detail below.

Subject Areas

The disciplines benefiting the most from Iowa's PDA purchases are the health sciences (20.5% of total purchases), sociology (10.2%), economics and commerce (8.3%), and education (7.6%). The costs align fairly well with the number of titles purchased in a given discipline; for every subject area identified in Table 2, the percent of total titles purchased in a given subject is within one percentage point of the percent of total costs, signifying a correlation between cost and the number of titles purchased (see Table 2).

Examining purchased titles and the risk pool by Library of Congress Classification (LC) can inform budget allocations and tell collection managers how many e-books in a given subject area are being bought through PDA. In addition, close examination of purchased titles can lead to discovering new areas of interdisciplinary research and study on campus. Interestingly, when purchased titles and the Iowa risk pool were compared by subject area, almost all subjects correlated within 1.5%, with the exception of health sciences and technology/engineering. Health science titles comprised 9.8% of the titles in the risk pool, but accounted for almost 20% of all purchases, showing that health science titles are highly used and needed. Conversely, 6.2% of the titles in the risk pool were in the area of technology and engineering, but purchases in that discipline accounted for only 3.2% of the total PDA purchases. Comparisons such as these help librarians project costs by subject area and highlight disciplines wherein the quantity in the risk pool does not directly correlate with the total ultimately purchased through patron use.

Publishers

Over 200 publishers are represented among Iowa's purchased PDA titles; almost half are university, society, or association publishers. Examining purchased titles by publisher reveals whose titles attract the most use and whose enjoy the highest average use per title (see Table 3). For example, Iowa bought 1,596 titles from Taylor & Francis (T&F) through the PDA plan, and those titles attracted 12,965 user sessions for an average of eight user sessions per title. By comparison, 58 purchased Princeton University Press (PUP) books enjoyed an average of 16 uses per title. PUP titles get more repeated use than the T&F ones.

This kind of information helps collection managers learn which publishers' titles are being purchased via PDA, but, most importantly, which publishers' titles the patrons find the most useful. The Iowa data show that their users value university press titles; so far, Iowa has bought PDA titles from 80 university presses. Further analysis could be undertaken to examine publishers by subject area, or to determine which publishers have the most expensive titles. By calculating average cost per user session for each publisher, librarians could decide to curb PDA expenses by dropping certain publishers with expensive, lower-use titles.

Publication Year

The array of publication dates for purchased titles highlights several informative elements of Iowa's PDA program. First, users *do* find older texts useful as evidenced by the purchase of over 2,300 titles with publication dates of 2008 or earlier (see Table 4).

When initially developing the PDA profile, Iowa librarians limited publication dates to the most recent two years (i.e., 2008 and 2009 at the PDA program's implementation in October 2009). Within the first year of

Table 2. PDA titles by subject class, number of titles purchased, and expenditures (October 2009–July 2014).

LC class	Class description	No. of titles	% of total titles	Cost	% of total costs
A-AZ	General works	4	0.1%	$375	0.1%
B-BD/BH-BJ	Philosophy	160	2.7%	$16,289	2.8%
BF	Psychology	259	4.4%	$24,409	4.1%
BL-BX	Religion	175	3.0%	$18,346	3.1%
C-CT	Aux sciences of history	22	0.4%	$2,357	0.4%
D-DX	History (excl. Americas)	203	3.4%	$21,943	3.7%
E-F	History. Americas	127	2.2%	$9,577	1.6%
G-GF	Geography (general)	42	0.7%	$5,004	0.8%
GN-GT	Anthropology	71	1.2%	$7,447	1.3%
GV	Recreation & leisure	96	1.6%	$11,271	1.9%
H-HA	Social sciences (general)	44	0.7%	$4,256	0.7%
HB-HJ	Economics & commerce	492	8.3%	$43,785	7.4%
HM-HX	Sociology	604	10.2%	$64,284	10.9%
JA-JZ	Political science	210	3.6%	$22,409	3.8%
K	Law	16	0.3%	$962	0.2%
L-LG	Education	447	7.6%	$40,720	6.9%
M-MT	Music	92	1.6%	$8,894	1.5%
N-NX/TR/TT	Visual arts, photography	92	1.6%	$6,679	1.1%

Code	Subject	Count	%	Amount	%
P-PQ, PT	Languages & literatures	501	8.5%	$51,929	8.8%
PR-PS	English lit., American lit.	179	3.0%	$16,432	2.8%
Q	Science (general)	21	0.4%	$2,368	0.4%
QA	Mathematics & computer sci.	170	2.9%	$15,409	2.6%
QB-QC	Astronomy & physics	80	1.4%	$9,751	1.7%
QD	Chemistry	65	1.1%	$10,439	1.8%
QE	Geology	13	0.2%	$1,194	0.2%
QH-QT	Biological sciences	246	4.2%	$28,247	4.8%
R-RZ	Health sciences	1210	20.5%	$115,320	19.6%
S-SK	Agriculture	14	0.2%	$1,972	0.3%
T-TP/TS/TX	Technology & engineering	191	3.2%	$22,197	3.8%
U/V	Military & naval science	20	0.3%	$1,791	0.3%
Z-ZA	Bibliography, library & info. sci.	38	0.6%	$2,706	0.5%
TOTAL		5904	100.10%	$588,762	99.9%

Table 3. Top 20 publishers represented in PDA purchases (October 2009–July 2014).*

Publisher	No. of titles	No. of sessions after purchase	Avg. use per title
Taylor & Francis	1596	12965	8
Wiley	835	8080	10
Cambridge University Press	605	4651	8
Elsevier	326	4598	14
Palgrave Macmillan	317	2331	7
Oxford University Press	141	1221	9
Sage	139	1075	8
Guilford Press	128	2170	17
McGraw-Hill	108	3735	35
Bloomsbury Publishing	103	623	6
ABC-CLIO	94	812	9
Springer	65	805	12
Jones & Bartlett Learning	61	832	14
Princeton University Press	58	931	16
Lawrence Erlbaum	57	551	10
MIT Press	53	503	9
Information Age Publishing	52	548	11
Duke University Press	48	625	13
Ashgate Publishing Group	47	211	4
World Scientific Publishing Co.	47	223	5

*Publishers in bold have been limited by publication date to exclude some years during which Iowa purchased front file titles directly from the publisher. Excluded years: Wiley (2007–2009), Elsevier (2006–2014), Springer (2006–2013).

the program, librarians modified the publication date parameters twice, first moving it to 2005, and then eliminating it altogether. The reason: patrons value seminal works republished as e-books and publishers assign the original print publication date rather than the reprint date to many of these titles. A few examples from older publications in the PDA collection include books in standard series, such as Volume 2 of *Advances in Experimental Social Psychology* (1965, Academic Press), and titles such

Table 4. Publication dates of purchased, short-term loaned (STL), and unpurchased PDA titles.*

Publication date	No. of PDA titles	% of PDA titles	No. of risk pool titles	% of risk pool titles
1958–1979	9	0.15%	9	0.05%
1980–1989	13	0.22%	14	0.07%
1990–1999	47	0.80%	37	0.19%
2000–2004	151	2.56%	23	0.12%
2005	536	9.08%	24	0.12%
2006	617	10.45%	136	0.70%
2007	446	7.55%	192	0.99%
2008	522	8.84%	302	1.56%
2009	469	7.94%	1032	5.33%
2010	750	12.70%	1731	8.94%
2011	1191	20.17%	3328	17.18%
2012	1335	22.61%	5345	27.59%
2013	684	11.59%	5280	27.26%
2014	105	1.78%	1912	9.87%

*PDA titles represent purchased and one-day short-term loan titles rented or purchased between October 2009–July 2014; risk pool represents unpurchased PDA titles on May 27, 2014.

as *Aesthetics of Change* (1983, Guilford Press) or *Life and Thought in the Early Middle Ages* (1967, University of Minnesota Press). The library holds most of these reprint titles in their original print editions; use of the PDA e-book equivalents indicate that patrons prefer the electronic versions enough to trigger purchases.

The second notable element of the publication year analysis reveals that the majority of annually purchased titles cluster in the publication years 2011 and 2012. The data show that patrons definitely use recent content the most; the lower number of purchased PDA titles in 2013 and 2014 reflects the time it takes for a book to receive enough use to trigger a short-term loan or purchase. The data in Table 4's risk pool columns show that recent titles make up the bulk of the content in Iowa's profile.

KEEPING PDA SUSTAINABLE

By now the reader has discerned that there are several ways to manage PDA costs. This section discusses the three main components for controlling and managing costs: managing the risk pool (the unpurchased titles), modifying the PDA profile, and using short-term loan options.

Managing the Risk Pool

E-book PDA programs vary considerably in the size of the risk pool offered for discovery and purchase. For example, the University of Texas at Austin has a range of 60,000–110,000 titles in its risk pool (Dillon, 2011). Iowa has a range of 16,000–22,000 titles, and many libraries have risk pools of 10,000 titles or fewer. The correlation between the size of a risk pool and PDA expenditures is important; the more titles in a risk pool, the higher the PDA costs will be because patrons have a larger array to discover and use. Analyzing basic data about the risk pool suggests ways to cull it as a way to regulate expenditures.

The author generated a report of 19,370 titles in the Iowa risk pool in May 2014. YBP price data for a single-user license indicated a total value of $1.9 million for these titles, with an average cost of $98 per e-book. The report identified 337 titles above the price cap of $225, indicating that e-book inflation regularly occurs after titles have been loaded in the catalog. The total cost of these over-price-cap titles exceeded $94,000, suggesting that routinely reviewing the risk pool for overpriced titles is an important task. At Iowa, these titles were immediately removed from the PDA program.

In addition to attending to problems that come up unexpectedly, such as the price increases noted above, it also is prudent to cull the PDA risk pool periodically. In January 2015, librarians implemented a five-year "moving wall" for annually removing titles that have remain unpurchased for five years; this activity will remove about 3,000 titles (15% of the risk pool) per year, or about $300,000 of content. At the University of Texas at Austin, staff annually remove titles that have "received no use over the past twelve to twenty-four months" (Dillon, 2011, p. 163). When books are removed from the risk pool, subject librarians may be interested in seeing a report of the deselected titles.

Modifying the PDA Profile

Modifying publication date and price cap parameters or selecting specific publishers for exclusion are simple ways to refine a profile. Iowa has a very broad profile in terms of subject coverage; however, other elements of the profile have been modified over time. For example, librarians changed the publication date parameters to increase access to older publications and also reduced the price cap in an effort to manage price increases that take effect after titles enter the risk pool. In addition, whenever Iowa buys a publisher's frontlist package, librarians ask YBP to modify the profile to exclude that publisher for a particular year. Regular examination of purchased titles for out-of-scope content may reveal holes in the profile that need adjusting.

Using Short-term Loans

Short-term loans are a mechanism by which libraries can rent an e-book when a patron makes significant use of it. Different vendors offer different loan periods and different trigger events. Each different rental period, such as one day or one week or one month, correlates with a different percentage of an e-book's list price; publishers set these percentages, which can vary considerably. For example, one-day STL percentages for ebrary titles currently range from 5% to 40% of a single-user license price; percentages can reach 60% for seven-day STL for some publishers' books.

Librarians often select the STL model when configuring a PDA program; they choose both the loan length and the number of loan trigger events before the next trigger event results in a purchase. In Iowa's case, the program started in 2009 with the initial significant use triggering an immediate purchase. It was not until October 2013 that librarians activated the STL option; the first significant use now triggers a one-day loan and the second one triggers the purchase. One of the main reasons Iowa chose to try the STL model was the evidence that many purchased PDA titles seldom received significant subsequent use. As Table 5 shows, 905 titles have had only one additional user session since they were purchased and, of those, 271 (30%) had an additional user session before 2012. By activating the STL option, Iowa librarians hoped to save money by renting rather than immediately purchasing titles that might be used only once.

Table 5. Number of user sessions for purchased PDA e-books (October 2009–July 2014).

No. of user sessions	No. of titles	Total titles (%)
1	905	15%
2	907	15%
3-5	1714	29%
6-10	1145	19%
11-20	722	12%
21-30	220	4%
31-40	87	1%
41-50	51	1%
51+	153	3%

There is no doubt that a library can save money by using short-term loans, especially in the first year or two of activating the option (see Table 1). However, Figure 1 shows exponential STL price increases; in just one year, the average cost of a short-term loan in Iowa's PDA program jumped from $11.00 to $24.11 per e-book. This is an increase of more than 119%; the author anticipates that the average STL cost will continue to rise.

Given this trend, the author will gather more data on STLs in the future to decide whether to end the STL option altogether or whether to block selected publishers with the highest STL costs from the PDA program. This evaluation will consider the average cost per book from each publisher in conjunction with the short-term loan percentage of the list price.

By 2015, some librarians began wondering about the long-term sustainability of the short-term loan model. As more libraries employ the STL model, many publishers have become increasingly uncomfortable with it. Swords (2011b) touted short-term loans as "the single most important capability in successful PDA programs" (p. 177), but many things have changed since he wrote that. Many publishers attribute considerable revenue losses to the STL model, evidenced by some publishers' regular (and steep) STL price increases in apparent efforts to recoup lost income. Increases of 10%

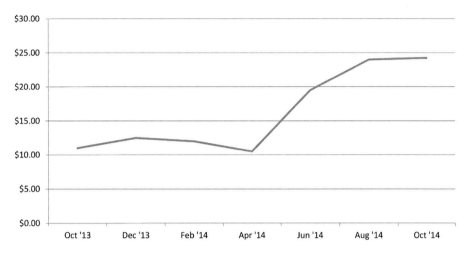

Figure 1. Average short-term loan cost per e-book at the University of Iowa Libraries (October 2013–October 2014).

to 20% are common, but some publishers have increased the one-day STL loan fee from 10% to 40% of list price. In 2014, ebrary reported STL price increases from 27 publishers that affect Iowa's PDA program. In sum, STLs can save a library money, but it is important to be aware that the savings will diminish as STL prices rise. When librarians use the STL option, librarians should monitor reports carefully and regularly.

THE PROVEN VALUE OF PDA

Since about 2010, PDA e-book programs have become a common service used by academic libraries to supplement traditional collection development. Numerous articles and conference papers present data and anecdotal evidence confirming that PDA works well when librarians set up and manage these programs carefully. At Iowa, the PDA program not only saved money, but also served as another tool in the collection management toolbox. Iowa patrons' use of PDA e-books proves that the program helps the library meet a demonstrated need by renting and then buying titles that patrons actually use, rather than perpetuating the traditional model of librarians buying books that they think their patrons will use. Table 6 shows that the majority (61%) of Iowa's PDA e-books have received between three and 20 user sessions since the purchase date; 9% of the titles enjoyed 21 or more user sessions per title.

During nearly five years, the e-books purchased through Iowa's PDA program accrued 54,426 user sessions (an average of nine user sessions per book), over one million page views, and nearly 600,000 chapter downloads. By late 2014, the average cost per PDA e-book reached $99.72 (down from $106.51 during the first year in 2009). These impressive use figures coupled with reasonable costs prove the value of committing library resources and also provide accountability for library expenditures to university and college administrators.

The data demonstrate the quality of the e-books purchased through user selection; a close examination of the purchased titles and their cumulative use over time shows that even those titles with only a single user session to date are titles that are appropriate to the collection. Identifying those titles with the highest number of sessions and page views reveals a breadth of subject coverage, a range of prices and publication dates, and variety of publishers (see Table 6). Although many people do not yet consider e-books ideal for deep reading due to interface challenges and digital rights management issues, the data support the fact that patrons' use of e-books offered through PDA plans results in adding quality library content.

Having a smoothly functioning PDA program allows collection managers to focus more on identifying and collecting specialized content rather than on the more routine selection of mainstream titles. This change should be welcome to collection managers who are increasingly pulled in directions other than selection, such as for outreach to faculty and students, instruction responsibilities, or working on scholarly communication efforts.

CONCLUSION

As PDA programs become a staple in academic libraries' collection management practices, librarians would greatly appreciate improved use reports from their e-book vendors. Currently, vendor reports on PDA activity and use do not completely meet librarians' requirements for analyzing the data needed to manage PDA programs effectively and efficiently. For example, COUNTER's Code of Practices for E-Resources should improve the Book Reports to include publication year and cumulative use data (Project COUNTER, 2012). Books are used and evaluated differently than journals, but since the e-book reports are modeled so closely on their e-journal counterparts, critical elements are missing. Librarians must be proactive in requesting (and evaluating) the

Table 6. Examples of most-used PDA titles at the University of Iowa Libraries (October 2009–July 2014).

Title	Publisher	Year of publication	Purchase date	Price	Page views	User sessions
Masculine jealousy and contemporary cinema	Palgrave Macmillan	2007	11/21/2010	$90.00	968	487
Current diagnosis and treatment: Pediatrics (19th Ed.)	McGraw-Hill	2008	2/18/2010	$72.95	6268	321
First aid for the USMLE step 3 (2nd Ed.)	McGraw-Hill	2008	12/29/2009	$39.95	9348	293
Roman games: Historical sources in translation	Wiley-Blackwell	2005	8/30/2010	$91.95	10734	237
Conspiracy theories: A critical introduction	Palgrave Macmillan	2011	9/1/2012	$80.00	3869	227
Frederick Douglass: A biography	ABC-CLIO	2011	10/17/2011	$35.00	5016	219
Invisible hook: The hidden economics of pirates	Princeton University Press	2009	1/21/2011	$24.95	3827	207
Applied logistic regression (3rd Ed.)	Wiley	2013	5/8/2013	$130.00	3420	190
Delivering health care in America: A systems approach (4th Ed.)	Jones & Bartlett	2008	1/22/2013	$129.95	5934	181

reports they receive from their PDA e-book vendors. Quality reports on PDA use, the risk pool, costs, and purchased titles should be considered fundamental tools for administering a successful and effective PDA program.

Using the University of Iowa Libraries' experience, this chapter outlined the basic elements of setting up a PDA e-book program as well as effective techniques for managing it. It explained how data analysis informs librarians about their users, assists in identifying new interdisciplinary areas of interest on campus, and allows collection managers to shift their attention from routine selection tasks to activities involving more interaction with their users to determine resource needs.

In the relative dawn of e-book PDA, there are still many issues under development, such as available content, digital rights management, pricing, reports, and sustainable PDA models. As shown in this chapter, PDA is not something that runs on its own. Like a print approval plan, it requires regular oversight and engagement. Most academic libraries are in financial situations that require diligent stewardship of collections funds. No longer can librarians continue building book collections by using the traditional speculative mode for buying the majority of their monographic acquisitions. PDA offers a solution that ensures that librarians meet users' needs effectively and instantly, while simultaneously building collections with demonstrated value.

REFERENCES

Anderson, K., Freeman, R., Hérubel, J-P., Mykytiuk, L., Nixon, J., & Ward, S. (2010). Liberal arts books on demand: A decade of patron-driven collection development, part 1. *Collection Management, 35*(3/4), 125–141. http://dx.doi.org/10.1080/01462679.2010.486959

Bracke, M. (2010). Science and technology books on demand: A decade of patron-driven collection development, part 2. *Collection Management, 35*(3/4), 142–150. http://dx.doi.org/10.1080/01462679.2010.486742

Dillon, D. (2009). Untitled talk and PowerPoint slides. Paper presented at the CIC Center for Library Initiative Conference, Bloomington, Indiana. http://www.cic.net/downloads/conferences/library2009/DennisDillon2009.pptx

Dillon, D. (2011). Texas demand-driven acquisitions: Controlling costs in a large-scale PDA program. In D. A. Swords (Ed.), *Patron-driven acquisitions: History and best practices* (pp. 154–167). Berlin/Boston: Walter De Gruyter. http://dx.doi.org/10.1515/9783110253030.157

Goldner, M., & Birch, K. (2012). Resource sharing in a cloud computing age. *Interlending & Document Supply, 40*(1), 4–11. http://dx.doi.org/10.1108/02641611211214224

Hodges, D., Preston, C., & Hamilton, M. J. (2010). Patron-initiated collection development: Progress of a paradigm shift. *Collection Management, 35*(3/4), 208–221. http://dx.doi.org/10.1080/01462679.2010.486968

Fischer, K., Wright, M., Clatanoff, K., Barton, H., & Shreeves, E. (2011). Give 'em what they want: A one-year study of unmediated patron-driven acquisition of e-books. *College & Research Libraries, 73*(5), 469–492. http://dx.doi.org/10.5860/crl-297

Lugg, R. (2011). Collecting for the moment: Patron-driven acquisitions as a disruptive technology. In D. Swords (Ed.), *Patron-driven acquisitions: History and best practices* (pp. 7–22). Berlin/Boston: Walter de Gruyter. http://dx.doi.org/10.1515/9783110253030.7

Nixon, J., Freeman, R., & Ward, S. (2010). Patron-driven acquisitions: An introduction and literature review. *Collection Management, 35*(3/4), 151–161. http://dx.doi.org/10.1080/01462679.2010.486963

Nixon, J., & Saunders, E. S. (2010). A study of circulation statistics of books on demand: A decade of patron-driven collection development, part 3. *Collection Management, 35*(3/4), 119–124. http://dx.doi.org/10.1080/01462679.2010.486957

Nixon, J., Ward, S., & Freeman, R. (2014). Selectors' perceptions of e-book patron-driven acquisitions. In K. Bridges (Ed.), *Customer-based collection development* (pp. 27–47). Chicago, IL: American Library Association.

Project COUNTER. (2012). Code of practice for e-resources: Release 4. Retrieved from http://www.projectcounter.org/code_practice.html

Swords, D. (Ed.). (2011a). *Patron-driven acquisitions: History and best practices.* Berlin/Boston: Walter de Gruyter. http://dx.doi.org/10.1515/9783110253030

Swords, D. (2011b). Elements of a demand-driven model. In D. Swords (Ed.), *Patron-driven acquisitions: History and best practices* (pp. 169–187). Berlin/Boston: Walter de Gruyter. http://dx.doi.org/10.1515/9783110253030

Tyler, D. C., Falci, C., Melvin, J. C., Epp, M., & Kreps, A. M. (2013). Patron-driven acquisition and circulation at an academic library: Interactions and circulation performance of print books acquired via librarians' orders, approval plans, and patrons' interlibrary loan requests. *Collection Management, 38*(1), 3–32. http://dx.doi.org/10.1080/01462679.2012.730494

8 | Use and Cost Analysis of E-Books: Patron-Driven Acquisitions Plan vs. Librarian-Selected Titles

Suzanne M. Ward and Rebecca A. Richardson

ABSTRACT

Many academic libraries have experimented with e-book patron-driven acquisitions (PDA) plans as small projects to test the concept of offering users thousands of titles, yet only paying for them as they are used. At the same time, many librarians continue traditional patterns of buying e-book titles the same way they bought print books for decades—purchasing titles based on their belief that these selections will be ones that local users need. This study shows that many librarian-selected e-book titles suffer the same fate as the traditional model of librarian-selected print books: many receive little or no use. The PDA model is far more effective, both by making large numbers of titles available and by leveraging tight collections budgets. This paper analyzes cost and use factors of three years of data from the Purdue University Libraries' PDA plan, and examines the same factors for librarian-selected e-books during the same time period. The authors conclude that it may be time to consider moving PDA from its current role as a small ancillary collection development tool to become a major component of an academic library's monograph collection development program and to suggest that selectors modify their title-by-title selection habits for e-books.

THE USE OF PRINT BOOKS

Most academic librarians are aware of the flood of articles starting in the 1960s demonstrating that high percentages of librarian-selected books were seldom or never used. One of the earliest and most widely cited studies is Trueswell's (1969) "Some Behavior Patterns of Library Users: The 80/20 Rule," which concluded that 20% of an academic library collection receives 80% of the use. Numerous later studies conducted in different sizes and types of academic libraries all confirmed some variation of Trueswell's findings: a relatively small percentage of a collection accounts for the lion's share of the use. Some authors also reported that large percentages of their collections received no use during the first few years after acquisition, after which the likelihood of any circulation activity was extremely low (Bulick, Sabor, & Flynn, 1979, pp. 9–18; Hardesty, 1981, p. 266). Rather than take the space to cite these studies here, the authors suggest that interested readers consult Ward's (2015, pp. 25–29) summary of these and other reports of use studies over the past 50 years. It is worth noting, however, that this phenomenon is not limited to the distant past. As recently as 2010, Nixon and Saunders (2010, pp. 151–161) reported that 46,996 (33%) of the 141,112 books purchased for the circulating collection of a large research library between 2000 and 2009 were never checked out. However, the authors also reported that during this same time period, patrons subsequently checked out 82% of the books purchased through their library's interlibrary loan (ILL) print PDA service following the first use by the requesting ILL patron.

This last finding dramatically underscores the point that patrons are good judges, at least in the short and medium term, of choosing titles that other patrons will use. Use studies for librarian-selected and patron-selected print books confirm that patrons are in fact better judges than librarians when it comes to identifying books that will meet the needs of the local user population.

Does this phenomenon also hold true now that academic libraries have embraced the e-book?

THE RISE OF E-BOOKS

Most academic librarians would agree that e-books are here to stay, even if they do not completely replace the need for print books. From the librarians' perspective, e-books are easy to buy (either singly or as part of packages), require no space, never wear out, never become lost, solve the challenge of serving patrons at a distance, and provide 24/7 access to content. Librarians enjoy the ease of buying e-book packages, especially when publishers and aggregators offer attractive pricing for multiple packages, commitments over multiple years, or consortial deals. Publisher and vendor products such as e-book packages and profiled slip plans have made it possible for academic librarians to abandon much of the title-by-title selection that consumed so much time in the past.

But have librarians really learned from past lessons with print books that selecting individual titles in the hopes that users will choose them is not the most effective approach? In the past, such activity might have been at least partially justified by the fact that books went out of print quickly; if librarians did not buy certain titles soon after publication, it then became even more expensive in terms of time and price to buy needed titles later. E-books, however, do not go out of print, and the print-on-demand services used by more and more publishers mean that many print books never go out of print either. There is decreasing need to buy any but the most obvious high-use titles immediately upon publication; the fear that there may not be a future opportunity to obtain them now hardly exists.

PDA plans (sometimes called demand-driven acquisitions, or DDA) offer librarians the option of adding thousands of librarian-profiled e-book titles to their catalogs or discovery layers. PDA plans involve a preselected number of short-term loans (STLs; essentially rental fees) until patron use reaches a certain threshold, at which point the next patron use triggers the title for purchase. Librarians can thus offer far more titles than they could ever afford to buy outright and pay only for what their patrons actually use. Patrons remain unaware that PDA e-book titles are any different from other e-books that their library offers. Based on the analysis of print PDA plans, typically linked with interlibrary loan requests, it is reasonable to predict that patron-selected e-books also will enjoy both high subsequent use and better overall use than librarian-selected titles.

Yet despite the early promising results of e-book PDA services, librarians seem reluctant to abandon the traditional activity of title-by-title selection in cases when there is no pressure to acquire books before the moment of need. Thousands of e-book titles are candidates for cost-avoidance, or at least cost-deferment. Instead of buying these books now, librarians can wait for the future moment when a user actually demonstrates a need for a particular title. If the title is part of an e-book PDA plan, the need is fulfilled instantly and possibly only at a low rental fee (STL) if the title is only needed once or twice.

The authors hypothesized that their library's e-book PDA plan was a cost-effective method to:

- meet patrons' immediate needs for occasional use of many titles (STLs)
- add relevant e-book titles to the permanent collection based on patron use (autopurchases after three STLs)
- add relevant titles to the collection that demonstrate a strong tendency to enjoy further use after purchase.

The authors also wanted to examine librarians' single title e-book buying patterns and patrons' use of those selections. They wondered if they would encounter similar overall results as with print books, that is, that patron-selected e-books would on average enjoy higher use than librarian-selected titles. Although patron satisfaction as evidenced through use was the most important outcome, the authors also were interested in looking at the costs involved in the two models.

PURDUE UNIVERSITY LIBRARIES E-BOOK PDA PROGRAM

The Purdue University Libraries started its e-book PDA program in March 2011 with an initial pool of 11,255 titles published from 2009 onward. Purdue chose EBL for its PDA plan and worked through its book vendor YBP to establish the profile. An average of about 160 new titles meet the profile and are added every week. No titles have been weeded to date, bringing the total number of PDA titles to 38,549 at the end of February 2015.

For the purposes of this study, the authors focused on the e-book PDA titles added between March 2011 and February 2014 (32,988 titles). When they conducted the analysis in January 2015, they looked at the *costs* for titles added during this three-year period and looked at *use* for these titles during the period March 2011 to August 2014 (three and a half years).

METHODOLOGY

The authors consulted EBL reports to determine costs and use. LibCentral, EBL's administrative site that collects pertinent information unique to each institution, supplied most of the reports; however, the authors also requested a custom EBL report to obtain data unavailable from LibCentral.

To analyze the costs associated with PDA and librarian-selected titles, the authors used EBL's Sales Report. This report contains the invoice date,

EBL ID, title, publisher, e-ISBN, purchase type, cost, and other pertinent bibliographic information. Using the Sales Report, the authors determined the number of STLs and autopurchases and the costs associated with them, as well as purchase information for the titles purchased outright.

To analyze use, the authors pulled EBL's Use Report. This report contains detailed use information, such as reader duration, the number of pages read, as well as if the use was from a PDA title versus a title purchased outright. The report also identifies uses as browses or loans. Browses are always free (no charge to the library). For PDA, browses are defined as any use under five minutes during which the user does not copy, cut, print, or download. Copying, cutting, printing, and downloading during this five-minute period triggers a use, or STL—Purdue librarians set this loan period as 24 hours. Publishers determine the STL cost as a percentage of the list price; this percentage can vary from 5% to 30% or more. Purdue found the average STL to be about 10% of the list price.

Browsing longer than five minutes also triggers an STL. On the fourth loan, titles are autopurchased, also noted on the report. After purchase, patrons have an option of longer checkout periods. These settings are unique to Purdue; each library determines how many STLs to allow before autopurchase. Only titles with use appear on the report, so the authors also were able to determine which titles had no use (browses or loans) at all.

It is important to note when looking at the Use Report that not all browses are equal. Some are standalone browses, meaning that the use did not trigger an STL. When a use triggers a loan or an autopurchase, it is always preceded by a browse, meaning that the use report shows *two* activities that the patron would consider a single use.

To determine what the cost of the librarian-selected titles would have been had they been added as PDA, the authors consulted EBL's Use Report and Sales Report. EBL allows 10 minutes of browse time for titles that have already been bought before triggering an "owned loan" (compared with five minutes of browse time for unpurchased titles). Using the browse duration information contained in the Use Report, the authors could identify browses under five minutes and browses over five minutes. Browses under five minutes would still be considered browses, and browses over five minutes would have triggered STLs. Based on this information, the authors were able to identify, hypothetically, the number of STLs per title and calculate their costs using an estimated 10% of the list price, pulled from the Sales Report.

EBL also provides COUNTER reports, which can be used to analyze use, although they do not contain browse and loan information or provide detailed use activity, such as the number of pages read, reader duration, and so forth.

PDA USE

Table 1 summarizes the use and cost data for the 599 e-books autopurchased during the PDA plan's first three years. The Purdue PDA plan allows three STLs before the fourth use triggers an autopurchase. The number of STLs and autopurchased titles (and thus total program costs) rose each year. This was not surprising; not only did the total number of available titles increase with new additions each year, but also because patrons became more accustomed to using e-books, based on the rising numbers of titles used each year. Rising average costs of both STLs and autopurchases probably stem from publishers adjusting costs for STLs and list prices as they learned how the PDA model affected their revenue.

Table 2 takes a closer look at the 16,237 titles that entered the PDA plan in its first year (March 2011–February 2012) and analyzes the amount of use they had received as of August 2014 (three and a half years). Seventy percent of the titles received no use at all during this time (no browses and no loans); their list prices value these 11,438 titles at over $1.2 million, but the cost to the library was zero. Thirty percent or 4,799 unique titles were used at least once; the value of these books totaled a little over $533,000. Overall, the library paid an average of $5.72 for each use (including browses, STLs, and autopurchases) for a total of $93,371.

In one sense, the library "saved" nearly $440,000 by paying only for the titles that patrons used ($533,000 total value of books used minus $93,000 actual costs paid for STLs and autopurchases), or even "saved" $1.66 million ($1.753 million total value of all PDA books minus $93,000 actual costs for use). In reality, these are phantom savings. The library would never have been able to afford buying the Year 1 pool of all 16,237 e-books and would in fact have been reckless to do so even if it had had the budget; the librarians would have known from past experience that only a small percentage of the titles would receive any use. As Table 1 shows, the cost for STLs exceeded the cost of autopurchases for two of the first three years studied. Having a large pool of potentially relevant e-books available for patrons to choose

Table 1. Cost summary of PDA e-books: March 2011–February 2014.

Year	Auto-purchases	Auto-purchases: Total cost	Auto-purchases: Average cost	STLs	STLs: Total cost	STLs: Average cost	Total cost by year
Year 1 (March 2011– February 2012)	111	$8,747	$78.80	1850	$16,875	$9.12	$25,622
Year 2 (March 2012– February 2013)	192	$18,298	$95.30	2424	$22,873	$9.44	$41,171
Year 3 (March 2013– February 2014)	296	$32,509	$109.83	3358	$33,127	$9.87	$65,636
TOTAL	599	$59,554	$94.64	7632	$72,875	$9.47	$132,429

Table 2. Use of PDA e-books added during Year 1: March 2011–February 2012 (use between March 2011 and August 2014).

Use*	Titles	Percent	List price	Library cost
No use (not touched)	11,438	70%	$1,219,711	$0
1 use	2395	15%	$271,523	$10,534
2 uses	921	6%	$103,535	$8,512
3 uses	497	3%	$56,718	$7,271
4 uses	291	2%	$32,734	$10,002
5-9 uses	481	3%	$49,435	$33,550
10+ uses	214	1%	$19,195	$23,502
TOTAL	16,237	100.0%	$1,752,851	$93,371

*Use includes browses and loans.

from means that many of the occasional uses, whether quick browses or longer STLs, met many patrons' needs. Although there is no way to quantify them, at least some of those $5.72 average costs per use avoided the need for a slower and more expensive interlibrary loan transaction.

How do these figures play out over the March 2011–February 2014 three-year period? During that time, the library loaded 32,988 PDA titles with total list price value of almost $3.3 million. Users touched 7,233 unique titles (22% of the titles in the entire pool) valued at total list price of about $784,000 (about 24% of the total value). These titles received a total of 21,015 uses (some browses, some STLs, and some autopurchases (see Table 3).

Table 3. PDA titles: Totals and value/cost: March 2011–February 2014.

Value	Cost
Total value of 32,988 PDA titles	$3,291,531
Value of 7,233 unique titles used	$784,274
Cost to library for 21,015 uses	$132,429

Table 4 takes a closer look at the details of the different types of uses over these three years. Browses accounted for 27% of the total use. Short-term loans cost the library almost $73,000, while autopurchases cost about $59,500, or

55% and 45%, respectively, of the total cost of about $132,000 over the three years. It is interesting to note that "owned loans," that is, subsequent use of titles that have been autopurchased, accounted for 34% of the total use. This important figure means that, in general, the titles that patrons use enough to trigger autopurchases are also ones that receive significant subsequent use.

Table 4. Overall PDA summary: March 2011–February 2014.

Type of use	Number	Cost	Percentage of use
Browses (free use)	5703	$0.00	27%
STLs (1-3 uses)	7632	$72,875	36%
Autopurchases (4th use)	599	$59,554	3%
Owned loans (5+ uses)	7081	$0.00	34%
TOTAL	21,015	$132,429	100%

Subsequent use is an important measure to determine a PDA program's success. It is also a measure that can only be determined after a PDA plan has been in place over a number of years. The authors took a closer look at the 599 autopurchases that were triggered by patron activity between March 2011 and February 2014, but they evaluated the activity that occurred between March 2011 and August 2014 (three and a half years), thus allowing the most recently purchased titles as of February 2014 at least six months more time for further activity. A few titles (7%) received no further use after the four uses that resulted in the autopurchase. The remaining 93% of titles received subsequent use, including 148 titles that clocked 11 or more uses past the autopurchase point. This is the "proof in the pudding": the titles that patrons use enough to reach autopurchase are almost all titles that will receive further use. These are the "right" books that meet the ongoing learning and research needs of the local patron community, at least in the short and medium term. Starting from a pool of 16,237 titles, these 599 are the ones that patrons need most at Purdue University. It would have been impossible for librarians to predict more than a few of them correctly. Table 5 summarizes post-autopurchase activity.

This brings the discussion to the point of librarian-selected e-books and how well these titles meet patrons' needs.

Table 5. Titles autopurchased between March 2011–February 2014 with activity through August 2014.

Use	Titles	Percentage
4 uses (no subsequent use after purchase)	42	7%
5-9 uses	276	46%
10-14 uses	133	22%
15+ uses	148	25%
TOTAL	599	100%

LIBRARIAN-SELECTED E-BOOKS

Purdue librarians have been buying e-books on a title-by-title basis through YBP's GOBI database since early 2010. The advent of the e-book PDA plan in March 2011 did not change this activity; librarians continued to select e-books from EBL and other aggregators through YBP, the difference being that the EBL titles were ones that did not fit the PDA plan profile. In March 2012, YBP added a feature that allowed librarians to move selected e-book titles into the PDA pool "manually" rather than buying them outright.

The authors looked at librarian-selected EBL titles for the same time period that they examined the results of the PDA plan: March 2011 through February 2014, and calculated activity from March 2011 through August 2014 to allow the titles at least six months of activity. The librarians bought 684 EBL e-books on a title-by-title basis during the three-year period at a total cost of almost $72,000; 189 (28%) of them (list price almost $18,000) had no use during the three and a half year period. A further 149 (22%) of them (list price about $14,500) had only one use. At the other end of the spectrum, 225 (33%) of the titles (list price $26,310) enjoyed four or more uses (see Table 6).

These results show how difficult it is for librarians to predict which titles their patrons will actually use. One can argue that in the end, use is the only metric that really matters; adding "good books" that nobody consults may not add much real value to a collection from the users' perspective. If use is the critical metric, then, in this case, librarians only made very good choices a third of the time. Despite their best intentions, 28% of their choices were not helpful ones from the patrons' point of

Table 6. E-books selected by librarians between March 2011–February 2014 (use between March 2011–August 2014).

Use*	Librarian-selected titles	Percent	List price
No browses, no loans = zero use	189	28%	$18,717
1 use	149	22%	$14,519
2 uses	78	11%	$7,736
3 uses	43	6%	$4,419
4+ uses	225	33%	$26,310
TOTAL	684	100%	$71,701

*Use includes browses and loans.

view, because no one even browsed these books during this time period. How can librarians be persuaded to alter a lifetime's habit of buying books "just in case" when PDA offers a "just-in-time" model that defers expenditure of library funds until the moment someone actually needs a certain title?

This raises a very delicate issue; one does not want to give the impression of making negative remarks about colleagues' professional judgment, knowledge of their subject areas or constituencies, or their collecting habits. After all, the selections were all appropriate additions in terms of subject matter and treatment; it just turned out that, as has been shown with print book purchases over the decades, patrons do not choose to use all of them. It is an awkward point because collection managers often are delighted when colleagues choose e-books over print books, but the managers also hope that selectors will adjust their selection habits to avoid cluttering cyberspace with e-books that nobody uses in the same way that many academic library stacks are crammed with print books that no one reads. PDA provides a way in which a library can offer thousands of relevant titles, but only buy selected ones when sufficient patron use indicates which ones are the good choices for the local collection.

The authors decided to illustrate the value of PDA over the outright purchase of seemingly appropriate titles by taking an in-depth look at the 684 e-books that their colleagues had bought and examining a "what if" scenario. What if these 684 books had all been available to add to the PDA pool at the moment that the librarians wanted to buy them? The authors know that this was not in fact possible because YBP did not offer the option of manually adding titles to the PDA pool until partway through this time period. But if these titles had been added to the PDA pool, how would they have been affected by the actual use that patrons made of them?

Table 7 shows the categories of actual patron use and the costs associated with them for the 684 books that the librarians bought outright. If these had actually been PDA books, for example, the 189 books with no uses and the 135 books with only browsing use would not have cost the library anything. The bottom line is that the total cost to the library of all the PDA activity with these titles would have been about $28,500. Comparing this with the nearly $72,000 that the librarians actually spent to buy these books, adding them to the PDA pool instead of buying them outright would have "saved" the library about $43,500 over three years.

Table 7. "What if" scenario: If librarian-selected books had been moved into the PDA pool instead (March 2011–February 2014).

Use*	Titles	Percent	Library cost
Titles with zero use	189	27%	$0
Titles with browses only (browses under 5 minutes)	135	20%	$0
1 use (any browse over 5 minutes and loans = "STL")	129	19%	$1,420
2 uses "STLs"	42	6%	$732
3 uses "STLs"	26	4%	$790
4+ uses ("autopurchase")	163	24%	$25,588
TOTAL	684	100%	$28,530

*Use includes browses and loans.

The concept of saving money is a little slippery in the PDA context; it really means that overall the library would have deferred some of the costs and avoided others. If a librarian buys a $100 book today, the library pays

$100. If the title drops into the PDA pool and if nobody uses it until five years later and then only for one STL, the library pays, say, $15 for the STL at that time. If, on the other hand, the book reaches the point of autopurchase within a few months, the library pays $145 (three STLs at $15 each plus the $100 list price). Since relatively few books reach the autopurchase stage, and since most autopurchased books enjoyed healthy subsequent use, collection managers would rather pay more for those specific titles that their patrons use rather than list price for hundreds of titles that are used seldom or not at all.

Another way to look at the "what if" scenario is to limit the view to the books that librarians bought in the first year (March 2011–February 2012) and then assess their actual use over the next three and a half years (to August 2014). As Table 8 shows, librarians bought 331 books in Year 1 for about $33,000. Thirty-six percent (118) of them (list price about $10,000) had no use; 88 (27%) of them (list price about $10,500) had four or more uses. Table 9 breaks out the use and costs for these 331 e-books if they had been in the PDA pool; the library would only have paid about $8,600 for 84 titles with STL activity and 14 autopurchased titles. This $8,600 first-year cost is only 26% of the $33,000 that the library actually paid when librarians bought 331 titles outright.

Table 8. Librarian selected e-books in Year 1: March 2011–February 2012.

Use*	Titles	Percent	Library cost
Titles with no browses, no loans = zero use	118	35%	$10,411
1 use	67	20%	$7,171
2 uses	36	11%	$2,950
3 uses	22	7%	$2,328
4+ uses	88	27%	$10,562
TOTAL purchased between March 2011– February 2012 (Year 1)	**331**	**100%**	**$33,422**

*Use includes browses and loans.

Table 9. "What if" scenario: If Year 1 librarian-selected books had been moved into the PDA pool instead: March 2011–February 2014 (use as of August 2014).

Use*	Titles	Percent	Library cost
Titles with zero use	118	36%	$0
Titles with browses only (browses under 5 minutes)	42	13%	$0
1 use = STL	70	21%	$717
2 uses = STLs	23	7%	$405
3 uses = STLs	10	3%	$276
4+ uses = autopurchase	68	20%	$11,342
TOTAL	331	100%	$12,740

*Use is browse over 5 minutes plus loans—would equal an STL in PDA.

PDA PLAN ENHANCEMENTS

Like most other digital products and services, the PDA plan options that YBP now offers include features that build on the "plain vanilla" version that the Purdue University Libraries launched in March 2011.

In March 2012, YBP introduced the manual demand-driven acquisitions (DDA) option. This option allows selectors to move e-book titles that do not match a library's PDA profile into the library's PDA pool. Although these books do not meet the profile criteria, a librarian may judge them to be of potential interest to users. Rather than buying these titles outright in the hopes that patrons might eventually use them, librarians can now transfer these titles to the PDA pool where no payments are assessed unless patrons access the books. This is an excellent way for librarians to exercise their skills in collection building while deferring costs until patrons use the books (or avoiding costs completely if patrons do not select them). It is interesting to note that in the list of Purdue's top 10 most-used autopurchased titles, three of the books were manually added librarian choices, including the top title with 1,146 uses (see Table 10).

Two other major vendors, ebrary and ESBCO, also offer PDA titles using slightly different models than EBL. Although all three vendors offer some of the same titles (often with price variations), other e-books appear on only one or two of these three vendors' lists. The Purdue University Libraries added a "cascade" of vendors in August 2014, setting

Table 10. Top 10 most-used autopurchased titles, March 2011–February 2014.

Title	Total uses	Publisher	EBL category
Handbook of Human Factors and Economics*	1408	John Wiley	Engineering: Civil; Engineering
The Morality and Global Justice Reader	1107	Westview Press	Philosophy, Political Science
Why We Hate the Oil Companies: Straight Talk From an Energy Insider	239	Palgrave Macmillan	Business / Management
Cultural Codes: Makings of a Black Music Philosophy	193	Scarecrow Press	Fine Arts
Behind the Beautiful Forevers: Life, Death, and Hope in a Mumbai Undercity*	184	Scribe Publications	Social Science
Environmental Health and Hazard Risk Assessment: Principles and Calculations	153	CRC Press	Social Science; Health; Environmental Studies
Advances in Human Aspects of Healthcare*	151	CRC Press	Medicine
Concepts in Syngas Manufacture	146	World Scientific Publishing	Engineering; Science: Chemistry; Science; Engineering: Chemical
Understanding Japanese Society	145	Taylor and Francis	Social Science
Thinking in Systems: A Primer	121	Taylor and Francis	Computer Science / IT, Mathematics, Environmental Studies

*A librarian manually added this title to the PDA pool.

preferences about vendor order for cases in which more than one holds a title. This action increases the PDA pool by adding more relevant titles and also potentially increases costs if patrons choose books that would not have been available had the library stayed with a single e-book PDA vendor.

PDA'S PLACE IN COLLECTION DEVELOPMENT

In many academic libraries, PDA started as a small experiment. In the original model, autopurchase occurred the first time a patron opened an e-book, even if only for a minute or two to review the table of contents. The experiences of early adopters helped shape the current model in which librarians can choose a number of short-term loans before autopurchase so that, as in Purdue's case, relatively few books receive enough use to trigger autopurchase. In these plans, libraries sometimes spend more money on STLs for occasional use than they do on autopurchases. This outcome is acceptable; the library supports meeting the needs of patrons who want occasional access to a large number of books, and also spending money to buy those few hundred titles out of tens of thousands that their patrons find valuable enough to consult more often, including after autopurchase.

Is e-book PDA the only way or the best way to build a collection? Not at all. PDA complements the large e-book packages or subscriptions that libraries buy or lease (libraries can exclude their package publishers' titles from their PDA plans). It also complements the print collections that libraries still develop. PDA cannot replace book selection in foreign languages or from publishers who do not participate with PDA vendors. But many librarians may want to consider letting PDA enjoy a bigger role than it has currently played in their libraries. PDA is a win-win solution for libraries and their users; users enjoy a far larger choice of titles than their libraries could possibly afford to buy outright, and the libraries only pay for the books that the patrons use. Studies like this one confirm that patrons have a solid track record of using titles that other patrons will also consult.

SELECTORS' CHOICES IN THE DIGITAL AGE

In the same way that the authors understand that PDA, although useful and effective, is not the only option for building an e-book collection, so also do they understand that selectors' experience and choices make a vital difference in shaping that collection. Collection managers usually solicit input from selectors when setting up the PDA profiles that generate both the initial title pool and the weekly new additions. Selectors join discussions about the shift away from print books and about choosing e-book packages that meet campus learning and research needs.

How is the selector's role changing when it comes to choosing books title-by-title? Fifty years of published research demonstrate that a high percentage of librarian-selected print books were never or seldom used. Before the advent of e-books, it was understandable that librarians would make best guesses to buy the print books they thought their patrons would use before those books went out of print. Today, however, any particular e-book title will be available for the foreseeable future, so in most cases, there is no need to buy it now just in case someone might use it; the purchase can be deferred until the moment, perhaps some years from now, when someone actually does want it. This study shows that when librarians buy a single e-book, the chance of use is relatively low, just as it has been for decades with print books. PDA offers the cost-saving option of presenting the titles for patrons to discover and then deferring costs until the moment of use. It does, however, require that selectors shift their habits from making outright purchases to moving relevant and eligible titles into the PDA pool instead.

There are some titles that are obvious acquisitions needed to support a particular library's clientele, for example, books used in courses, a title requested by an instructor, or a statesman's much-anticipated memoir; these should be purchased and ready for patron use. The authors suggest, however, that buying many just-in-case titles can be deferred until the moment of patron need, ideally by offering the titles through e-book PDA plans, but also through rapid print fulfillment services. In many cases, the practice of deferring purchase until use means that certain books are never bought because patrons never use them. The money that would otherwise have been spent on them can be deployed for other purchases or used to replenish the PDA budget.

CONCLUSION

Years of analysis of librarian-selected print purchases in many libraries have shown that it is impossible for librarians to predict what books their patrons will need with a high degree of accuracy. This analysis of librarian-selected e-book purchases reveals the same tendency. However, the environment has changed enough with the advent of e-books that librarians need not re-create the same scenario in an electronic world. With PDA plans, academic librarians now have the tools to avoid the decades-old pitfall of buying in the hope of future use and then seeing 30% to 50% of their purchases languish untouched. However, as the authors' investigation revealed, old habits die hard. Selectors need to hear from their colleagues with responsibilities in collection management, acquisitions, and electronic resources that making titles discoverable is usually a much sounder fiscal practice than buying them outright. Using the data that e-book PDA vendors provide, collection managers can determine whether their patrons use librarians' individually selected e-books at significantly lower rates than PDA titles and then calculate how much money can potentially be saved or deferred by moving titles into the PDA pool rather than buying them immediately. The results may be illuminating and lead to some tough but interesting conversations with colleagues about modifying e-book selection practices.

REFERENCES

Bulick, S., Sabor, W. N., & Flynn, R. R. (1979). Circulation and in-house use of books. In A. Kent, J. Cohen, K. L. Montgomery, J. G. Williams, S. Bulick, R. R. Flynn, & N. Mansfield (Eds.), *Use of library materials: The University of Pittsburgh study* (pp. 9–55). New York, NY: Marcel Dekker.

Hardesty, L. (1981). Use of library materials at a small liberal arts college. *Library Research, 3*(3), 261–282.

Nixon, J. M., & Saunders, E. S. (2010). A study of circulation statistics of Books on Demand: A decade of patron-driven collection development. *Collection Management, 35*(3/4), 151–161. http://dx.doi.org/10.1080/01462679.2010.486963

Trueswell, R. W. (1969). Some behavior patterns of library users: The 80/20 rule. *Wilson Library Bulletin, 43*(5), 348–461.

Ward, S. M. (2015). *Rightsizing the academic library collection*. Chicago, IL: ALA Editions.

9 | E-Books Across the Consortium: Reflections and Lessons From a Three-Year DDA Experiment at the Orbis Cascade Alliance

Kathleen Carlisle Fountain

ABSTRACT

For the last several years, the Orbis Cascade Alliance consortium has successfully run a consortium-wide demand-driven acquisitions (DDA) program to provide broad access to e-books. This program has ensured jointly owned and shared electronic books, secured core resources at a reasonable cost, and challenged the interlibrary loan prohibitions of e-book licenses. After three years of funding and managing the program, the Orbis Cascade Alliance experience provides lessons for operating at the consortium level. This chapter will describe the program and its history, provide an analysis of program data, and discuss the evolution of the program.

HISTORY

Since July 2011, the Orbis Cascade Alliance consortium has successfully run a consortium-wide DDA program for purchasing e-books. Designed as a method to share a core set of e-books collectively, this program facilitates access to about 17,000 titles a month and has purchased more than 1,900 titles in common for the consortium.

The Orbis Cascade Alliance is an academic consortium of 37 libraries in Oregon, Washington, and Idaho. Its members vary in size and type, with community colleges, small liberal arts universities, and large public research institutions on equal footing with one another within the organization. The Orbis Cascade Alliance's 21-year history is steeped in supporting resource sharing through its Summit system. A shared catalog, a

145

shared courier, and a commitment to sharing physical items provided the foundation for fostering a variety of collaborative collection development initiatives within the consortium. The Alliance's Collection Development and Management Committee (CDMC) led efforts to coordinate collections decisions across the member libraries. In the years just prior to the launch of the DDA program, it spearheaded several notable projects illustrating the consortium's commitment to shared collections. One project, initiated in 2007, created a distributed print repository for journal titles held in JSTOR. This committed selected members to retain specific journals as a light archive, thereby allowing other libraries to withdraw their copies of the same journals. In 2011, this project formed the basis for the creation of the Western Regional Storage Trust (WEST).

Another CDMC project focused on reducing "unnecessary duplication" of new monographs. The committee established a voluntary maximum copy threshold for the consortium in 2010 (Collection Development and Management Committee, 2010). This policy's goal was to increase the acquisition of titles not yet owned in the consortium without additional budget funds. In essence, the CDMC wanted to increase the availability of the monographic "long tail" within the consortium and facilitate cost-effective resource sharing of those titles through the Alliance's Summit program. To establish the threshold of three copies, the CDMC worked with YBP, the Alliance's preferred book vendor, to identify rates of acquisition for the consortium. YBP's data demonstrated that the most common rate of duplication was four copies, so dropping that number would be a modest goal that focused the librarians' attention on cooperative collection building.

The growth of member library e-book acquisitions and their attendant licenses prohibiting interlibrary loan presented a significant challenge to resource sharing. On the one hand, access to e-books permitted local student use at all hours of the day. On the other hand, those same resources could no longer be available to students across the consortium. As Jim Bunnelle noted, "Building up robust, locked-down localized e-book collections is totally counterproductive and hurts the Alliance's consortial leveraging power" (Emery, 2012, p. 3). The Alliance's governing council began planning for a method of sharing e-books across the Alliance in 2009 (McElroy & Hinken, 2011, p. 34). The planning groups evaluated purchasing models and eventually recommended the implementation of a DDA approach. In

2011, the council charged a new Alliance group, the Demand-Driven Acquisitions Pilot Implementation Team (DDAPIT), to "create an entirely new e-book purchasing model that allows consortium-wide access to titles purchased by individual member libraries" (Bunnelle, 2012, p. 24). Oversight was later transitioned to the E-Book Working Group. The council expected the Pilot Implementation Team to challenge the e-book acquisition status quo, expand access rights to e-books, and support an ownership approach.

PROGRAM OVERVIEW

The six-month DDA pilot launched on July 1, 2011, with a budget of $231,000 ("Demand Driven Acquisitions Pilot Funding," 2011). The titles included within the DDA program were determined by a profile, administered by YBP, and provided on the Ebook Library (EBL) platform. The team selected EBL through a request for information (RFI) process in 2011. As McElroy and Hinken (2011) noted in their pilot summary, EBL had a proven DDA model, was currently in use by member libraries locally, and offered robust data for pilot evaluation. They worked well with YBP and had the best potential to work well with the Alliance (McElroy & Hinken, 2011, p. 38). The initial discovery pool included 1,700 titles with 2011 imprints from 12 publishers (Bunnelle, 2012). By June 30, 2014, the end of the consortium's fiscal year, the Alliance had access to 19,000 titles, owned 1,771 e-books, and devoted $1,000,000 a year to the cost of the program.

The team partnered with YBP at the outset of this project because YBP's profiling and GOBI3 acquisitions data provided ways to protect earlier efforts to foster collaborative collection development. For example, within GOBI3, member library staff could see whether a title they wished to purchase was currently included in the consortium's DDA discovery pool. Additionally, YBP's historical acquisitions data detailed rates of duplication across the consortium. This information proved helpful when negotiating the purchasing cost with publishers.

Content

Throughout the life of this program, the profile remained steady. All subjects from selected publishers were included. This arrangement allowed access to the diversity of titles needed by the Alliance's liberal arts, professional, law, and medical communities. One significant change affecting the discovery pool has been based on imprint date. The initial load of 1,700 titles included only titles from 2011. After the DDAPIT group observed the pilot's slow rate of spending in late 2011, they added titles from 2009 and 2010. Conversely, in 2014, all titles published before 2012 were removed to compensate for the increased cost of short-term loans (STLs) in 2014.

A second change affecting the discovery pool was a change in the list of publishers in the YBP profile. During fiscal year (FY) 2014, the E-Book Working Group sought to address members' requests for additional content in the discovery pool. The budget at the time allowed the team to respond to those concerns by adding six new publishers to the program. As of this writing, there are 18 participating publishers: ABC-CLIO, Ashgate, Brill, Cambridge University Press, Earthscan, Hodder Education, John Benjamins, John Wiley & Sons, McFarland, Morgan & Claypool, New York University Press, Oxford University Press, Pharmaceutical Press, SAGE, Taylor & Francis, the Policy Press, the University of California Press, and the University of Minnesota Press.

Short-Term Loans and Autopurchases

The Demand-Driven Acquisitions Pilot Implementation Team and EBL negotiated a flexible autopurchase trigger for the program that continues today. The team sets the trigger point as needed to respond to expenditures or meet purchasing targets. When the pilot launched, the trigger was 10 STLs before triggering an autopurchase. Since that time, the trigger has ranged from a low of five (to stimulate the rate of purchasing) to a high of 15 (to slow the costs of purchasing). The maximum purchase price was capped at $250 since the list price dictated the STL fees and the total cost of an e-book upon autopurchase. Each STL cost the Alliance an average of 14% of list price. The consortium paid five times the list price at the point of autopurchase, but then each title became available in perpetuity to all member libraries.

Funding

Participation in the DDA program became a requirement of membership; all Alliance member libraries contributed to a central fund that paid for the E-Book Program. During the pilot phase, the council assigned a tiered flat fee based on the size of the institution. The DDAPIT recommended and the council accepted a revised funding structure that assessed each library a portion of the budget. The formula adopted split 30% equally among all member libraries, based a further 35% on full-time equivalent (FTE) enrollment, and based a final 35% on the materials budget.

PROGRAM EVALUATION

Over the last three years, DDAPIT and the E-Book Working Group relied on EBL-provided data to evaluate use and expenses. The E-Book Working Group also conducted routine surveys of the Alliance membership to ascertain their satisfaction with the program. These data allowed the group to respond to the needs of the members and recommend changes to the Alliance's governing body. The E-Book Working Group routinely reviewed data both for the overall program and by library. At the programmatic level, overall data helped the group keep within budget and monitor the program's return on investment. What follows are examples of how the E-Book Working Group used EBL's monthly and annual data to evaluate the E-Book Program.

Use of the Collection

The team analyzed trends over time from EBL's monthly and annual use reports. In general, total use has grown 83% from FY 2012 to FY 2014. The monthly use showed a continuous growth during the first year but definite cyclical trends in each successive year. Figure 1 shows spikes in use occurring during academic midterm periods of October, November, and April.

EBL tracked four distinct types of use: "unowned browse," "unowned loan," "owned browse," and "owned loan." A browse described a use of less than five minutes that did not involve any printing or downloading. A loan or STL either exceeded five minutes in duration or included printing or downloading. Of the four types of use listed above, only an "unowned loan" results in a charge to the Alliance.

One of the program's specific goals was to increase consortial ownership of titles that member libraries' patrons deemed useful as demonstrated by high use. The data suggest that the Alliance is meeting this goal. Ownership provides free transactions for all post-purchase use, which represents considerable savings if a title has long-term value to students and scholars. One method of evaluating whether the program met its goal is to review the number of owned uses over time, both as a total number and a percent of

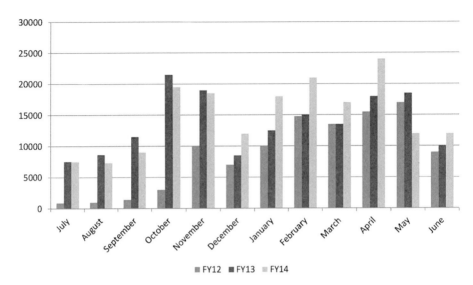

Figure 1. Monthly use, FY 2012–FY 2014.

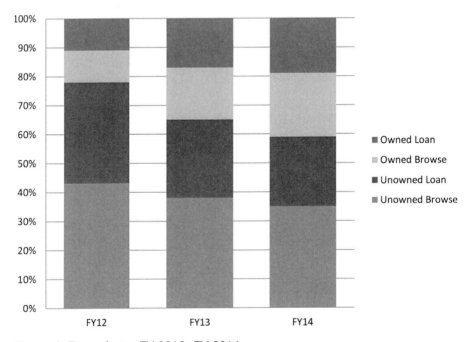

Figure 2. Type of use, FY 2012–FY 2014.

total transactions during a year. Figure 2 shows the comparative percentage of use by type and the growth of all owned use. In FY 2012, owned use constituted 23% of all use, but it grew to 41% in FY 2014.

The program's overall return on investment increased over the three-year period. In each successive year, the E-Book Program saw higher use and costs. However, as Table 1 indicates, the increase in "owned loans" means that the cost per use declined over the three-year period from $4.91 per use to $3.64 per use.

Table 1. Program cost per use, FY 2012–FY 2014.

	FY12	FY13	FY14
Use	102,912	155,672	188,534
Expenses	$505,338.45	$677,564.03	$686,360.97*
Cost Per Use	$4.91	$4.35	$3.64

*Does not include the cost of direct purchases.

Anecdotal evidence suggests that the Alliance preserved access to content and saved on STL costs through purchasing. Linda Di Biase (2014), the E-Book Working Group chair, reviewed the five titles with the most loans in FY 2014. Of those, three were no longer available from EBL for loan or sale. As purchased books, however, they remained available for use by the consortium's patrons. Further research is needed to examine the return on investment for post-purchase use.

Expenses

In three years, the Alliance spent $2,085,783 on the DDA program. The cost per purchased title averaged $517 between 2011 and 2014, owing to the purchase multiplier of five. Including initial STLs in the cost figure brings the average total spent per purchased title to $1,016. The mean cost of an STL was $14.57.

The DDA program required considerable financial oversight to keep it under budget. Unlike traditional collection development where librarians spend against an established budget, DDA programs must estimate expenditures based on the size of the discovery pool, the potential cost of the titles, and the rate of use. Larger discovery pools, higher average list prices of titles, and higher rates of use all drive costs up. The Orbis Cascade Alliance program observed each of these trends.

Autopurchase Trigger

When the pilot launched in July 2011, the DDAPIT had few models to inform its program. As a result, they kept the initial title pool small and made subsequent adjustments based on the resulting patterns of use and expense. The team agreed in September 2011 to lower the STL trigger from 10 to five to accelerate purchasing. They feared that the pilot would reach its expiration date without a purchase if left at 10 for the duration, and owning titles collectively was a primary goal for the project.

Since that initial pilot period, DDAPIT and the E-Book Working Group moved the trigger as necessitated by financial realities. At the close of FY 2013, for example, they moved the trigger from 10 to 15 to further delay autopurchases that would have put the program over budget. The trigger remained set at 15 STLs during the entirety of FY 2014, the third year of the program. It has been the only time that the trigger remained steady through an entire fiscal year. As a result, the Alliance reduced its rate of autopurchase for the year and spent more money on STLs than in previous years, as Figure 3 shows.

Multiplier

In consortium-based DDA programs, publishers charge a multiplier to the list price upon purchase. A multiplier of five is equivalent to buying five copies. Publishers viewed consortium programs as undermining the possibility of multiple local library purchases, so they wished to charge a fee that represented buying multiple copies consortially. In negotiations with publishers, YBP data proved essential to demonstrate the low rate of average duplication within the Alliance and reduce the final multiplier to five times the list price.

This multiplier makes consortial DDA a substantially more expensive project than when administered at a single institution. Delaying purchasing by increasing the autopurchase trigger increased the overall cost of a purchased title because more charges would occur before purchase, but it reduced the frequency of those large budget expenses. Kari Paulson of EBL conducted a spending analysis for the Alliance to model spending in various scenarios. In that analysis, she found that the Alliance would own an

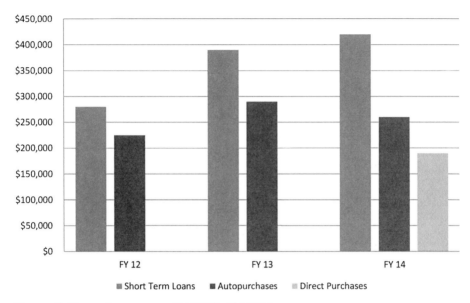

Figure 3. Type of expenses, FY 2012–FY 2014.

additional 2,982 titles if it kept its trigger steady at five STLs throughout the duration of the program, but it would have increased its total spend by 83% (K. Paulson, personal communication, July 26, 2014).

Library Costs and Use

Since participation is mandatory for all Alliance members, libraries want to see the DDA program serve their communities well. Most but not all libraries showed increased use (counting all use) over the three-year period. The median use per library grew from 1,522 in FY 2012 to 2,791 in FY 2014. Four libraries had more than 10,000 uses per year for each of the last fiscal years, which skewed the mean use for the consortium (see Table 2).

Although the overall return on investment increased over the three years, not all libraries enjoyed the same benefit. In each successive year, the governing council increased the program budget, thus increasing costs for each member library. Use also increased each year, but not at a rate that compensated for the council's assigned contribution. Although the libraries' mean cost per use declined from FY 2012 to FY 2014, Table 2 shows dramatic disparities between the maximum and minimum cost per use each year.

Table 2. Libraries' use and expenses, FY 2012–FY 2014.

	FY12			FY13			FY14		
	Total use	Total costs	Cost per use	Total use	Total costs	Cost per use	Total use	Total costs	Cost per use
Mean	2,781	$12,833.00	$7.16	4,207	$25,814.92	$8.62	5,095	$26,850.22	$8.04
Median	1,522	$10,000.00	$6.12	2,361	$16,580.00	$7.06	2,791	$17,074.00	$7.25
Max	16,162	$30,000.00	$17.64	27,193	$130,074.00	$24.50	39,880	$131,032.56	$27.70
Min	0	$5,000.00	$1.52	510	$10,184.00	$2.99	387	$10,718.50	$2.80

These data substantiated private concerns that the E-Book Working Group received from member libraries regarding the cost and scope of the program. One library stated that it had to eliminate firm orders in order to afford its DDA obligations; another simply did not think the content suited its students well. In reviewing the data, the group also found many libraries had very low use compared to their costs even though they reported satisfaction with the program.

Responding to these issues, the E-Book Working Group recommended an adjustment to the program's funding formula. Funding for the DDA program had evolved from a tiered approach in FY 2012 to the funding formula approved for FY 2013 and FY 2014. As mentioned earlier, the fee was assessed based on splitting 30% of the cost equally and then basing 35% on FTE and 35% on each library's materials budget. Since the program showed growing evidence of use across institutions (and increasingly stable records management in the consortium),[1] the E-Book Working Group recommended that the council introduce "use" as a component of the funding formula. The revised formula approved by the council called for 20% of the cost to be based on use, with the remainder divided into 20% of the total equally, 30% based on FTE, and 30% on budget.

PROGRAM AFFORDABILITY

The DDA pilot transitioned into a permanent program in July 2012 and received two years of successive budget increases; however, the council made it clear that the $1 million budget allocated in FY 2014 would not be increased again in the near term. This required the E-Book Working Group to consider the best sustainable solution to providing e-books within this budget to the consortium's patrons over time.

The E-Book Working Group considered a variety of options to increase content, a primary request of the membership, while managing costs in FY 2014. First, EBL's team presented alternative pricing structures. They suggested a limited use option, colloquially called the NovaNET model[2] after the Canadian consortium's pilot. This plan would have limited the number of post-purchased loans permitted without purchasing additional copies, reduced the multiplier for the initial purchase cost, and preserved consortial ownership. Another option included a shared pool of funding for STLs but local purchasing when an individual library reached a smaller autopurchase trigger. The E-Book Working Group weighed these options as well as the possibilities of adding a subscription e-book collection or jointly purchasing a DRM-free e-book collection.

As the year progressed, the number of viable options shrank. Publishers rejected widespread adoption of the NovaNET model because it would have substantially reduced their revenue. The distributed purchasing option would have preserved shared access but undermined the concept of shared ownership. A joint direct purchase of e-book titles proved prohibitively expensive. All that remained in that moment was the addition of an e-book subscription collection available for the entire consortium.

This decision-making process coincided with a series of publishers' STL rate increases that EBL began announcing in May 2014. Although the program had reduced costs by increasing the autopurchase trigger and was expected to end the year under budget, the rate increases projected overruns in FY 2015. The first set of publishers to raise their rates accounted for 81% of the titles and 91% of the STL charges in the Alliance.

The E-Book Working Group began planning to contain costs for FY 2015 by removing some titles from the discovery pool. In the course of evaluating titles for removal, the group analyzed the use of unpurchased titles. It selected 268 books that had 12 or more STLs at six or more libraries and purchased them directly from EBL. For the remaining titles selected for removal, the group provided use data that helped librarians identify titles that it might be useful to purchase locally.

DDA Program to E-Book Program

The moment served as a significant philosophical shift for the program from ownership to access. The titles selected for removal were all dated 2011 and earlier, which effectively turned the discovery pool into a frontlist purchasing tool for the consortium. Since the group had already started considering an e-book subscription, they recognized the value of the subscription as an affordable way to supplement the current collection with backlist titles from academic publishers. Further, an e-book subscription plan would add content from more publishers than were available to the consortium through DDA.

After comparing subscription e-book products and hosting informational sessions for consortium members, the E-Book Working Group recommended using DDA program funds to subscribe to an e-book collection for the consortium. The council approved, and the Alliance finalized a subscription to ebrary's Academic Complete in September 2014. Over the following year, the group will actively assess members' satisfaction and use of the collection. This information will help inform future directions for the Alliance E-Book Program.

Lessons Learned

Over the course of the Orbis Cascade Alliance's three-year experiment with a DDA model, the consortium successfully facilitated access to e-books at all 37 member libraries. Heavily used titles now belong permanently to a centrally owned collection, and some titles see significant post-purchase use. Owned book use will grow every year and improve the return on investment of the program over time. The program's cost per use declined each year, but the data showed varying use intensity across libraries. As a result, the local cost per use varied widely and necessitated a change in funding structure to compensate.

Publishers viewed DDA programs like the Alliance's as experiments of their own, which required modifications over time. The increased STL rates, the first significant response to declining publishers' revenues, required adjustments from the consortium to manage the budget implications. The first step was the removal of titles, but future action may include dropping the maximum price per title, renegotiating the autopurchase multiplier, or diversifying the included publishers. More importantly, the DDA program as originally conceived evolved to include additional e-book acquisition approaches. Central direct purchases, local purchasing informed by DDA use data, and e-book access through subscription have proved valuable ways to complement the DDA program and provide additional content to the membership.

The E-Book Working Group will continue to evaluate and modify the Orbis Cascade Alliance's E-Book Program to best serve the membership.

NOTES

1. Although not addressed in this chapter, the Alliance's challenges with records management across the consortium are worth noting. Initially, each library used a record feed from OCLC's WorldShare Collection Manager to import discovery records and update purchased records. This process was not uniform across

libraries, as some added only purchased records and others added all records. As the E-Book Working Group reevaluated the funding formula, the Orbis Cascade Alliance was in the middle of a consortium-wide adoption of Ex Libris's Alma integrated library system and Primo discovery service. This centralized management of records eliminated discrepancies among libraries and created more uniform opportunities for discovery and use.

2. NovaNET is a consortium of academic libraries in Nova Scotia, Canada. When proposed, EBL consistently referred to the limited use option as the "NovaNET model."

REFERENCES

Bunnelle, J. (2012). Pilot to program: Demand driven e-books at the Orbis-Cascade consortium, 1 year later. *Against the Grain, 24*(5), 24–27.

Collection Development and Management Committee. (2010). Unnecessary duplicate threshold. Retrieved from https://www.orbiscascade.org/file_viewer.php?id=1403

Demand driven acquisitions pilot funding. (2011) Retrieved from https://www.orbiscascade.org/file_viewer.php?id=985

Di Biase, L. (2014). Ebook program update [PowerPoint slides]. Retrieved from https://www.orbiscascade.org/alliancesummer2014

Emery, J. (2012). The demand driven acquisitions pilot project by the Orbis Cascade Alliance: An interview with members of the demand driven acquisitions implementation team. *Library Faculty Publications and Presentations.* Paper 52. http://dx.doi.org/10.1080/00987913.2012.10765440

McElroy, E., & Hinken, S. (2011). Pioneering partnerships: Building a demand-driven consortium ebook collection. *Against the Grain, 23*(3), 34, 36, 38.

10 | The Simplest Explanation: Occam's Reader and the Future of Interlibrary Loan and E-Books

Ryan Litsey, Kenny Ketner, Joni Blake, and Anne McKee

ABSTRACT

In spring 2011, members at the joint meeting of the Greater Western Library Alliance Resource Sharing/Document Delivery and Collection Development committees discussed the growing "silo-ization" of e-books behind different universities' local databases and access portals. The group formed a subcommittee to investigate the possibility of developing a software system that would allow the interlibrary loan (ILL) of e-books. Two employees of the Texas Tech University (TTU) Libraries explored the question: "What is the simplest way for libraries to lend e-books to each other?" Together, three members—Texas Tech, the University of Hawai'i at Mānoa, and the Greater Western Library Alliance (GWLA)—formed the Occam's Reader Project. Each institution began developing different components of the software. Hawai'i designed the public viewer, and Texas Tech designed the software that would handle the e-book conversion, transmission, and hosting. Occam's Reader offers a unique solution in which the intellectual content of the book is made available for the patron to read, but it is stripped of the additional features and links of the full e-book. The philosophy is similar to offering the level of access of printed books, but with quicker delivery. By spring 2014, the Occam's Reader project entered a pilot program with the publisher Springer to test the Occam's Reader software with other GWLA members.

BACKGROUND

The Greater Western Library Alliance (GWLA) is a consortium of 33 research libraries located in the central and western United States. At the 2011 GWLA annual meeting, the heads of collection development and resource sharing from member libraries held a joint session to discuss topics of mutual interest. The collection development librarians emphasized their growing collections of e-books; interlibrary loan (ILL) colleagues expressed concerns that e-books meant that large parts of the collections would be unavailable for consortial sharing. How could the tradition of ILL be maintained when increasing numbers of requested titles are locked behind local authentication barriers?

GWLA's Resource Sharing and Document Delivery (RSDD) Committee, comprised of interlibrary loan librarians, rose to the challenge of continuing their tradition of finding innovative solutions for interlibrary lending. The RSDD Committee historically has been very proactive; its members maintain close contact and are always ready to help during times of institutional crisis. For example, RSDD members assisted Colorado State University after a flash flood damaged parts of the library in 1997; this disaster resulted in the creation of the Rapid ILL service. The group rallied again after a flood at the University of Hawai'i at Mānoa in 2004. This history of cooperation and problem solving laid the groundwork to generate and support innovative ideas like Occam's Reader, a solution to the challenge of e-book lending.

As a result of the 2011 GWLA meeting discussion, librarians from Texas Tech University (TTU) pondered the question: "Why not develop a method to lend e-books via interlibrary loan?" A library-developed method for lending e-books had not been attempted before. Because libraries are sensitive to the issues of their profession, the GWLA members wanted to develop a system that remained true to the long-standing traditions of ILL, while simultaneously respecting the contracts and copyright issues that surround the use of and access to e-books. With these issues in mind, the TTU Libraries, led by the first two authors (the head of document delivery/interlibrary loan and the software development manager, respectively), along with colleagues at the initial group of Washington State University and the University of Hawai'i at Mānoa, formed a working group to create a method to lend e-books via interlibrary loan.

THE DEVELOPMENT HISTORY

In the initial development stages, the team at TTU discussed using existing library technologies to accomplish the task of allowing another university temporary, limited access to a specific e-book requested via the interlibrary loan process. Discussions centered on an existing system called EZproxy, which is used by many academic libraries to control patron access to their electronic collections. Investigation with EZproxy revealed an unintended consequence. It was possible to generate a URL that could be shared amongst institutions, but with one major flaw: although EZproxy is very good at granting access, it is very hard to restrict that access once it is granted. This approach failed to restrict access to only the single ILL request. A clever patron receiving the URL and allowed access to a single title at another institution could potentially backtrack along the URL to gain access to the entire collection or e-database. The team did not want to proceed down the potential rabbit hole of security issues, so it met with colleagues to discuss other options.

A new question inspired the vision for the whole project: "What is the simplest way to lend an e-book securely between one institution and another?" From this question was born the system known as Occam's Reader. The name Occam's Reader is a reference to the idea of Occam's Razor—all things being equal, a simple explanation is preferred to a more complex one. The challenge was building a system that not only integrated with existing ILL procedures, but also allowed the exchange of e-books via secure interlibrary loan channels. By spring 2012, the team had assembled the first working model of Occam's Reader (explained in the next section of this chapter), and in March presented a very early build of the system at the GWLA deans and directors meeting. Next, the team built a prototype to demonstrate at the fall 2012 meeting. At that meeting, the deans and directors saw the first working system of Occam's Reader. The first test was a book sent from TTU to the University of Hawai'i at Mānoa and vice versa. With an effective working model, the team began to refine the programming and prepare for piloting.

PROGRAMMING AND WORKFLOW

During the development of the system, the TTU development team decided to build what amounts to a "neutral zone" for e-books, in which staff at the lending library use Occam's Reader to take a photo of each page of the e-book, compress the file, and send it to a web server. Staff at the borrowing library then access this server using password-protected authentication and are able to view each page of the e-book in a viewer designed by the University of Hawai'i at Mānoa. Creating a neutral system in this way allows the necessary flexibility to integrate with existing ILL workflows. Early versions were built to integrate with ILLiad, the popular Atlas Systems software product used by many academic libraries and by all GWLA libraries. Using a series of ILLiad add-ons, the team has been able to integrate the Occam's Reader system into the standard ILL workflow at consortial universities.

Simplicity in encoding and presentation of e-books was the focus throughout designing Occam's Reader. Most of what publishers or third-party vendors provide with e-books are "bells and whistles" beyond what can be done with a physical book. For example, native e-books and e-books scanned with optical character recognition (OCR) provide a means for electronic search of the full text. Full-text search is something unique to e-books, along with hyperlinked metadata such as in a table of contents, text highlighting, copy and paste of text, and other functions. Since these functions are not possible with a physical book, the development team decided to dispense with them in this simple e-book lending model. And, since the loans do not compete with their full e-book feature set, publishers and e-book vendors would likely adopt a friendly attitude toward the project as well. So far this has been the case.

The vision of mimicking a physical book as a simple e-book drove the core feature set selected for the Occam's Reader e-book viewer. Basically, the Occam's Reader e-books are collections of image files, one per page of the physical book. These image files can be rotated, zoomed, panned, advanced next and previous, and jumped to a specific page. In other words, the functionality enables one to do what one can do holding a physical copy of the book. The image file format Portable Network Graphics (PNG) was selected because of its high text readability, universal display capability in web browsers, good compression, capability for transparent backgrounds, and rich history as an image standard.

Behind the scenes on the interlibrary loan staff side of the system, the goal was to preserve the current ILL workflow with minimal disruption. To that end, the Occam's Reader System was written as an ILLiad add-on. All ILLiad add-ons consist of LUA script files and XML configuration files written in a pattern determined by Atlas Systems. To learn the design patterns of the ILLiad add-on, the team at TTU consulted with staff at Atlas Systems and at the Information Delivery Services (IDS) Project, the developers of the popular Getting It Systems Toolkit ILLiad add-on. With advice from both groups, the TTU Libraries development team created one of the most sophisticated ILLiad add-ons available today.

Another compelling reason for the decision to create an ILLiad add-on rather than a standalone system is that all 33 GWLA libraries use ILLiad in their daily work. The ILL staff members at the GWLA institutions required training to install, configure, and practice using the Occam's Reader system, but they provided positive feedback regarding the minimal disruption to their workflow. Establishing this good working relationship early at the point of installation at each institution proved helpful during the test and production phases.

Additional configurations such as permissions, modification of the system path variable, and location of work folders are all guided by the initial training process after the software prerequisites are installed. The team at TTU spent a significant amount of time performing this initial configuration and training with participating institutions. The team at University of Hawai'i at Mānoa led the documentation effort to create a user manual for ILL staff. The time spent training and documenting was worth the expense to increase the adoption and use of Occam's Reader.

The actual image conversion process is accomplished through an external program launched from the ILLiad add-on that runs on each ILL staff computer. The ILLiad add-on and the image conversion software communicate important information to each other, such as a unique number identifying the ILL request. This is true generally within the Occam's Reader system; it contains many distinct parts that must communicate with one another without ambiguity.

The image conversion software is a .NET executable written by the TTU Libraries development team, and it requires three open-source software prerequisites, all freely available online. ImageMagick, Ghostscript, and 7-Zip must be installed on each ILL staff machine that processes Occam's Reader requests. The image conversion software takes input from the user regarding which e-book file to convert and what image conversion settings to use and returns a single archive file of PNG images for uploading to the Occam's Reader web server. The currently available image conversion settings include image quality settings and an option to do grayscale or full color images. Notably, the current ILL industry standard for electronic items is grayscale. Occam's Reader users are happy to have a full color option for electronic items.

The converted e-books are uploaded to the Occam's Reader web server through the ILLiad add-on interface. This portion is a PHP webpage rendered within ILLiad by the add-on. The upload page returns a confirmation that the file was received along with an automatically generated e-mail for the lending library to pass along to the borrowing library. This e-mail will be sent from the borrowing library to the end user who placed the request; the e-mail contains instructions for the customer, a copyright notice, and a link to the Occam's Reader web viewer with a randomly generated token that grants access to the book while it is still on the server. Currently, e-books remain on the server for 14 days, after which they are automatically deleted.

The customer accesses the e-book from the link in the e-mail sent by the home institution, the borrowing library. Developed by the team at University of Hawai'i at Mānoa, the viewer implements the feature set of basic e-book navigation described earlier: rotate, zoom, pan, previous, next, and jump to page. The viewer is built on the widely used technology stack of PHP, HTML 5, and JavaScript. The main reason for selecting these technologies is to create a viewer that works well in most combinations of browser, operating system, and hardware device. As consumers move more toward tablets and phones as their primary reading devices, this goal becomes even more important to meet.

The Occam's Reader web viewer went through one major revision on its path to the current product. It was rewritten to use the open-source OpenSeaDragon image display tool that the developers learned about at the Code4Lib 2013 conference in Chicago. The result is a faster and more stable image viewer than the previous attempt. The viewer also automatically detects every page in the book to create the navigation. The thoughtful team at University of Hawai'i at Mānoa also created a feedback form to solicit comments from users of the viewer. Some users lament the missing bells and whistles like metadata, full-text search, and copy/paste of e-book text. The occasional complaint about image quality points to the inevitable time/quality tradeoff at the point of image conversion at the lending library. However, most customers are simply happy to read a good quality copy of the book they sought. Data collected through December 2014 suggest that customers actually are reading the e-books they borrow through Occam's Reader.

TESTING AND PILOT PROJECT

The first round of testing began with the University of Hawai'i at Mānoa in fall 2012. This testing gave the team an opportunity to address critical errors and streamline the process so as to be ready for a large-scale deployment. In fall 2013, GWLA brought the system to the attention of the Springer International Publishing Group. The history between Springer and GWLA has been positive, and licensing agreements were in place for a pilot project.

The licensing history is worth examining in detail. When GWLA launched a fledgling Collection Development committee in 2000, members emphasized that fair use should never be surrendered in electronic content negotiations, licenses, or contracts. In negotiating for electronic content with publishers and content providers, GWLA staff has never waived the right to provide interlibrary loan and has in fact walked away from several offers when publishers refused to allow resource sharing in their licenses.

Balancing the philosophical demands of the members with the proposed licensing terms from vendors meant that the first few years in GWLA's licensing programs were rocky ones. Thus, the GWLA program officer, in consultation with the RSDD Committee, developed a key phrase that is used in all GWLA licenses: "The Consortium may supply a single copy of an individual document, chapter or book derived from the Licensed Materials to an Authorized User of another library utilizing the prevailing technology of the day." It was a natural progression to begin using this clause in all licenses for electronic content, regardless of the medium. When presented with this wording for e-books, the publishers would frequently chuckle and say, "But there is no platform to enable ILL for e-books." One day in November 2013, GWLA's program officer asked the Springer representative, "But what if there were such a platform?" Springer showed a keen interest and suggested a pilot project among the GWLA libraries for one calendar year using Springer content within the Occam's Reader system. Some of the key points of the agreement with Springer actually laid the groundwork for important lessons learned from the pilot.

One of the first terms negotiated was the length of time that e-books would be available to patrons. Since no one had ever sent an e-book via interlibrary loan, no one was sure what would be an appropriate amount of time to read an e-book. The team eventually settled on 14 days. In many ways, this is an arbitrary number and is still debated amongst the group.

A second key point in the negotiations was sharing e-book lending statistics with Springer. This has turned out to be one of the most important and interesting components of the agreement. When librarians read about sharing the lending data with a publisher, they are understandably worried about patron security and patron confidentiality. They can rest assured that no patron information is shared between the Occam's Reader project and Springer International. The data shared with the publisher are limited to information about the titles requested by each library and which libraries supply those books. This type of business intelligence is a level of detail yet to be provided to publishers, but it can be a powerful purchasing and selling tool.

A third important feature of the agreement with Springer describes how the e-books are displayed to the patron. One of the balancing acts is remaining faithful to the tradition of interlibrary loan while also allowing universities access to e-books they could not previously share and to a type of content where even the very nature of ownership is still hotly debated. When beginning to build the pilot system, it was necessary to decide how much of the content of the e-book to send in the transmission to the web server. Discussion centered primarily on whether or not the metadata (hyperlinks, OCR, bells and whistles) would accompany the Occam's Reader e-book. As part of the negotiations for access to lend the content, an agreement was reached to remove any metadata or extra content provided by the publisher. This is certainly a compromise. However, the arrangement still maintains the ILL tradition of sending a "book in a box" to another university. One of the interesting aspects of the development of Occam's Reader is that it has expanded the discussion about the meaning of "ownership" of e-books and whether or not that includes metadata.

By the time the terms of the agreement were reached, the team had developed a very good working relationship with Springer that helped immensely when the pilot project encountered its first big problem. It was very difficult for users to find the e-books they wanted to borrow. Discoverability is a real issue for lending e-books, due to the innumerable ways in which individual libraries catalog their e-books. Some add records in OCLC while others do not; some include them in their local catalogs while others keep them within their e-databases. It often is difficult for library staff to know which e-books their own institution holds.

The need to come up with a way to make discoverability as simple as possible led to the second most interesting innovation to come from the pilot: the shared discovery layer using data files provided from Springer. In exchange for the previously mentioned ILL data, Springer was willing to provide the Occam's Reader project with lists of which universities owned which Springer titles. This was exactly the boost needed to make a functional pilot system. Using the Springer data files, the team was able to construct a discovery layer that integrates into ILLiad, so that ILL staff can locate the Springer e-books for which they are searching. The discovery tool is a PHP webpage embedded in the Occam's Reader ILLiad add-on; it is powered by a Microsoft SQL Server database hosted at TTU. The discovery tool supports searches by title and ISBN, and it returns basic bibliographic information along with a link to the e-book at the host institution and a lending string necessary to generate the borrowing request in ILLiad. The discovery layer also alerts ILL staff if their library already holds a particular e-book. This approach has worked well for the Springer e-books held by GWLA libraries, and could potentially work with other libraries and publishers in the future.

The pilot project launched in March 2014. It has produced some very interesting results. From the beginning, the pilot included a usability feedback survey in both the e-mail that goes to the patron and as a sidebar link on the viewer. By December 2014, approximately 700 e-books had been shared via Occam's Reader and there have been over one million page views. The analytics for OccamsReader.org demonstrate interesting facts about the viewer and the webpages. Once again, there is no tracking of individual patron information. There are only typical web analytics such as page views and time spent on each page. The most-viewed page in terms of total number is the discovery layer, which is not surprising given the heavy use of the system by ILL staff. The second interesting analytic is the behavior of a typical user. The data show an average of about 35 minutes spent per visit to OccamsReader.org. The average user views 15 pages per session at just over two minutes per page. These metrics demonstrate that visitors are actually reading the e-books through the viewer. So far in the pilot project, which will conclude in March 2015, both staff and patrons are successfully using Occam's Reader to lend and read e-books.

FUTURE DEVELOPMENTS

The piloting and testing of Occam's Reader suggest new avenues of research and exploration. Libraries have an opportunity to address matters that were only theoretical until the creation of a working model of ILL for e-books.

The first new avenue of research is what the Occam's Reader project team calls "content collaboration." Content collaboration means using publisher-provided content in a library-developed system. Why is this a new field and something that is important for librarians to talk about? First, libraries must leverage the long tradition of respecting patron confidentiality to fulfill their role in society by providing a secure place for patrons to view e-books unhindered by potential marketers. The recent news about Adobe Digital Edition eReader user data being gathered and used by Adobe demonstrates the importance of this trust (Coldewey, 2014). Second, if libraries continue to allow third-party vendors to provide the viewer platforms for their digital content, eventually patrons may ask themselves, "Why use a library at all when I can get an individual account from a vendor like OverDrive?" With content collaboration, libraries can use their tradition of patron security to provide a trusted viewer through which publishers can provide content to patrons. This is a win for users, libraries, and publishers.

The pilot phase also identified the need for a standalone version of Occam's Reader as an area of future investigation. The team initially developed Occam's Reader as a system integrated with both ILLiad and OCLC. Although this worked well for the GWLA libraries, there is a need to establish a version that can function across a variety of platforms as the project expands beyond one consortium. A standalone system can also help both international and American users. With these goals in mind, the team has begun to brainstorm a standalone version of Occam's Reader to meet the needs of a larger user base.

A third avenue of future research centers on the idea of the relationship between the publisher and the library. Occam's Reader has shown a type of relationship that can be beneficial both to libraries and to publishers, a relationship that is more collaborative and less vendor-and-buyer. Through this model, libraries can approach publishers with a collaborative mindset and work with them to establish a way to leverage the fair use of digital content. Although librarians recognize that publishers are generally for-profit businesses and libraries are usually non-profit, there are still areas of possible collaboration. Occam's Reader demonstrates a successful collaborative approach with both the discovery layer and the web viewer.

The final avenue of research is the discussion of policies and procedures that govern the e-book ILL exchange. Because the fair use questions encountered during the project remain unanswered, many e-book interlibrary loan policies and procedures remain in flux. How long should a patron have access to a borrowed e-book? GWLA members choose 14 days, but is that enough? Should content license agreements be rewritten to include lending e-books? Are there certain national or international standards relevant to the system that need to be developed or adapted? Many of these questions remain unanswered. They can be solved as e-book ILL grows in popularity.

CONCLUSIONS

Occam's Reader's success is a watershed moment at the intersection of interlibrary loan and e-content. It has brought to the forefront many of the issues libraries currently face when thinking about e-books and their role in the libraries of the future. The authors hope that it is the beginning of a conversation demonstrating that it is possible for libraries to remain true to their traditional core values while at the same time embracing new ideas and new ways of providing services in a digital environment as successfully as they have done for decades by mailing physical books to meet the learning and research needs of other libraries' users. Occam's Reader demonstrates the usefulness of publisher and library collaborative partnerships. The Occam's Reader developers think that they have accomplished that goal and, as they move forward to Phase 2, they see a bright future in which libraries continue offering information services in new ways using innovative technology.

The Occam's Reader web viewer is the most widely known piece of the Occam's Reader system. View a demonstration of the web viewer at Occams Reader.org.

REFERENCES

Coldewey, D. (2014, October 8). Adobe to issue software fix after report of leaking user reading habits. *NBC News*. Retrieved from http://www.nbcnews.com/tech/security/adobe-issue-software-fix-after-report-leaking-user-reading-habits-n220506

11 | Developing a Global E-Book Collection: An Exploratory Study

Dracine Hodges

ABSTRACT

Collection development of e-books for international and area studies, specifically for non-English language content, is challenging. This chapter will provide insight into acquisitions by looking at vendor/publisher issues, reviewing insights from The Ohio State University Libraries' area studies subject librarians on the market culture issues, discussing the Title VI federal funding changes, highlighting logistical barriers, and describing existing and emerging cooperative collection development models.

INTRODUCTION

Academic libraries have largely embraced the pursuit of e-book content as a priority because of user demand and shifting collection philosophies. As a result, the challenges surrounding e-book collection development activities continue to unfold. Such challenges of the e-book marketplace include variability of acquisition models and uncertainties related to standards and publisher and vendor practices. One particular aspect in need of exploration concerns e-book collection development for international and area studies, specifically non-English language content.

Research libraries have doggedly pursued print collection development in international and areas studies for decades. Globalized collection development has always presented challenges, ranging from identifying and sourcing scholarly foreign language materials, to acquiring and shipping materials from overseas, to finding personnel with language expertise to process and catalog them. The critical need for research libraries to develop scholarly collections of international and area studies content continues to be a priority in an increasingly globalized world.

Globalization is not a new phenomenon, but like most facets of 21st-century culture, it has accelerated due to technology. The world is becoming a smaller and more interdependent place even with a population of 7 billion people occupying 196 sovereign states spread over 57,000,000 square miles. This interconnectedness stems from world-changing technological advancements, including civil aviation, personal computing, the World Wide Web, mobile phones, and other devices. Distance and time, formerly formidable obstacles, have been neutralized by the impact of an Internet connection. Globalization has moved beyond the borders of geopolitics to encompass economic, telecommunication, environmental, health, and cultural infrastructures. The impact of technology on globalization also can be seen in the shifting priorities of academic libraries.

The Ohio State University Libraries (OSUL) has a strategic focus directive to increase the scale and scope of digital collections that support teaching and research priorities. This focus identified the need for more expansive e-book content. Significant progress has been made in most disciplines with the notable exception of international and area studies. OSUL currently holds over 802,000 e-books of which only 36,500 (5%) are in non-English languages. The majority of these (59%) are titles in Romance and Germanic languages including French (6%), German (22%), Italian (9%), Latin (16%), and Spanish (6%). Glaringly underrepresented in this group are e-books in key non-Roman script languages, including Chinese, Japanese, Korean, Russian, Arabic, Turkish, and Hebrew. OSUL holds a woefully modest 275 e-books representing East Asian, African, Eastern European, and Middle Eastern languages (see Figure 1). E-book content from these regions is critical because of growing economic power, emerging public health threats, diverse natural resource availability, and far-reaching political, ethnic, and religious conflicts. Teaching, learning, and research focusing on the nations, cultures, and regions associated with each area studies discipline rely heavily on content in the vernacular languages. Though many of these cultures have been studied and written about by outsiders, there is an imperative to provide researchers with content by local experts and scholars who write in vernacular languages. Even if some small percentage of content is available in translation, original texts may be preferred because of the nuances and context that can be lost in translation. Although academic research libraries want to develop e-book collections in area studies vernacular languages, little is currently held. There are many logistical reasons.

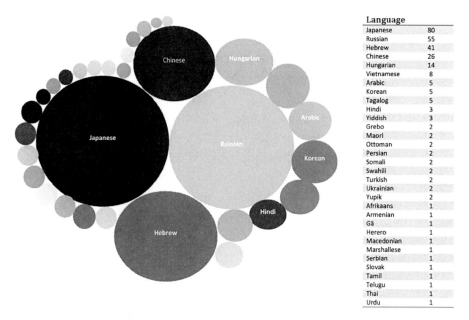

Language	
Japanese	80
Russian	55
Hebrew	41
Chinese	26
Hungarian	14
Vietnamese	8
Arabic	5
Korean	5
Tagalog	5
Hindi	3
Yiddish	3
Grebo	2
Maori	2
Ottoman	2
Persian	2
Somali	2
Swahili	2
Turkish	2
Ukrainian	2
Yupik	2
Afrikaans	1
Armenian	1
Gã	1
Herero	1
Macedonian	1
Marshallese	1
Serbian	1
Slovak	1
Tamil	1
Telugu	1
Thai	1
Urdu	1

Figure 1. Numbers of OSUL area studies e-books representing East Asian, African, Eastern European, and Middle Eastern languages.

This chapter will: 1) look at a selection of vendors/publishers providing international and area studies e-book content; 2) obtain insights from OSUL area studies subject librarians for perspectives on the e-book market culture in their respective disciplines; 3) discuss the financial retrenchment of Title VI federal funding for libraries; 4) highlight logistical barriers to affordable vernacular e-book access and distribution; and, 5) describe scenarios where existing and emerging cooperative collection development models expand non-English language e-book access. This information will provide practitioners with greater insight into acquisitions models for developing area studies e-book collections, highlight challenges to acquiring and accessing vernacular e-book content, and identify issues for further study.

EXPLORING TOP PUBLISHERS' NON-ENGLISH LANGUAGE OFFERINGS

Libraries work with many publishers to purchase or lease content that will support teaching, learning, and research objectives. Alongside this mission, librarians also take into account practicalities that support efficient workflows. A look at the offerings of the "big four" academic publishers and the top e-book aggregators provides a logical place to begin the exploration of non-English e-book providers. All of these companies are headquartered in the Western world, but their footprint is relatively global. The big four consist of the following academic publishing companies: Elsevier; Springer; Taylor & Francis; and Wiley. These publishers are considered the biggest because of their profit margins, volume of content, and robust distribution and service support. They also share a characteristic focus on science, technology, engineering, and mathematics (STEM) content. Unfortunately, this leaves the rich cultural scholarship of the social sciences and humanities in other world regions unaddressed.

Elsevier, a company specializing in science, technology, and medical (STM) content, has offices in many geographical locations encompassed in area studies. The network includes China, India, Japan, South Korea, Russia, and South Africa, as well as offices throughout Asia and in the West. These locations reflect not only the Elsevier consumer market, but also the many non-English languages in which it publishes. Elsevier publishes content in Western languages including English, German, French, Spanish, Italian, and Portuguese, and additional languages including Polish, Japanese, Hindi, and Chinese. However, it appears that non-English language content is more prevalent in journal than e-book content.

Springer, like Elsevier, has offices on six continents in countries including South Africa, China, India, Japan, South Korea, the United Arab Emirates, and Turkey. Springer content is also largely focused on STM areas. Despite its global presence and consumer market, Springer's non-English language e-book content is primarily focused on German and Italian with a small number of e-books in Spanish and French. This seems logical upon review of Springer's 2013 revenue reports which show 28% of its profits coming from Germany, Austria, and Switzerland, 24% from North America, 23% from the rest of Europe, and 17% from the Asia Pacific region (Springer, 2014). The Asia Pacific region includes many area studies locations and perhaps points to a growing consumer market. However, the rest of the world, including

Latin America and the Middle East, accounts for only 8%. This small revenue percentage is not an incentive to a publisher with a bottom line.

Taylor & Francis (T&F) has a smaller global footprint with offices primarily in the United Kingdom and the United States, but offers a more diverse content portfolio. Publications cover not only STM but also include the humanities, social and behavioral sciences, and law. T&F has identified area studies subject content that specifically allow consumer browsing on its e-book platform. However, the nearly 6,500 e-books with international and area studies content are English language, not vernacular language, materials.

Finally, John Wiley & Sons (Wiley) is an academic publisher also focusing primarily on STEM content and like the others has offices primarily in the United States and Western Europe with newer locations in Dubai and China. Though much of its content is English language, Wiley is growing not only the consumer market, but also content development in area studies regions. The company's (Wiley, 2014) narrative history states the following:

> Over the past decade, Asia has emerged as both a dynamic market and a vital source of Wiley content. China is now the second-largest consumer of Wiley Online Library content, as well as the second-largest source of articles for Global Research journals. India, a well-established market for Wiley, is also developing into an important source of content.
>
> In the Middle East, Wiley opened an office in Dubai in 2010 to take advantage of the region's rapid growth of higher education opportunities; in 2012, Wiley established Brasil Editora LTDA, based in Rio de Janeiro, Brazil. As a global company, Wiley is able to create consolidated centers of excellence at locations sited strategically around the world and, in turn, achieve cost savings and efficiencies that make room for ongoing investments to develop the business. ("Creating Global Centers of Excellence" section, para. 2)

The big four academic publishers principally focus on the sale and distribution of their own concentrated content. Conversely, e-book aggregators assemble content from hundreds of publishers, including the big four, covering all academic and professional subject disciplines. Despite their more comprehensive catalogs, only a few aggregators offer non-English language e-books. A number of the major aggregators like ebrary and EBL (both owned by ProQuest) offer non-English language e-books. EBL's non-English language coverage includes German, French, Spanish, and Dutch materials. ebrary offers Spanish, Portuguese, German, and more recently a Nordic collection featuring Danish, Finnish, Icelandic, Norwegian, and Swedish language content. Credo Reference offers e-book content in Chinese, French, Polish, Spanish, and Urdu. EBSCO has a diverse offering of non-English e-books in over 20 languages, including Arabic, Chinese, Dutch, French, German, Italian, Japanese, Latin, Portuguese, Spanish, and Welsh, to name a few. In addition, EBSCO launched the *Arab e-Marefa* database in 2013. This database does not currently include e-book content, but it is comprised of full-text Arabic language journals and statistical reports from 18 Arabic-speaking countries. The database also includes over 7,000 book reviews that librarians and scholars can use to identify additional titles for collection development. It can be seen as a potential acquisitions model for purchasing or leasing collections of non-English area studies e-book content facilitated by the distribution and service infrastructure of a well-established vendor like EBSCO.

AREA STUDIES LIBRARIAN INSIGHTS AND TITLE VI FUNDING

It is clear that major publishers and aggregators are expanding their non-English language e-book content. However, it is a slow progression and not particularly robust for area studies. A brief survey, including informal interviews, was conducted with the six OSUL area studies subject librarians to obtain their perspective on the availability of e-books in their respective disciplines. OSUL has subject librarians for Chinese and Korean Studies, Eastern European and Slavic Studies, Japanese Studies, Jewish Studies, Latin American and Iberian Studies, and Middle Eastern Studies. The area studies librarians, like general subject librarians, support students and faculty with their research and teaching activities. This work includes selecting library materials, providing reference and consultations, and instruction on the research tools and methods in their subject areas and languages. Most area studies librarians do these activities in English as well as in languages related to the study of their geographic regions.

Academic libraries are developing new strategies in response to changes and shifts in higher education. One of those major shifts has been the ongoing transition from print to electronic collection development. Even with this directive, only half of the OSUL area studies librarians consider the e-book format when selecting materials in their discipline vernaculars. The Jewish and Middle Eastern Studies librarians attributed this to the lack of a platform available in the United States that provides access to Hebrew, Arabic, Persian, and/or Turkish e-books. Both acknowledged an awareness of limited e-book availability within countries in their area disciplines.

All of the area studies librarians noted that they were more likely to select the e-book format for vernacular content when presented with the option. Many noted the desire to pursue more electronic collection development because of benefits such as meeting a noted preference for the format by linguistics students and faculty, accessibility, opportunity to reduce the physical footprint of collections, and ease of use in both face-to-face and distance learning classroom settings. Area studies librarians at OSUL rely heavily on approval plans with booksellers or vendors based overseas to locate vernacular content in print format. Having access to vernacular e-books could potentially alleviate the challenge of securing a copy of a title in what are usually very limited print runs. Non-English area studies e-books are fairly unmapped territory for both acquisitions and subject librarians alike. Several OSUL area studies librarians revealed they are actively educating themselves about the availability of e-books and paying attention to what colleagues at other institutions are doing. The Middle East Studies librarian noted her discovery of a Lebanon-based Arabic language e-book publisher, Al Manhal. However, she pointed out that its specialization is currently medical and science textbooks. This is a significant issue because local demand for vernacular language materials is often STEM-based, whereas U.S. academic library demand for vernacular language materials is focused heavily on content in the humanities and social sciences. As reflected in the brief overview of publishers carrying non-English e-books, Spanish was one of the more abundant languages to be found. The Latin American and Iberian Studies librarian remarked that there are emerging players in what is a fast-growing Spanish language e-book market. However, he noted that the same is not true for Portuguese language e-books, which are almost nonexistent. The Jewish Studies librarian identified two prominent university presses in Israel that are beginning to offer Hebrew language e-books.

Many of the OSUL area studies librarians felt that the few opportunities for obtaining access to vernacular language e-books were complicated by acquisitions models requiring the purchase or subscription to an entire package or collection. Some noted the additional challenge of vernacular language e-book content being primarily available in the commercial market. This market largely accommodates individual buying and not institutional access. Like other librarians with collection development responsibilities, OSUL area studies librarians have limited budgets. They often must take into account the currency exchange rate and strength of the U.S. dollar. This has been beneficial to some, like the Chinese and Korean Studies librarian who is acquiring Chinese language print materials for a fraction of what his Japanese Studies colleague pays for her materials. Shipping charges also can be a major cost for area studies print materials.

To understand the challenges of pursuing vernacular language e-books for area studies, one must also take into account the acceptance of the format by both the culture producing the content and the potential audience of scholars. Several area studies librarians expressed concern that some teaching faculty members were still uncomfortable with the use of the e-book format in their research. In addition, the Middle East Studies librarian explained that the majority of the Middle East is currently very much a print-based reading culture. In juxtaposition to this is the eager adoption of e-books in the technologically sophisticated Japanese culture, along with the proactive e-book movement among Japanese Studies librarians. The OSUL Japanese Studies librarian has taken advantage of Japanese language e-books offered by EBSCO and is looking at *Maruzen eBook Library,* launched in Japan in 2013. This long-established company provides electronic resources in the humanities, social sciences, and sciences from academic institutions and libraries in Japan. In addition, the Maruzen Company is working with EBSCO to make its e-book metadata searchable in the EBSCO Information Services database.

The OSUL Japanese Studies librarian also pointed out experimentation with customized patron-driven acquisitions (PDA) programs for Japanese language e-books. Currently, two separate patron-driven or demand-driven e-book acquisitions programs are being piloted with EBSCO by nine campuses in the University of California system and at the University of Pittsburgh. As forward-looking as this type of activity is for area studies librarians, it has points of frustration as well. For example, the full range of trigger options is not currently available for EBSCO's Japanese language e-books. Short-term loans, a popular option in general subject PDA, are currently not allowed.

In addition, the Japanese Studies librarian noted many discussions among her peers on the JpnLibLiaisons listserv regarding the difference between the Maruzen and the EBSCOhost user interfaces. The EBSCO hosted content is experienced through a typical academic research database with keyword and advanced faceted search options. The Maruzen content interface is easy to use, but does not lend itself to serendipitous or focused browsing. This could be helped with improved Japanese language meta-data standards that are currently being examined by Japanese booksellers working with OCLC. These issues are not unique to area studies, but rather are experienced by all librarians evaluating electronic content on new and evolving platforms.

One concern unique to area studies librarians is the defunding of government programs that support international and area studies, usu-ally referred to as Title VI. Title VI of the National Defense Education Act of 1958 was approved in response to the launch of *Sputnik* and the U.S. government's recognition that a stronger and broader capacity in foreign language and area studies was needed. It was later incorporated into the Higher Education Act of 1965 (U.S. Dept. of Education, 2011). Widely known Title VI programs include language area centers, or National Resource Centers (NRCs), Foreign Language and Area Studies Fellowships (FLAS), and funding for International Research and Studies (IRS). These programs have been the cornerstone of the federal government's structure to increase acquisition of understudied languages, develop capacities to understand evolving global trends, and encourage cross-cultural teaching and learning. Of primary relevance are NRCs associated with universities. The Ohio State University's resource centers include the Center for African Studies (CAS), Center for Latin American Studies (CLAS), Center for Slavic and East European Studies (CSEES), East Asian Studies Center (EASC), and the Middle East Studies Center (MESC). OSUL area studies librarians regularly work with the centers on outreach and engagement to support teaching and research as well as programming with the goal of extending what is frequently referred to as global competencies.

In addition, most of the centers designate portions of their Title VI grant funding to OSUL in support of collection development and library services directly related to their international areas. Several of the area studies librarians rely on this funding for flexibility in their selection of material. Some use it to fill in gaps or add depth to the collection when a new degree program or curriculum in the area is created. Others use it to purchase rare or primary source materials or to participate in cooperative collection development with consortial or peer institutions. In some instances, they use it to trial new electronic resources or simply to make ends meet during a time when library materials budgets are stretched thin.

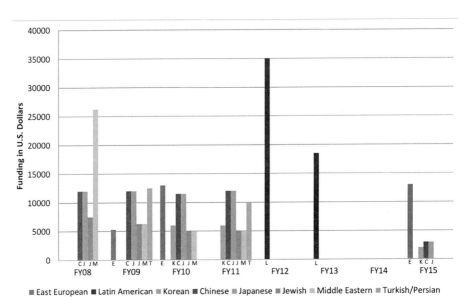

Figure 2. OSUL Title VI funding from centers.

A review of Title VI financial support received by OSUL confirms an irregularity and/or absence of support over the last eight years. Funding classifications correlate with OSUL's subject disciplines in the acquisitions budget structure and cover fiscal years, which run July 1 through June 30. Looking at Figure 2, one of the first things to note is the absence of funding available from the Center for African Studies. This center has not received Title VI funding and, therefore, has been unable to support OSUL area studies collections and service development directly. Fiscal year 2007–2008 saw no funding for Eastern European or Latin American Studies, but it was the peak year of funding for Middle East Studies. In fact, Latin American Studies did not receive Title VI funding in fiscal years 2008 through 2011. However, it was the sole area to receive funding in fiscal years 2011–2012 and 2012–2013. The most consistently funded area is East Asian Studies, specifically Chinese and Japanese. Korean Studies has been funded sporadically, but may be on the verge of a renaissance with new funding received in fiscal year 2014–2015. There was no Title VI funding for any of the area studies in fiscal year 2013–2014. This was likely the direct result of the U.S. Congress' decision to cut the Department of Education's funding during the critical 2011 budget negotiations (U.S. Department of Education, 2011). According to Brown (2014), this translated into a 48% reduction in budgets for all NRCs. Figure 3 shows total OSUL Title VI funding by area over the last eight years. Overall, East Asian Studies has benefited from the largest percentage of funding. Middle East Studies follows with slightly more than

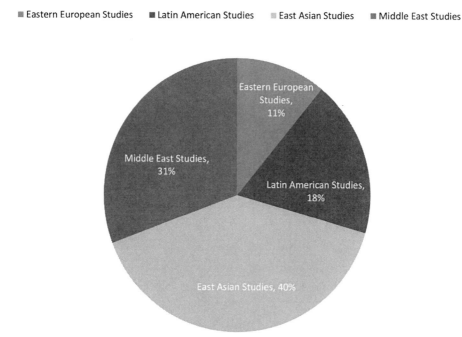

Figure 3. Cumulative Title VI funding by area.

a quarter of the funding while Latin American and East European Studies claim the remainder. Title VI funding is highly desirable for area studies e-book collection development. It has been a significant incentive in collaborations between research libraries and NRCs. However, funding is not always the greatest obstacle to developing a global e-book collection.

SIGNIFICANT BARRIERS TO ACCESS AND MODELS

Acquiring print area studies materials published in pertinent geographic locations can be challenging because of many logistical factors. These materials usually have very short print runs, with local demand absorbing most or all copies. Physical pieces must traverse long distances sometimes via unstable government-run postal services or through conflict areas. They may accrue additional costs and delays gaining clearance through U.S. Customs. E-books could be the ideal solution to some of these challenges as well as provide convenient accessibility and meet increased user demand for electronic content. However, a potential transition to the e-book format could be stalled by any one of several factors. As discussed earlier, the non-English area studies e-book market, currently in its infancy, is not robust enough to affect a tipping point amongst the major academic publishers and aggregators. In addition, impediments related to licensing, value-added taxation (VAT), trade embargoes, and copyright law interpretation dim enthusiasm for a non-English e-book marketplace.

The majority of electronic content of any type requires some form of a license agreement. Area studies electronic content is the same, but has the potential complication of licensing content from a publisher in another country where the governing laws differ. Often each party in a license agreement prefers the jurisdiction or constituted legal authority of their home country in the event of a dispute. In addition, if resolution cannot be achieved due to lack of jurisdiction, then copyright laws come into play. For libraries like OSUL that are part of a publicly funded university system, this can be a significant challenge. Public universities and their libraries are subsidiaries of the state and subject to its administrative and legal oversight. Many domestic publishers and vendors will often concede jurisdiction to the library's governing state or remain silent on the issue. In instances where this is not agreeable, there are potential solutions. One is the use of the Berne Convention for the Protection of Literary and Artistic Works, an international copyright treaty, if the home countries are signatories (Harris, 2009, pp. 29–30). According to the Berkman Center (2010), the Berne Convention, signed by 168 countries, calls for participating nations to comply with the following three principles: 1) national treatment or bestowing residents of member countries the same rights under the copyright laws given to their own residents; 2) independence of protection or protection of foreign works in accord with protections given to domestic works; and 3) automatic protection or the removal of legal formalities for persons from member countries. More specifically, this requires a single copyright registration in the home country. The Berne Convention still presents a complicated system, but it attempts to provide a common framework to navigate copyright and licensing. If both parties agree, perhaps a reasonable license alternative is the Shared Electronic Resource Understanding (SERU). SERU is a recommended best practice from the National Information Standards Organization (NISO) that forgoes legal terms for a common understanding of use, privacy, service performance, and perpetual access (NISO SERU Standing Committee, 2012). The 2012 recommended practice update of SERU specifically expanded its scope to other electronic resources including e-books.

Another issue that poses a challenge to developing non-English e-book markets in many countries is the trade embargo. A trade embargo or ban is the prohibition of specific or all commerce (imports and exports) to another country. This can sometimes include informational and/or published materials of scholarly interest. Trade embargoes are frequently used by a country to impose sanctions on another in protest against a moral, political, or environmental practice (Shambaugh, n.d.). One example is the longstanding trade embargo imposed by the U.S. against Cuba, a Latin American Studies-related country under communist rule. This embargo, in place since 1960, imposes strict sanctions on almost all import and export activity between the U.S. and Cuba. Additional sanctions were added later to deter foreign companies doing business with Cuba from doing business with the United States. Although thawing of diplomatic relations between the U.S. and Cuba is under discussion, any change in the trade embargo would require passage of new legislation through Congress, a typically lengthy process. Embargoes are also put in place by the United Nations to restrict trade with countries involved in malicious armed conflict and/or human rights violations. This issue will continue to thwart the development of a robust non-English language e-book market for vernacular area studies scholarship, particularly in regions connected to Middle East and African Studies.

Publishers have shown an inclination to rally against such sanctions that aggressively block or attempt to control the exchange of ideas in the publishing industry. One such demonstration was seen in 2004 when the Association of American University Presses (AAUP), PEN (an organization of writers and editors), and other trade publishing organizations sued the U.S. government. The suit was brought specifically against the Office of Foreign Assets Control (OFAC) of the Department of the Treasury, charged with enforcing trade sanctions. The suit accused OFAC of narrowly interpreting "informational materials" protected under the 1988 Berman Amendment. The amendment was originally intended to limit Executive Branch power under the Trading with the Enemy Act (TWEA) of 1917 and the 1977 International Emergency Economic Powers Act (IEEPA). Both TWEA and IEEPA were created to restrict trade with foreign countries hostile to the United States and its interests. The Berman Amendment specifically limited the president's "authority to regulate or prohibit, directly or indirectly, the importation from any country, or the exportation to any country, whether commercial or otherwise of publications, films, posters . . . or other informational materials" (Association of American University Presses, n.d.). However, AAUP also notes OFAC began issuing "a series of interpretive rulings that made clear that publishers were prohibited from engaging in standard publishing activities in connection with works written by authors in embargoed nations unless granted a special license from OFAC" (Association of American University Presses, n.d.). OFAC specifically prohibited "collaboration on and editing of the manuscripts, the selection of reviewers, and facilitation of a review resulting in substantive enhancements or alterations to the manuscripts" (Liptak, 2004, para. 15).The suit was dropped in 2007 when OFAC removed its special license requirement and its editorial restrictions for U.S. citizens working with Cuban, Iranian, and Sudanese authors (Association of American University Presses, 2007). However, it appears this issue may be on the rise once again. Elsevier distributed a notice to its staff explaining that American editors or reviewers must not handle manuscripts written by an employee of the Iranian government. According to Marshall (2013), additional instructions were later issued to reject a manuscript if a non-American was not available to handle it because of additional sanctions approved in 2013. These sanctions are limited to scholarship on the development of nuclear technology, which is believed to be the target, but they have been indifferently applied to scholarship as far afield as the treatment of schizophrenia (Zarghami, 2013, pp. 1–4). Publishers have a financial bottom line and are thus obliged to act lawfully to avoid a breach of international trade sanctions. Challenges of this magnitude frustrate and discourage potential authors and diminish publishing opportunities for vernacular language e-books from countries of interest to U.S. academic library area studies programs.

One final barrier to growing an audience and content creators for vernacular language e-books concerns the VAT, a consumer tax added to the purchase price of goods or services in the European Union (EU) and in non-EU countries that use a similar system. It is an alternative to the sales tax system used in the United States. Just as sales tax rates can vary from state to state, so can VAT rates vary from country to country. Print books are subject to VAT, but many countries including the United Kingdom, Germany, and France apply a reduced rate to this format. The reduced VAT rate for print books in Germany is 7%, which is significantly less than the standard 19% rate. Print books in the United Kingdom are zero rated, which exempts them from VAT, but allows the publisher to claim taxes on production costs. However, e-books present a more complicated picture. EU VAT rules define e-books as a digitally supplied service instead of a book. Countries like France and Luxembourg have defiantly chosen to apply a reduced VAT to e-books in accord with the reduced print book rates. However, policymakers in the United Kingdom argue, "a reduced rate cannot be applied to digital or electronic supplies, or supplies of text via the Internet, as they are classed as supplies of services rather than physical goods. There is therefore no scope in the principal VAT directive to apply a reduced rate on e-books" (Jones, 2011, para.3). In accordance with this stance, the United Kingdom applies the standard VAT rate of 20% to e-books. International publisher groups have lobbied for reduced e-book rates. However, the fast-growing e-book market along with other digital services represents a significant income stream for government.

In an effort to bring practices in sync, the EU has called for e-book publishers and aggregators to charge consumers the standard, not reduced, VAT rate of their residential country in 2015. This point is significant because some e-book providers like Amazon took advantage of a loophole that allowed them to charge consumers the VAT rate of the country in which they are based. Amazon's European headquarters are based in Luxembourg. For a time, U.K. residents were able to purchase e-book content at Luxembourg's 3% VAT instead of the standard 20% used in the United Kingdom. Like individual consumers, libraries in many EU countries pay the standard VAT rate. A few EU countries have refunded VAT to libraries or made them VAT-exempt altogether. For instance, "Danish government libraries are VAT-exempt; Austrian and Swedish libraries are annually reimbursed for their VAT expenditures; and, in the U.K., certain libraries that have outsourced parts of their operations can reclaim percentages of their VAT. Further, national consortia in the Czech Republic and Lithuania allow libraries to obtain resources without paying VAT" (de Vos, 2008, p. 10). These rates do not affect the U.S. libraries directly, but indirectly it makes the international e-book market smaller and less able to scale up for sustainability. In the end, EU countries represent a substantial portion of the potential audience for vernacular language area studies e-book content. As discussed earlier, EU countries provide more than 50% of the revenue stream for the big four publishers. Obstacles such as these make it unlikely that publishers will invest in high-risk and high-cost area studies e-book content. Publishers may address this concern by setting prices higher to offset VAT costs, with the result of putting additional pressure on limited library budgets. In response to the implications of VAT, European librarians frequently advocate for equality in the treatment of print and electronic books particularly in the context of scholarship, public access, and cultural preservation.

POSSIBILITIES FOR COOPERATIVE COLLECTION DEVELOPMENT

Despite the quagmire of challenges, there remain opportunities to develop vernacular language e-book collections further. Libraries have long been bastions of cooperation and collaboration. Prominent examples of this are interlibrary lending, cooperative cataloging, collaborative collection development programs, consortial memberships, and integrated library systems. Notable collaborative collection development programs targeting area studies include the Association of Research Libraries (ARL) Foreign Acquisitions Project, the Association of American Universities (AAU) Research Libraries

Project, and the joint AAU/ARL Global Resources Program. Jakubs (2000) asserts that all three programs served "to improve access to international research resources for scholars and students, especially through cooperative structures and new technologies, and to help libraries contain associated costs" (p. 255). In addition, the Library of Congress has run the Cooperative Acquisitions Program (CAP) since 1962. It maintains "offices abroad to acquire, catalog, preserve, and distribute library and research materials from countries where such materials are essentially unavailable through conventional acquisitions methods" (Library of Congress, n.d., para. 1). Its primary audience has been academic research libraries. There is also the Center for Research Libraries (CRL), self-described as the world's largest and most longstanding cooperative collection development enterprise, whose emphasis is to acquire and preserve global materials in print and electronic formats. CRL has given significant focus to regions of the world tied to area studies. The consortium has progressively looked for ways to obtain electronic access to primary resources or digitize at-risk print materials from these regions. After the transfer of the Global Resources Program from ARL to CRL in 2006, it became the Global Resources Network (GRN). The GRN cultivates partnerships with other organizations to identify and digitize resources focusing on news; law and government information; the history and economics of agriculture; and the history of science, technology, and engineering. For example, CRL has partnered with the Law Library Microform Consortium to preserve scholarly access to primary historical U.S. and foreign legal publications not captured in commercial databases. CRL also provides oversight for the Area Materials Project, which again focuses on the six major regions of area studies. These projects bring together CRL members with collection interests in those regions to identify uncommonly held physical format content for digital preservation and collection building.

All of these examples show a common thread of collaboration and partnership. Individual libraries might consider leveraging partnerships with like institutions in area studies countries on a peer-to-peer basis. The Ohio State University has made the development of global knowledge-based collaborations a priority. In so doing, the university has developed "global gateways" by opening offices in Brazil, China, and India. Related to these initiatives, the OSU Libraries began a staff exchange program with the Shanghai

Library, the second largest library in China. The exchange involves librarians from each institution traveling to the other to enable cross-cultural learning and participation in practitioner knowledge sharing. A visit from Shanghai Library librarians in 2014 resulted in OSUL receiving access to the Window of Shanghai e-book platform, an ambitious cultural exchange e-book project. The Shanghai Library worked with Chinese publishers to provide e-books to both their library patrons and international partners, including OSUL. The platform includes thousands of e-books in Chinese and other languages including Arabic, German, Indonesian, Mongolian, Russian, Spanish, Vietnamese, and bilingual Chinese-French and Chinese-English works. All of the content is from Chinese publishers. OSUL was granted access to these e-books gratis. It presents a fascinating model of exchange and sharing between two institutions. It also presents an opportunity for the Chinese and Korean Studies subject librarian to compare the strengths and challenges of United States/European e-book platforms to one based in China.

CONCLUSION

Pursuing e-book content in support of teaching, learning, and research is a priority for academic libraries. Libraries are shifting their collection development philosophies to prefer e-formats in response to increased demand from users and to meet the practicalities of budget and staffing limitations. The progressing e-book market is complex and many of its facets are unsettled territory. The professional literature and debate surrounding e-books have been primarily focused on general English language content. However, area studies collection development is an important priority and investment for academic libraries. U.S. research libraries have played a significant role in acquiring foreign language materials and making them available to students and scholars. The e-book revolution will affect area studies as its audience of scholars and the countries and cultures they study evolve in their consumption and distribution of information and adoption of technology.

The constant flux of the globalized world makes it prudent to support production and availability of vernacular language scholarship, particularly during moments of crisis or conflict. Publishers and aggregators must have indications that investing in international e-book content will result in a relatively stable academic audience and allow for the potential to scale up with more robust offerings. Of course, it is not solely the responsibility of publishers. Libraries are also in a position to leverage existing programs and initiatives to make inroads into digitizing retrospective materials or producing and sharing new content as well. There are opportunities to form strategic partnerships with peer institutions or to participate in consortia with active area studies collection development agendas. As Jakubs (1996) writes, "To do this will mean, in many areas, changing our acquisition patterns. Like any cooperative approach, it will mean fostering interdependencies among institutions, and providing expedited access to the materials needed by researchers" (p. 52). What better vehicle for expedited access than e-books?

Obstacles like Title VI defunding, licensing, trade embargoes, and unfavorable tax directives are difficult challenges. It is important for librarians to be aware of the issues and options to formulate value statements that might influence the creation of better models or, at the very least, educate policymakers on the vital role of libraries and scholarship in support of area studies research and diplomatic relations. Area studies librarians in particular must provide some leadership for developing a vernacular language e-book market. They sit at the crossroads of expertise about the subject, the format, and the users. There are many possibilities for future research in this migration from print to digital. More in-depth study can be undertaken, especially for countries with vital domestic e-book markets. This should include the cultural understanding of copyright and licensing. In addition, the practicalities of e-book platforms can be explored in relation to discovery and access, including the functionality of translating English language publications to other languages. There will continue to be many unknowns and uncertainties about the global e-book market, but global citizenship calls for libraries to forge ahead in this next frontier.

REFERENCES

Association of American University Presses. (2007, October 1). Government issues new regulations on publications from Cuba, Iran, and Sudan. Retrieved from http://www.aaupnet.org/news-a-publications/news/archived-press-releases/329-aaup-ends-litigation-against-ofac

Association of American University Presses. (n.d.). OFAC lawsuit background. Retrieved from http://www.aaupnet.org/policy-areas/intellectual-freedom/suit-against-ofac-regulations/367-ofac-lawsuit-background

Berkman Center for Internet & Society at Harvard University. (2010). Copyright for librarians [website]. Retrieved from http://cyber.law.harvard.edu/copy rightforlibrarians/Module_2:_The_International_Framework

Brown, N. J. (2014, October 30). In defense of U.S. funding for area studies. *The Washington Post.* Retrieved from http://www.washingtonpost.com/blogs /monkey-cage/wp/2014/10/30/in-defense-of-u-s-funding-for-area-studies/

de Vos, L. (2008, January). European libraries feel effects of VAT on e-publications. *Elsevier Library Connect Newsletter, 6*(1), 10.

Harris, L. A. (2009). Licensing digital content: A practical guide for librarians. Chicago, IL: American Library Association.

Jakubs, D. (1996). Modernizing Mycroft: The future of the area librarian. Retrieved from http://hdl.handle.net/2022/3071

Jakubs, D. (2000). The AAU/ARL Global Resources Program. *Journal of Library Administration, 29*(3/4), 255–313. http://dx.doi.org/10.1300/J111v29n03_17

Jones, P. (2011, December 23). UK government holds firm on e-book VAT. *The Bookseller.* Retrieved from http://www.thebookseller.com/news/uk-government -holds-firm-e-book-vat

Library of Congress. (n.d.). Cooperative acquisitions program. Retrieved from http://www.loc.gov/acq/ovop/

Liptak, A. (2004, February 28). Treasury Department is warning publishers of the perils of criminal editing of the enemy. *The New York Times.* Retrieved from http://www.nytimes.com/2004/02/28/national/28PUBL.html

Marshall, E. (2013, May 3). Scientific journals adapt to new U.S. trade sanctions on Iran. *ScienceInsider.* Retrieved from http://news.sciencemag.org/2013/05 /scientific-journals-adapt-new-u.s.-trade-sanctions-iran

NISO SERU Standing Committee. (2012). SERU: A shared electronic resource understanding: A recommended practice of the national information standards organization. Retrieved from http://www.niso.org/publications/rp/RP-7-2012_SERU.pdf

Shambaugh, G. (n.d.). Embargo. *Encyclopedia Britannica.* Retrieved from http:// www.britannica.com/EBchecked/topic/185507/embargo

Springer. (2014). Springer facts and figures: Springer Science + Business Media. Retrieved from http://static.springer.com/sgw/documents/1413855/application /pdf/SSBM_facts_figures_May2014_EN.pdf

U.S. Department of Education. (2011, January 21). The history of Title VI and Fulbright-Hays: An impressive international timeline. Retrieved from http:// www2.ed.gov/about/offices/list/ope/iegps/history.html

Wiley. (2014). Narrative history. Retrieved from http://www.wiley.com/WileyCDA
/Section/id-301697.html

Zarghami, M. (2013). Illogical and unethical scientific sanctions against Iranian
authors. *Iranian Journal of Psychiatry and Behavioral Sciences, 7*(2), 1–4.

Users' Experiences

12 | A Social Scientist Uses E-Books for Research and in the Classroom

Ann Marie Clark

ABSTRACT

In this chapter, a political science professor describes and evaluates her experiences with e-books in the classroom and for research. E-books are delightful resources for quick use, but for this user they have certain drawbacks when considered for sustained scholarly reference and teaching purposes. The author also considers the perspectives of students and colleagues. Some discomfort with e-books may be generational and may fade with the emergence of students and researchers who have grown up as "native users" of e-resources.

WHERE DO E-BOOKS FIT IN THE SCHOLARLY LIFE?

I was invited to write about my work-related uses of e-books as a university professor. In research and teaching, e-resources, including e-books, differ from traditional library resources in the possibilities they offer for acquisition, use, and information retention. The general point I make in this chapter is that e-books are delightful resources for quick use, but they still have certain drawbacks when considered for sustained scholarly reference and teaching purposes. Some of these drawbacks are practical issues that are likely to diminish as e-book technology adapts to suit the humans who use it. For now, humans must adapt to e-books to use them effectively. For people like me who did not grow up with e-reading technology, e-books are rarely optimal reading tools. Difficulties related to human cognitive development might diminish for people who learn to e-read as children, but from what I can gather as a nonexpert, scientists are conservative about that prospect. I address the main desirable qualities of e-books below, followed by a section on e-books in use, incorporating some impressions I have gathered informally from colleagues and students. I then add some reflections on how the strengths and limitations of e-books may vary along with differences in the ways that we use e-books.

Below, I refer to all available online research tools as e-resources, e-books being a subset. E-resources, to me, are invaluable. I still subscribe to the major print periodicals in my academic field, international relations/political science, although many of my colleagues no longer acquire the journals in print that are so easily available online through a research library. Still, the hard-copy journals are stable and dependable ways to keep up with the topics of greatest professional interest to me, and to have them at hand.

I don't regret that electronic reference resources have more or less replaced physical reference books for current social science sources. For research, I search electronically. Then, if I am near my journals, I go to the hard copy. Like books, journal issues are easy to read, easy to file, and will stay neatly in order on a shelf until I need them. They are stable and dependable. However, I use my paper journals less frequently than I used to unless I am reading deeply, since it is so easy to go straight to a link for almost any article found in a search.

I went to school, to college, and began graduate school in the pre-web era. As an elementary school student in the 1970s, I recall a special class visit to a high school library, where we were taught how to slog through the *Readers' Guide to Periodical Literature*. It was full of strange codes and hard to handle physically. No wonder children today get excited about using iPads for school research (Barger & Notwell, 2013). As an undergraduate, I attended Earlham College, known for its top-notch library education (Information Literacy, 2014), but the same challenges applied then and even later in my academic training when approaching the *Social Science Citation Index*, *The New York Times Index*, international and national government documents indices, and other reference tomes. There was no choice but to use these heavy volumes filled with fine print. On good days the thrill of a successful search was its own reward, but on bad days searching social science reference materials was like taking medicine. In contrast, even though there is a learning process associated with the efficient use of electronic reference sources, research with electronic databases can be done relatively easily, and from the comfort of the office, coffee shop, or sofa. No heavy lifting required.

AVAILABILITY, SPEED, AND PORTABILITY

In my view, three characteristics of scholarly e-resources, including e-books, give them notable advantages over physical library materials for research and teaching: availability, speed of use, and portable access.

Availability

For availability of materials in a research library context, nothing beats electronic resources. Initial background research with all e-resources is simpler and more efficient than the old way. Heretofore, I have mainly used electronic databases and retrieval services for journal articles, rather than for books, but as libraries acquire more e-book holdings, I use them, too.

As of this writing, I have purchased exactly one e-book for professional use. That decision was a matter of availability. I had already bought and extensively annotated a paper copy of the book, but had misplaced or loaned it—in true absent-minded professor fashion—I am still not sure which. (Okay, I admit that reveals an obvious disadvantage of paper books, but let's not talk about that right now.) I needed the text right away to prepare for the next graduate seminar session in a course I was teaching. Needless to say, I preferred to avoid purchasing a second copy. Our library did not hold the e-book version of the text, a university press book. The physical copy was checked out from the library. Technically, since it was a text adopted for course use, I could have requested a desk copy from the publisher, but time was too short for that. The university press did not distribute its own e-books, but only paper. On the publisher's website I learned that the e-book was available for purchase through Amazon. At Amazon, the e-book was cheaper than the paper version and immediately available for download. And so it happens that, by accident, I learned what it is like to acquire and (re)read deeply and thoroughly using an e-book, even though I would not have ordinarily done so. I discuss the outcome of my natural experiment below in the section on e-book use, after first pointing out other desirable qualities of e-books.

Speed

After an electronic search, getting hold of the actual items, if they are electronic and available, is almost instantaneous. Speed of acquisition was a second, separate factor in my decision to purchase the e-book course text. The speed of e-resource access means that I can quickly get the lay of the land on a new topic, or update myself on ongoing research directions. I more often use e-books to *rule out* potentially useful sources quickly than to work at length with those sources.

If material is electronically available, I can take a quick peek and then either download it or request the physical copy for later perusal. I could use Google Books for a quick online look at some parts of most books, but the e-book format is a lot more accommodating. I particularly appreciate the ability to view e-books quickly if I am thinking about buying a paper copy, since well-stocked academic bookstores are hard to find. The speedy access to e-books is also great for students doing course-related research. One caveat is that an electronic word search rarely replaces a good index in a scholarly book, and it would be sad were e-publishers to begin skimping on e-book indexing.

Portability

You would think that portability would be one of e-books' greatest advantages. It is, if you are a student or do your work in more than one location. Students appreciate not having to lug lots of books around during a day on campus. Professors, if they have a workspace at home as well as on campus, and especially if they most often walk or bike to work as I do, potentially benefit from portability, too. However, there is still the little matter of how many devices and platforms are associated with that supposed portability. If I need to read one book, I would rather carry that single book to and fro than my tablet, especially if I also have to carry my laptop. Committed users of laptops for reading—or of tablets for writing—would not face this two-device problem, but I am not one of them.

Because of my overall preference for plain old books, the main instances when I am more likely to appreciate the portability advantage of an e-book are when I am temporarily away from the office and might need to carry one or more devices with me anyway. Then, for that kind of use, the portability of e-book supplements is really helpful.

No mid-career scholar really wants to sound like (or actually be) an old fogy, so among ourselves we either pronounce upon how much we know about the latest technology or cavil regarding how much we really, on principle, hate all this newfangled technology. Sometimes the same people do both. I have friends of any station in life who will break out the latest issue of *The New Yorker* on their iPhone during an unexpected wait in the dentist's office, and I suppose this could work with scholarly e-books, but who conducts research or course preparation in a dentist's office?

In any case, I first bought a portable device, a tablet, when I took an off-campus sabbatical in 2010. The principal reason was that I did not want to carry lots of photocopies with me. Before I left, a savvy colleague showed me an app, iAnnotate for iPad, which would permit me to receive and comment on my students' dissertation chapters using the tablet rather than print them or use a word processor (Branchfire, 2014). With this app I can type or write freehand on a PDF document, a process that replicates my usual hard-copy process *and* allows me to save my own copy and send it back to the student electronically. The notes are saved with a PDF version of the document. This works so well for me that I have retained these particular uses in large part because the app is great for interacting with students over e-mail about their writing. I also have begun using it when asked to review manuscripts for professional journals, and sometimes even book manuscripts for university presses. I used it to read and edit drafts of this very chapter. In an article-length paper, the somewhat slower reading and note creation demanded by the app can be offset by the convenience, eco-friendliness, and storage options achieved by *not* using paper. But even the relatively young editor who last asked me to review a book manuscript admitted that he, too, reads the long form faster and more efficiently on paper.

For general professional reading, I concede that it is nice to have a couple of things loaded on a tablet or phone in case one gets stuck somewhere and would like to feel productive, or alternately if one commutes by public transportation or travels frequently to professional conferences. In my quotidian experience, though, the portability of an e-book is overrated at the professional level. The availability and speed of access to e-books, for me, are a bigger draw than portability.

E-BOOKS IN USE

Now, on to describe the outcome of my e-book experiment. But first, where is that e-book now, several months after I purchased it? Is it in my iBooks app, which I thought of first, since I am mostly a Mac user? No. Is it in ebrary, the facility on our university library site for reading e-books (ebrary [ProQuest], 2014)? No, because the book did not come from the library. OverDrive (OverDrive, 2014), which is often used for e-books from public libraries? No, for the same reason. . . . Oh, here it is—in the Kindle app, because I purchased it through Amazon, and that is the only platform Amazon sells. Luckily, Apple's iTunes deigns to host a Mac version of Kindle, so I did not need to add a Kindle reader to my stable of devices.

The truth is, this proliferation of platforms is another major practical drawback for people who don't seek out e-books. Since the course ended about six months ago, I had forgotten where the file was. I had to figure out where I had bought the e-book first, then I had to remember that I had the Kindle app on my iPad, or that I could log into Amazon to find the book and my notes. What if they had disappeared in the meantime?

Taking Notes

For about 10 years I have used an electronic note-taking program, OneNote (Microsoft, 2014), for teaching-related review of course texts and often for research. This way, my detailed notes are saved and easily retrievable later for class, and whenever I teach the course again. If time permits, I do this whenever I am reading for class—it does make the note-taking process slower, but it also means that I think about what the author is saying, just as one does with paper-based notes. The saved notes can be synced to multiple devices; they also can be printed out, and PDF quotes from an e-source can be pasted into my notes record. Additionally, the notes can easily be revised and extended when I read a text again.

Several of my colleagues and students have gone entirely paperless, but I prefer to read a paper copy and take my notes with OneNote, which can be used either with a tablet or keyboard. Another colleague keeps her book notes in ebrary, but her unsaved notes have evaporated once or twice. As I do with my separate notes program, she appreciates the ability to bring up saved book notes for review within ebrary and to access them whenever and wherever she is online.

In my natural experiment, when I had no choice, using the e-book for class was not an entirely satisfactory fit with my work style. I tend to rely heavily on the text and my notes when teaching so, having no choice under the circumstances, I junked my usual practice and made notes on the e-book within Kindle. Otherwise, I would have faced another version of the two-device problem in order to take separate notes in my preferred way without cumbersome switching back and forth.

Notes in the Kindle app were not flexible enough for me. It is possible to highlight text and enter notes in Kindle, and the notes can be edited, but at the time I did not see a way to export them, print them, or sync them. Remember that I was a first-time user. A quick real-time Google search as I write this shows that, yes, I can use something called "Whispersync," apparently a feature of the Kindle app, to sync my annotations and the book itself to other devices. It was not obvious how I could print notes without first cutting and pasting them, and the electronic format was not particularly convenient for later reference purposes. In other words, I cannot treat the e-book like just another book. And, because of the different platforms, I cannot treat one e-book the same as every other e-book. Each requires a level of special treatment.

An electronic alternative I sometime use with articles in PDF form, if I am in a hurry or have just one screen, is to import the file to iAnnotate and make notes that can be saved as part of the PDF. As far as I can tell, that level of interaction with the text was not possible with my e-book. First of all, many e-books do not provide a facsimile version of the paper copy. Usually, any page view can be traced to the actual page number of the paper book, but since the actual views do not necessarily match a book's pages, it is not as easy to share references during text-oriented seminar discussion. Navigating the e-book and my notes was awkward.

Finally, the notes from my e-book experiment are not going to be easy to transfer to OneNote, where, as mentioned, I keep most of my research and teaching notes. There is a good chance that OneNote will be around for a while, since Microsoft produces it, but it is still true that if Microsoft stops producing it, I will be in trouble. An update is needed for the classic protest song (Dylan, 1990 [1962]): "How many platforms must one scholar adopt, before her records are washed to the sea?"

Deep Reading

At this point I probably do not need to say that, when a book's hard copy is readily available, I much prefer it to an e-book. The main reason why is that I find it easier to read on paper and take notes either in OneNote or right on the book, if I own it.

What I will call *cognitive fit* also affects my preferences when reading something lengthy. With books, especially, it is easier to sustain focus when I read on paper and easier to remember what I read. I like being able to flip back and forth inside the book if there is something I want to review. Now, I find that some of those intuitions about ease of use are supported by research summarized for a popular audience in a recent issue of *Scientific American* (Jabr, 2013). Apparently, the brain finds it more stressful to read on screen. The physicality of print on paper seems better suited to the object-oriented nature of human vision, according to one hypothesis. It is possible that we might change, as humans, as more of us are trained from birth to use screens. However, the ability to hold a book, to flip back and forth, and to reference passages easily, either alone or in discussion, without waiting for material to search or to load are all relevant features when comparing professional uses of e-books vs. paper books. And those features advantage paper books, for now. Of course, for some platforms, portions of a book can be printed out for reading, but throwaway printouts made from e-books are not an optimal solution because of the waste involved.

A friend in graduate school with me at the dawn of digitization used to call books "the ultimate multimedia tools." Books are easy to navigate, to open or close at will. Most are small enough to carry easily, with almost no obsolescence. I need not mention the need for an electric supply for long-term reading. You can use books off the grid. I have had the opportunity to carry out participant observation in several old but venerated research libraries recently: the most popular study spots are those with a plug nearby. For many uses of books, that does not matter.

A Sample of Student Perspectives

During a graduate seminar break one day several months ago, I talked with my graduate students about e-books. The issue came up in conversation before I was asked to be a part of this volume, and I had been thinking a lot about e-resources, because my natural experiment was conducted in that same class. In a later (anonymous) course evaluation comment, one student indicated appreciation of "technologically literate" professors. (He or she used that phrase! I was relieved that the student seemed to think that I belonged in this group.) Having had the in-class conversation, I got the impression that, at minimum, technological literacy included making sure that electronic versions of course books and articles are available whenever possible and, more importantly, understanding how e-resources can be helpful to students and how students use e-resources. I think students perceive professors who do not at least have a working knowledge of the technological universe as either failing to exert due diligence or out of touch, or both.

I believe that the expectation of course e-material access for students (all in accordance with intellectual property rights) is a reasonable and widely accepted standard of practice nowadays. If students cannot find course resources with a click, sometimes the materials will not be used. I am not surprised if the run-of-the-mill undergraduate is not thoroughly familiar with the physical use of the library. That has become something that educators will have to teach some students to do. Students *should* be taught to do it competently. As I like to tell my undergraduates, there is more to "research" than typing a question into Google.

It is natural that, just as I have gotten accustomed to fast delivery of research material, we all get used to the wonderful, speedy availability of electronic course materials. Electronic availability makes course preparation for students far easier and cheaper than trudging individually to the library to photocopy reserve material, or buying a course packet of photocopies from a third-party vendor. Now that we can avoid that, we should.

Several of my graduate students said they "love" e-books, and they prefer only to use their laptops or tablets. Grad students have no choice but to be heavy readers, and a few of my students said they still, like me, found physical books easier to navigate when reading deeply. This group included a couple of nonnative English speakers who, like me, seemed to find paper a better fit for their reading and annotation needs.

It is an obvious possibility that some generational differences exist and may wax or wane as people grow up with sophisticated reading devices. The national and global economic divide related to digital access is something beyond the scope of this particular chapter, but I will say that libraries and affordable versions of publications, whether paper or digital, are part of the solution.

Given that many of my students prefer, or do not mind, e-resources for their college texts, and they prefer affordable texts, I keep that option in mind when I choose course texts. For students and for myself, I believe it is necessary to keep up with evolving publication platforms. I admit, though, that in the short run e-books, in whichever version one uses them, seem less enduring and, for me, more cumbersome and less valuable than paper books.

APP FATIGUE

A number of colleagues gave e-books mixed reviews for additional reasons. My account is anecdotal and restricted to personal acquaintances, but several have said they prefer physical books because they are easier to read, faster to read, and you don't have to mess with the technology and wait for it to load. Also, given the large amount of screen time already logged, many frequent book readers may find a sense of physical relief and even pleasure when reading a regular book.

Although I appreciate the constant software updates associated with improvements in e-resource use, I also rue the time it takes just to keep up with latest versions, software updates, and the jumbled assortment of ways to access various e-content sources. This, and the issue of dealing with multiple and changing software platforms, have induced in me a kind of *app fatigue*. Keeping up with the pace of technical change can cut into productive research, teaching, and even free time. This is a real phenomenon that extends to e-book use for me, and possibly for other frequent digital users like me.

In addition, many people who use screens professionally all day just for writing and daily uses like e-mail have at one time or another experienced a related health issue. Such concerns include eyestrain and other aches and pains (Korkki, 2011). I have to agree with a colleague who mentioned that, in practical terms, adding e-book reading to existing screen time is not a particularly attractive prospect.

CONCLUSION AND CONFESSION OF AN E-AUTHOR

To conclude, given my usual preference for paper, when must I have a printed book and when will an e-book do? I want a book when I will be making extensive notes on it, and when I think I will be referring to it repeatedly or in depth. I also really need a paper book when the subject material is highly complex. This applies when I am using it in the classroom or as a key research text, when the subject matter requires deep thinking and concentration. The preference also includes potential uses *in extremis*, such as when I experience eyestrain or might lack either a charged device or Wi-Fi access. An e-book will often suffice when I am doing quick reference or searching for something in particular. Also, I often do find it convenient to read lighter fare on a screen.

On the whole, some practical benefits of e-books generally balance the drawbacks for many of my professional uses. I am very happy that libraries are beginning to include e-books in their holdings. Library access is extremely useful to me as a scholar. Still, I do not yet foresee a time when the physical book will be outmoded for my own use. If I buy a book, I prefer to spend money on a paper copy.

Finally, the incorporation of e-books into research libraries makes me more confident that if I suggest a book to individual students or colleagues, they will be able to peruse it without undue investment or inconvenience. My confession in this regard is that sometimes that includes library e-books that I myself have written. For good or ill, thanks to the presses that have published my work, I am now an e-author.

ACKNOWLEDGMENTS

For helpful comments, special thanks to my brother, George E. Clark, who happens to be a university librarian and is much more of a techie than I am. For supporting evidence of this, see http://people.fas.harvard.edu/~clark5/. Among those who shared some of their ideas about e-books with me, I particularly thank Elisabeth Jay Friedman, Kathryn Hochstetler, Jay McCann, and the members of Purdue University's spring 2014 graduate course in political science, "Theories and Practice of Justice in International Politics."

REFERENCES

Barger, B. P., & Notwell, M. (2013). The ebook hook. *Science and Children, 51,* 31–37.

Branchfire. (2014). iAnnotate. Retrieved from www.branchfire.com

Dylan, B. (1990 [1962]). Blowin' in the wind. Retrieved from www.bobdylan.com

ebrary (ProQuest). (2014). Retrieved from www.ebrary.com

Information literacy: A legacy of excellence. (2014). *Earlham College Libraries.* Retrieved from http://library.earlham.edu/c.php?g=82954&p=533029

Jabr, F. (2013). Why the brain prefers paper. *Scientific American, 309,* 48–53. http://dx.doi.org/10.1038/scientificamerican1113-48

Korkki, P. (2011, September 11). So many gadgets, so many aches. *The New York Times,* p. 56.

Microsoft. (2014). Microsoft Onenote for Mac. Retrieved from www.onenote.com

OverDrive. (2014). Retrieved from www.overdrive.com

13 | The User Experience of E-Books in Academic Libraries: Perception, Discovery, and Use

Tao Zhang and Xi Niu

ABSTRACT

E-books are being widely adopted as a new format of scholarly information to meet increasing educational and research needs in academic libraries. The advantages of e-books over print books from the libraries' perspective (e.g., cost and storage requirements) have been well discussed. Although a number of studies have reported faculty and students' perceptions and attitudes on e-books (e.g., Shelburne, 2009), there have been relatively few studies of actual e-book use and user behavior (O'Hare & Smith, 2012). Recent literature reviews on e-book-related research have identified several themes, including library adoption of e-books, the e-book market, supply side of e-books (publishers and aggregators), copyright and digital rights management (DRM), e-book readers, e-book acquisition models, promotion, and e-book cataloging (Kumbhar, 2012). These themes are useful in determining library acquisition strategies and designing e-book-related services, but there is a lack of emphasis on how users perceive and use e-books as part of their information-seeking behavior.

A few studies have examined specific e-book platforms (e.g., Heyd, 2010; O'Neill, 2009; Pierce, 2011; Shereff, 2010), but there is still a strong need for libraries and other stakeholders to understand better all aspects of the e-book user experience, including users' perception, discovery, and actual use. This paper outlines and discusses the key phases of using e-books in academic libraries from the user experience perspective. Understanding these phases and significant findings regarding user behavior can facilitate a user-centered approach to improving e-books and their use.

A CONCEPTUAL FRAMEWORK

User experience involves a person's perception, attitude, emotion, and behavior with a particular product, system, or service (Albert & Tullis, 2013). User experience is not a one-dimensional characteristic for complex systems like e-books, but should include multiple attributes: useful, usable, desirable, findable, accessible, credible, and valuable (Morville, 2006). It takes a broader view of the entire interactive experience and task flow than the concept of usability, which is essentially a quality attribute of a user interface, product, or service. As the complexity of technology grows, user experience becomes critical for system design and user acceptance. Although the idea of user experience has been discussed in previous studies of e-books under different terms, such as user friendliness and ease of use, there is a lack of conceptual framework of e-book user experience and systematic assessment methodology.

The authors review studies on various aspects of e-book user experience and align these findings in the course of major phases of user experience with e-books: perceiving e-books as a useful information resource, discovering e-books from library collections, and using e-books in different contexts (see Figure 1). Users' perceptions of e-books include their awareness of e-books as a resource as well as their attitude about and preference for using e-books (or not). Awareness, attitude, and preference jointly affect users' intentions to use e-books, which translate into the discovery and actual use. In the discovery phase, users search for relevant e-book titles and identify the ones that they will further examine. The results of discovery may affect users' perception of e-books as a potential resource. The actual use of e-books involves navigating within the e-book structure, seeking targeted information, and reading the content. Perception, discovery, and use of e-books are affected by users' interaction with the e-book interface and how the interface presents features and content to users. The assessment of these three phases from the perspective of user and e-book interaction could be helpful in understanding better the determinants of a quality experience.

USER PERCEPTION OF E-BOOKS

In user experience research, perception is the cognitive process or capability to attain awareness and understand a product or service by selecting and interpreting information from the task context. Perception has been

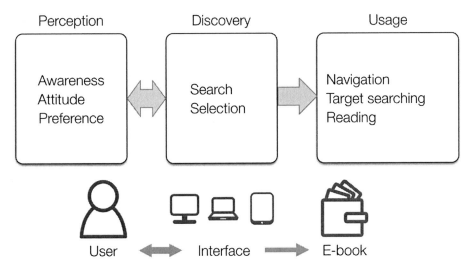

Figure 1. The e-book user experience conceptual framework.

considered as a fundamental cognitive measure and precedent of behavioral intentions. Studies of e-book perceptions have been focused on users' awareness of e-book resources, their attitude toward using e-books, and their preferences for e-books or print books for different tasks.

Many library users are not aware of the availability of e-books as library resources (Buczynski, 2010; Shelburne, 2009). Abdullah and Gibb's survey (2008a) found that e-book awareness and the level of e-book use among students was low: 57% of students were not aware of the availability of e-books from the library, and consequently, 60% of them had not used an e-book. Users' awareness of e-books varies across different disciplines. For example, Levine-Clark (2006) found that a significantly higher percentage of humanists were aware of e-books than users in general, probably because humanists rely more on books (and thus e-books) than researchers in other fields. Staiger (2012) found a wide range of percentage of e-book awareness reported in the literature and suggested that awareness is mostly dependent on how e-books are promoted at local institutions. In addition, users may not have a clear concept of e-books or which online resources are considered as e-books, since studies have found that students did not clearly distinguish among types of resources such as online journals, conference proceedings, and e-books (Hernon, Hopper, Leach, Saunders, & Zhang,

2007; Levine-Clark, 2006) and that they may be accessing e-books without knowing the exact type of the resources (Shelburne, 2009). The lack of awareness of the e-book concept and its availability may affect how users discover e-books in library resources and how they interact with the e-book features and contents (to be discussed in following sections).

Buczynski (2010) discussed the possible reasons for this lack of awareness, including: 1) not all e-books can be accessed through the library catalog, due to the lack of individual machine-readable cataloging (MARC) records; 2) the library catalog is not updated as frequently as the publishers' e-book platforms; and 3) publisher platforms may offer table of contents and full-text searching not available in the library catalog. The fragmented nature of e-book collections in libraries may result in missing titles in library catalogs and in user confusion. Recent developments in discovery tools could potentially mitigate the e-book discovery issue by indexing metadata from multiple collections. However, technical and access barriers still exist between e-book collections and discovery tools.

Users' attitudes toward e-books depend on their perceived value and utility, and more importantly, on the technical aspects of access to e-books. Previous surveys have shown that users view the convenience of online access and search functions as the most important advantages of e-books over print books (Jamali, Nicholas, & Rowlands, 2009). Users often regard e-books as a quick reference tool (Abdullah & Gibb, 2008b; Staiger, 2012). As a result, how e-books help users find relevant sections and extract information for further use affects users' attitude about using e-books as valuable information resources. Searching and navigation functions are thus critical to users' acceptance (Levine-Clark, 2006). Other e-book features, such as downloading, printing, text highlighting, annotating, copying, and pasting, have repeatedly been found important for users to develop positive attitudes toward e-books (Brahme & Gabriel, 2012).

In addition to surveys of users' attitudes, Chrzastowski (2011) conducted a diary study of user behavior with Elsevier e-books with 129 faculty and Ph.D. students at University of Illinois at Urbana-Champaign (UIUC). Participants' perceptions of the advantages of e-books included 24/7 online access, easy to search and navigate, downloading and storage, and off campus access. The top three behaviors with e-books reported by participants are brief look, reading from screen, and downloading PDF. Participants also regarded these behaviors as the value of e-books. Nearly 70% of participants rated e-books as "need to have" or "nice to have," showing the perceived usefulness of e-books.

From the usability perspective, a common concern affecting users' attitudes toward e-books is the perceived eyestrain or fatigue from reading or viewing information on a screen for an extended period of time (Kang, Wang, & Lin, 2009; Levine-Clark, 2006). E-books are sometimes limited in meeting users' requirements of text size and clarity, although this limitation could be reduced by new display technologies such as e-ink and high-resolution screens. Print books appear to enable better reading comprehension (Jeong, 2013), and more use of cognitive strategies in analyzing, rereading, comprehending, elaborating, and integrating are required in electronic reading (ChanLin, 2013). Other usability issues of e-books, such as the book layout with limited display area on the screen and slow response, might also affect students' willingness to read e-books online (Hernon et al., 2007).

Users' preference for book format (e-books or print books) is influenced by the context of their information need as well as individual differences. Abdullah and Gibb (2008a) categorized e-book use into four types: finding relevant content, selective reading, fact finding, and extended reading. In a follow-up study (Abdullah & Gibb, 2008b), most students preferred to use a print book for extended reading, although they preferred e-books for finding relevant information and selective reading. Students had no strong preferences for book format for fact finding. For selective reading, students who had used an e-book before preferred print books and students without experience of e-books preferred to use e-books. This finding suggests that students expected e-books to be more effective for searching information, but they were not satisfied with their experiences. Foasberg (2014) conducted a diary study of a small group of college students and concluded that students prefer to use print for academic and long-form reading, and to engage more deeply with the text. Electronic resources are preferred mostly for shorter and nonacademic reading. As for individual differences, Shrimplin, Revelle, Hurst, and Messner (2010) identified four distinct clusters of users: book lovers, technophiles, pragmatists, and printers. Book lovers are emotionally attached to print books; technophiles prefer e-books as a new technology; pragmatists tend to be comfortable with both print books and e-books depending on their availability; and printers like to print out e-books without restrictions for further reading.

DISCOVERY OF E-BOOKS

Discovery and access have been identified as significant barriers to extensive e-book adoption in libraries, particularly because many users have difficulty identifying the e-books they need and understanding where to locate them. Other feedback from users regarding the discovery and access of e-books include the irrelevancy of e-book search results, or the fact that e-books from the search results were no better than other resources (Chrzastowski, 2012).

Earlier studies raised concerns about e-books not being indexed by library catalogs and suggested including indexes and tables of contents in the catalogs to improve users' browsing and searching capabilities of relevant e-books (Abdullah & Gibb, 2008b). Shelburne (2009) further suggested enhancing the full-text search ability and bibliographic information for e-books in the same way that journal content can be searched and discovered. With recent technological development, libraries have implemented three major mechanisms for improving e-book discovery and access: e-book vendors' platforms, library catalogs (OPACs), and discovery tools. Walters (2013) summarized each mechanism's challenges in meeting users' e-book needs. Users may have to search and access e-books on multiple vendor platforms to identify a library's e-book holdings. E-book vendors' interfaces vary in appearance, layout, and functionality, creating additional learning requirements for the user. Presenting e-books in library catalogs has some common challenges, including limited availability of record metadata, lack of standardization, difficulties managing the addition and removal of titles, and the generally low quality of vendor-supplied records (Martin & Mundle, 2010). The challenges of e-book discovery tools include incomplete coverage, reliance on metadata from external sources, problems with subject headings and authority control, difficulties with guest-user access, and continuing dependence on vendors' platforms for access to full text. Without proper guidance on the incomplete coverage, users could have the false impression that all the library's e-books could be accessed from the discovery tool's single search interface. Users may be able to use a single interface for e-book discovery, but must still deal with a wide range of platform-specific display and control options at the access stage.

Analyzing transaction logs from catalogs and discovery tools is an effective way of studying users' e-book search behavior. Most transaction logs contain information elements such as the particular page requested by the user, the identity of the requesting user (IP address), the date and time of the request, and whether the request was successful. Transaction log analysis is an unobtrusive and inexpensive way of collecting large amounts of data about users' searching behavior. The authors collected and analyzed one month of transaction logs with over 50,000 search records from two discovery tools (VuFind and Ex Libris Primo) at the Purdue University Libraries (Niu, Zhang, & Chen, 2014). They found that the format (e-book and book) and availability (online and at the library) were among the most used facets in all search sessions. However, the use of facets in the discovery tools was low (8.4% of all searches in VuFind and 9.7% in Primo). Using transaction log analysis, Urbano, Zhang, Downey, and Klingler (2015) examined how the library catalog facilitates e-book discovery and use in patron-driven acquisitions (PDA). Their analysis showed that general keyword and title searches are most frequent for e-book searches. E-books accessed from the full bibliographic record pages in the catalog resulted in significantly higher use. This finding highlights the importance of providing the necessary information in the catalogs or discovery tools for users to identify relevant e-books from the search results.

In addition to searches in the catalog and discovery tools, how users select e-books and determine their usefulness before fully committing to reading is also a critical part of the discovery phase. McKay, Hinze, and colleagues (2012) analyzed a sample of transaction logs of 100 randomly selected browsed e-books and 100 e-books loaned to users. The data covered the period during which users were making a selection (i.e., before a loan was created) and includes all the pages users viewed to a maximum of 19 pages. The results of log analysis include the book features users viewed, the length of time users spent with books, and how users examined books and their features. The analysis identified the five most commonly viewed parts of the e-books: front matter, chapter headings, table of contents, the first page of content, and the introduction. Almost all users reviewed the front matter before initiating a more thorough investigation of the e-book. Users were seen to move page-by-page through the book (21% loaned, 14% browsed), flip to the middle of a section within the content (49%, 29%), and directly navigate to a chapter heading (51%, 55%). Users appeared to use the table of contents (ToC) navigation more often than they entered a page number into the top navigation (63 of 200 vs. 14 of 200). The conclusion and index seem to be used less often than in similar studies, possibly because users in the discovery stage might be focusing on the overall relevancy of the e-book and not on a particular piece of information. The e-book platform (EBL) in this study provided three navigation methods for the user: the ToC, pagination, and scrolling; however, there may be different interaction methods that would better support users' sampling of the e-book content.

Another study by McKay, Buchanan, and colleagues (2012) analyzed transaction logs from e-book publishers to determine which user interface elements affect users' selection behavior. The results demonstrated that flaws in the presentation of the covers and ToCs of e-books increased the volume of short time-span reading, and reduced the likelihood of long-span reading. Inconsistencies or errors in e-book covers and ToCs caused extended investigation of books without further significant reading. The log analysis showed that e-books with clearer and more consistent indicators of their content would either be examined briefly or read over an extensive period of time. Reducing errors in cover image and table of contents would make it easier for readers to determine which e-books are useful without having to engage further.

Although transaction log analysis can generate quantitative information about users' e-book search behavior, it fails to capture any information about the context in which the search event occurs. Behavioral observations complement the limitations inherent of logs by providing such missing contextual information. An exemplary study by Hinze, McKay, Vanderschantz, Timpany, and Cunningham (2012) observed the physical book selection process at the library shelves, and their findings have implications for designing e-book discovery and access systems. For example, when selecting books users tend to be close to the shelves in order to retain the context of their search. Hinze and colleagues (2012) suggested that e-book collections could provide users with richer context information (e.g., previous interaction history) to aid the search and selection process.

THE USE OF E-BOOKS

Users tend to have different use patterns for e-books and print books, the latter of which tends to be constant, frequent, or linear. E-books in academic libraries usually are used as online references to extract information for study and research (Folb, Wessel, & Czechowski, 2011; Staiger,

2012). For example, Hernon and colleagues (2007) studied e-book use by undergraduate students in economics, literature, and nursing. They found that students used ToCs to determine which chapters seemed relevant for browsing and scanning, and they did not read e-books entirely. The eBooks Observatory Project of the United Kingdom's Joint Information Systems Committee (JISC) found that course-related e-books were not being used as a substitute for print books. Most users spent less than one minute per page with the e-books tested, and they used e-books in a nonlinear, just-in-time manner (Estelle, Milloy, Rowlands, & Woodward, 2009). Therefore, McKay (2011) suggested that e-books are more analogous to journal articles or other scholarly publications with clear in-document navigation points such as title, abstract, and section headings. McKay's (2011) exploratory log analysis showed that academic e-book use involves nonsequential reading with frequent flipping back and forth at chapter headings and other breaks, similar to the use and reading behavior in other scholarly documents.

Although navigation is a key function for information retrieval, users struggle to navigate effectively in e-books with similar features of print books presented on screen. Berg, Hoffmann, and Dawson (2010) examined undergraduate students' information retrieval performance with print and e-books. Participants were asked to search for discrete facts and sections (i.e., "fact searching") within a print book or e-book. Their observation showed that participants used linear approaches to seek information in print books, from identifying keywords, looking for keywords in the ToCs and index, turning to the designated pages, and scanning for relevant content. However, participants' sense of linearity appeared to be lost with e-books, nor did they use the indexes in e-books. Participants used the physicality of print books to track their reading, but they were unable to make immediate observations of e-books such as point of entry, current position, length, and structure of the book. Berg and colleagues (2010) noted that compared to print books, moving through e-book pages was sluggish. Participants expected to interact with e-books in a way similar to navigating websites. For example, they expected that all chapter titles, keywords, indexed terms and page numbers would be hyperlinked, which was not true for the tested e-book platform. Finally, participants showed a strong preference for searching within e-books, but the nature and structure of the search function in e-books did not meet their expectations.

There may be a disconnection between users' experience of print and e-books. Berg and colleagues (2010) suggested that the e-books in their study did not facilitate the transfer of linear information retrieval skills from using print books. One example of this lack of transfer is that participants did not know of the existence of indexes in e-books. In addition, Liesaputra and Witten (2008) compared users' navigation within books in four formats (three online and one in print) and found that users had disorientations with e-books and could not determine the size of online documents. It is possible that the digital environment of e-books does not provide enough contextual information for users to orientate and navigate in e-books as they would with print books. As the respondents of Shelburne's (2009) survey noted, many e-books are designed for sequential access, which is not very efficient for reference and research work, such as flipping through pages in different chapters and cross-referencing. Without efficient and accurate navigation in e-books, it is a major challenge for users to develop cognitive maps as the basis of their critical thinking and deep understanding of the content (Thayer et al., 2011).

The disconnection between print and e-book user experience is probably caused by the lack of support in e-book interface for the effective navigation and information retrieval that is critical for nonlinear reading of scholarly publications. As an example, studies of information retrieval with e-books have identified the importance of navigational features other than ToCs and paginations provided upfront in most e-books. Abdullah and Gibb (2009) investigated the usability and information retrieval performance of three common searching and browsing features in e-books: back-of-the-book index (BoBI), ToC, and full-text search (FTS). Their data showed that BoBI was more efficient (i.e., shorter task time) and accurate than ToC and FTS for finding information in an e-book. This result highlighted the importance of a BoBI for information seeking in e-books even when an FTS tool is available. Compared to FTS, BoBI directly identifies important topics in the book and distinguishes those topics from simple occurrence of keywords in the FTS results. BoBI also supports cross-references of preferred and related terms, which could be more efficient than alternating keywords in the FTS tool and understanding the information organization in the ToC.

Transaction log analysis has identified three distinct e-book reading patterns: linear progression, contextual confirmation, and exploratory assessment (McKay et al., 2012). Linear progression involves readers paging through the initial parts of the book, before using the left-hand ToC navigation to jump forward in the book to the start of a chapter. Contextual confirmation represents a user jumping to the first page of a chapter before paging forward two to three pages, then jumping backward in the book to the final few pages of the previous chapter. Exploratory assessment shows the user jumping back and forward throughout the book, seldom looking at more than one page. Linear progression was most likely to be the only pattern used; the other two patterns were most commonly used in conjunction with other interaction patterns.

Academic reading is an active process of sense-making and knowledge development. A number of e-book features have been identified as crucial to support strategies of academic reading and ensure usability and user satisfaction. Features that most users would expect include download and offline use, text highlighting, copying and pasting, printing, and note-taking (Croft & Davis, 2010; Hernon et al., 2007; Lam, Lam, Lam, & McNaught, 2009). These features are implemented differently on different platforms (e.g., printing availability and access restrictions), which pose challenges for libraries to provide a consistent e-book user experience (Hodges, Preston, & Hamilton, 2010). It is also a challenge for users to be aware of all available features of e-book platforms (Brahme & Gabriel, 2012). Future studies should closely examine how users utilize e-book features in their reading process (i.e., human-document interaction), and how to improve those features for better reading efficiency and comprehension (Qayyum, 2008).

DISCUSSION AND CONCLUSION

There have been many studies of users' attitude, preferences, discovery, access, and reading of e-books. Unfortunately, those studies have not been interpreted and discussed in a user experience research framework. Furthermore, there are few sets of guidelines of optimizing user experience and task performance throughout the phases of using e-books in academic libraries. In general, librarians have observed that there is an issue of e-book awareness among users, whose attitudes toward and preference for e-books are dependent on the context of information needs. In the discovery phase, the fragmented nature of library resources affects users' ability to find relevant e-books; additionally, navigation features of e-book platforms influence users' assessing and selection behavior. This summary of e-book use studies indicates that users mainly extract discrete information from e-books, rather than perusing the content. This reading pattern has significant implications for the design of e-book navigation features. The authors also observed that users have high expectations of e-book features that can support their reading strategies, such as printing and downloading of sections, annotations, and copying and pasting of text. The different access and copyright restrictions from e-book vendors have hindered the creation of a consistent user experience.

To promote awareness of, and a positive attitude toward, e-books among users, it is important for librarians to integrate e-books in their information literacy and instruction efforts. Librarians should work with system providers to improve the coverage and metadata quality of e-books in the catalogs and discovery tools. Results of user studies on reading behaviors need to be converted into new interaction designs that address the disconnection of reading experience from print books, and support effective navigation and information retrieval in e-books. The authors believe that a structured, user-centered research and design methodology is fundamental to these directions. To understand users' interaction with e-books in different phases, traditional transaction log analysis should be integrated with behavioral research methods to generate a comprehensive assessment of users' information-seeking activities. Findings of user research must be utilized to drive the design of e-book features, and the overall interaction between users and the e-book system. Usability issues with supporting evidence identified from user evaluations should be fed back to interface design for iterative refinement and improvement. E-books with an engaging user experience will be a great addition to users' current scholarly information resources.

ACKNOWLEDGMENTS

This work is supported by a fellowship from the Electronic Resources and Libraries (ER&L) and EBSCO. The views and opinions expressed are those of the authors and do not necessarily reflect the views of the ER&L and EBSCO.

REFERENCES

Abdullah, N., & Gibb, F. (2008a). Students' attitudes towards e-books in a Scottish higher education institute: Part 1. *Library Review*, *57*(8), 593–605. http://dx.doi.org/10.1108/00242530810899577

Abdullah, N., & Gibb, F. (2008b). Students' attitudes towards e-books in a Scottish higher education institute: Part 2: Analysis of e-book usage. *Library Review*, *57*(9), 676–689. http://dx.doi.org/10.1108/00242530810911798

Abdullah, N., & Gibb, F. (2009). Students' attitudes towards e-books in a Scottish Higher Education Institute: Part 3—Search and browse tasks. *Library Review*, *58*(1), 17–27. http://dx.doi.org/10.1108/00242530910928906

Albert, W., & Tullis, T. (2013). *Measuring the user experience: Collecting, analyzing, and presenting usability metrics* (2nd ed.). Amsterdam, Netherlands: Morgan Kaufmann.

Berg, S. A., Hoffmann, K., & Dawson, D. (2010). Not on the same page: Undergraduates' information retrieval in electronic and print books. *The Journal of Academic Librarianship*, *36*(6), 518–525. http://dx.doi.org/10.1016/j.acalib.2010.08.008

Brahme, M., & Gabriel, L. (2012). Are students keeping up with the e-book evolution? Are e-books keeping up with students' evolving needs?: Distance students and e-book usage, a survey. *Journal of Library & Information Services in Distance Learning*, *6*(3-4), 180–198. http://dx.doi.org/10.1080/1533290X.2012.705109

Buczynski, J. A. (2010). Library ebooks: Some can't find them, others find them and don't know what they are. *Internet Reference Services Quarterly*, *15*(1), 11–19. http://dx.doi.org/10.1080/10875300903517089

ChanLin, L. J. (2013). Reading strategy and the need of e-book features. *The Electronic Library*, *31*(3), 329–344. http://dx.doi.org/10.1108/EL-08-2011-0127

Chrzastowski, T. (2011). Assessing the value of ebooks to academic libraries and users. In *Proceedings of the 9th Northumbria International Conference on Performance Measurement in Libraries and Information Services*. Retrieved from http://hdl.handle.net/2142/28612

Chrzastowski, T. (2012). Ebook users speak! Analyzing comment boxes from an ebook value survey. *Qualitative and Quantitative Methods in Libraries (QQML)*, *1*, 27–33.

Croft, R., & Davis, C. (2010). E-books revisited: Surveying student e-book usage in a distributed learning academic library 6 years later. *Journal of Library Administration*, *50*(5-6), 543–569. http://dx.doi.org/10.1080/01930826.2010.488600

Estelle, L., Milloy, C., Rowlands, I., & Woodward, H. (2009). Understanding how students and faculty REALLY use e-books: The UK National E-Books Observatory. In *ElPub2009—13th International Conference on Electronic Publishing*.

Foasberg, N. M. (2014). Student reading practices in print and electronic media. *College & Research Libraries*, *75*(5), 705–723. http://dx.doi.org/10.5860/crl.75.5.705

Folb, B. L., Wessel, C. B., & Czechowski, L. J. (2011). Clinical and academic use of electronic and print books: The Health Sciences Library System e-book study at the University of Pittsburgh. *Journal of the Medical Library Association, 99*(3), 218–228. http://dx.doi.org/10.3163/1536-5050.99.3.009

Hernon, P., Hopper, R., Leach, M. R., Saunders, L. L., & Zhang, J. (2007). E-book use by students: Undergraduates in economics, literature, and nursing. *The Journal of Academic Librarianship, 33*(1), 3–13. http://dx.doi.org/10.1016/j.acalib.2006.08.005

Heyd, M. (2010). Three e-book aggregators for medical libraries: NetLibrary, Rittenhouse R2 Digital Library, and STAT!Ref. *Journal of Electronic Resources in Medical Libraries, 7*(1), 13–41. http://dx.doi.org/10.1080/15424060903585693

Hinze, A., McKay, D., Vanderschantz, N., Timpany, C., & Cunningham, S. J. (2012). Book selection behavior in the physical library. In *Proceedings of the 12th ACM/IEEE-CS Joint Conference on Digital Libraries—JCDL '12* (pp. 305–314). New York, NY: ACM Press. http://dx.doi.org/10.1145/2232817.2232874

Hodges, D., Preston, C., & Hamilton, M. (2010). Resolving the challenge of e-books. *Collection Management, 35*(3), 196–200. http://dx.doi.org/10.1080/01462679.2010.486964

Jamali, H. R., Nicholas, D., & Rowlands, I. (2009). Scholarly e-books: The views of 16,000 academics: Results from the JISC national e-book observatory. *Aslib Proceedings, 61*(1), 33–47.

Jeong, H. (2013). A comparison of the influence of electronic books and paper books on reading comprehension, eye fatigue, and perception. *The Electronic Library, 30*(3), 390–408. http://dx.doi.org/10.1108/02640471211241663

Kang, Y.-Y., Wang, M.-J. J., & Lin, R. (2009). Usability evaluation of e-books. *Displays, 30*(2), 49–52. http://dx.doi.org/10.1016/j.displa.2008.12.002

Kumbhar, R. (2012). E-books: Review of research and writing during 2010. *The Electronic Library, 30*(6), 777–795. http://dx.doi.org/10.1108/02640471211282109

Lam, P., Lam, S. L., Lam, J., & McNaught, C. (2009). Usability and usefulness of ebooks on PPCs: How students' opinions vary over time. *Australasian Journal of Educational Technology, 25*(1), 30–44.

Levine-Clark, M. (2006). Electronic book usage: A survey at the University of Denver. *portal: Libraries and the Academy, 6*(3), 285–299. http://dx.doi.org/10.1353/pla.2006.0041

Liesaputra, V., & Witten, I. H. (2008). Seeking information in Realistic Books. In *Proceedings of the 8th ACM/IEEE-CS joint conference on Digital libraries—JCDL '08* (pp. 29–38). New York, NY: ACM Press. http://dx.doi.org /10.1145/1378889.1378896

Martin, K. E., & Mundle, K. (2010). Cataloging e-books and vendor records. *Library Resources & Technical Services, 54*(4), 227–237. http://dx.doi.org/10.5860 /lrts.54n4

McKay, D. (2011). A jump to the left (and then a step to the right). In *Proceedings of the 23rd Australian Computer-Human Interaction Conference—OzCHI '11* (pp. 202– 210). New York, NY: ACM Press. http://dx.doi.org/10.1145/2071536.2071569

McKay, D., Buchanan, G. Vanderschantz, N., Timpany, C., Cunningham, S. J., & Hinze, A. (2012). Judging a book by its cover: Interface elements that affect reader selection of ebooks. In *Proceedings of the 24th Australian Computer-Human Interaction Conference* (pp. 381–390). New York, NY: ACM Press. http://dx.doi.org/10.1145/2414536.2414597

McKay, D., Hinze, A., Heese, R., Vanderschantz, N., Timpany, C., & Cunningham, S. J. (2012). An exploration of ebook selection behavior in academic library collections. In *Theory and Practice of Digital Libraries* (pp. 13–24). Berlin, Germany: Springer. http://dx.doi.org/10.1007/978-3-642-33290-6_2

Morville, P. (2006). *Information architecture for the world wide web: Designing large-scale web sites* (3rd ed.). Sebastopol, CA: O'Reilly Media.

Niu, X., Zhang, T., & Chen, H. (2014). Study of user search activities with two discovery tools at an academic library. *International Journal of Human-Computer Interaction, 30*(5), 422–433. http://dx.doi.org/10.1080/10447318.2013.873281

O'Hare, S., & Smith, A. J. (2012). The customer is always right? Resistance from college students to e-books as textbooks. *Kansas Library Association College and University Libraries Section Proceedings, 2*(1), 35–41. http://dx.doi.org /10.4148/culs.v2i0.1615

O'Neill, L. C. (2009). *A usability study of e-book platforms.* Chapel Hill, NC: University of North Carolina at Chapel Hill.

Pierce, J. (2011). R2 Library: A review. *Journal of Electronic Resources in Medical Libraries, 8*(4), 430–440. http://dx.doi.org/10.1080/15424065.2011.626358

Qayyum, M. A. (2008). Capturing the online academic reading process. *Information Processing & Management, 44*(2), 581–595. http://dx.doi.org/10.1016/j .ipm.2007.05.005

Shelburne, W. A. (2009). E-book usage in an academic library: User attitudes and behaviors. *Library Collections, Acquisitions, & Technical Services, 33*(2–3), 59–72. http://dx.doi.org/10.1016/j.lcats.2009.04.002

Shereff, D. (2010). Electronic books for biomedical information. *Journal of Electronic Resources in Medical Libraries*, *7*(2), 115–125. http://dx.doi.org/10.1080/15424065.2010.482903

Shrimplin, A. K., Revelle, A., Hurst, S., & Messner, K. (2010). Contradictions and consensus—Clusters of opinions on e-books. *College & Research Libraries*, *72*(2), 181–190. http://dx.doi.org/10.5860/crl-108rl

Staiger, J. (2012). How e-books are used: A literature review of the e-book studies conducted from 2006 to 2011. *Reference & User Services Quarterly*, *51*(4), 355–365. http://dx.doi.org/10.5860/rusq.51n4.355

Thayer, A., Lee, C. P., Hwang, L. H., Sales, H., Sen, P., & Dalal, N. (2011). The imposition and superimposition of digital reading technology. In *Proceedings of the 2011 Annual Conference on Human Factors in Computing Systems—CHI '11* (pp. 2917–2926). New York, NY: ACM Press. http://dx.doi.org/10.1145/1978942.1979375

Urbano, C., Zhang, Y., Downey, K., & Klingler, T. (2015). Library catalog log analysis in e-book patron-driven acquisitions (PDA): A case study. *College & Research Libraries*, *76*(4), 412–426. Retrieved from http://crl.acrl.org/content/76/4/412.full.pdf+html

Walters, W. H. (2013). E-books in academic libraries: Challenges for discovery and access. *Serials Review*, *39*(2), 97–104. http://dx.doi.org/10.1080/00987913.2013.10765501

14 | E-Book Reading Practices in Different Subject Areas: An Exploratory Log Analysis

Robert S. Freeman and E. Stewart Saunders

ABSTRACT

Print books pose inherent difficulties for researchers who want to observe users' natural in-book reading patterns. With e-books and logs of their use, it is now possible to track several aspects of users' interactions inside e-books, including the number and duration of their sessions with an e-book and the order in which pages are viewed. This chapter reports on a study of one year of EBL user log data from Purdue University to identify different reading patterns or ways in which users navigate within different types of e-books—authored monographs vs. edited collections—and in e-books in different subject areas. The results of the analysis revealed a few differences in the reading patterns used for e-books of different types and subject areas, but more striking was the similarity in reading patterns across the e-books. Greater differences occurred between individual users, and these differences are best explained by differences in individuals' personal reading objectives. The analysis of reading logs for e-books is still very much a new venture. From this perspective, the findings are exploratory and descriptive rather than conclusive, and as much about the evolution of workable methodologies as they are about the results of the analysis. Log analysis reveals nothing about users' circumstances or intentions; however, if used in tandem with usability studies, and studies based on surveys, diaries, and interviews, it could contribute to a more objective understanding of users' interactions with e-books.

BACKGROUND AND INTRODUCTION

In the ancient world, reading was usually done out loud. In *A History of Reading*, Alberto Manguel (1996) recounts a story from the *Confessions* of St. Augustine in which Augustine tells of the time he paid a visit to Ambrose, the Bishop of Milan. Augustine observed Ambrose reading: "his eyes scanned the page and his heart sought out the meaning, but his voice was silent, and his tongue was still" (*Confessions*, 6, 3, as cited by Manguel, 1996, p. 42). This was remarkable to Augustine because reading silently was something out of the ordinary.

Like Augustine's observation, most objective descriptions of silent reading have focused on its physiognomic aspects (i.e., reading posture, facial expression, and movements of the hands, fingers, tongue, lips, and eyes). In the 19th and 20th centuries, many scientific studies of reading concentrated on readers' visual behavior or eye movements. Methods of tracking eye movements included the corneal reflection and the scleral observation methods, both of which required holding the subject's head in a fixed position. Other methods involved attaching monitors to the subject's eye while the subject scanned a page or read lines of text. Another study placed the reader in a darkened room with a text and a flashlight. "The use of a light is clearly somewhat unnatural for the reader," the educational psychologist A. K. Pugh (1977) noted, "but the restrictions on the subject are less than in most of the eye-movement recording methods" (p. 42). Pugh discussed a fundamental discovery resulting from Louis-Émile Javal's early eye-movement studies; when reading or scanning, human eyes do not move smoothly, but rather make jerky movements (saccades) and stop several times, moving very quickly between each stop (fixation). The movements measured in these experiments are very small, and the subjects read only relatively short texts (Pugh, 1978, p. 14). Marshall (2009) notes that, although eye tracking "provides important data about some aspects of reading—word and letter recognition, most importantly—it has not shed as much light on how people read in the wild," that is, read naturally (p. 101).

Other controlled reading studies give test subjects identical reading material with instructions, observe and record subjects' actions (e.g., through video recording), and, in some studies, ask them all the same series of questions. User studies often are conducted to inform improvements in the design of products, including printed and digital documents and webpages. A study by Liesaputra and Witten (2008) compared users' interactions with print books and different e-book formats, including one that simulated a 3-D book with realistic page turning. Still, the nature of silent reading makes it difficult to study and measure in the laboratory. The fact that the act of observing affects the behavior being observed means that such research can only go a short way toward describing reader behavior. Reading researchers have long recognized the need for observations or field work in natural situations.

In *Reading and Writing the Electronic Book*, C.C. Marshall (2009), who has observed natural reader behaviors for Microsoft Research, identifies the following kinds of field studies: surveys and questionnaires, interview and diary studies, and studies using instrumenting software that logs details of user interactions with digital technologies such as e-books.

Since the advent of e-books, academic librarians have been conducting surveys to determine how well e-books are catching on with students and faculty. Among the larger surveys of students and faculty by librarians are Levine-Clark (2006), who received 2,067 responses at the University of Denver; Nicholas and colleagues (2008), who received 1,818 responses at University College London; Li, Poe, Potter, Quigley and Wilson (2011), who received 2,569 responses from the University of California; and Corlett-Rivera and Hackman (2014), who received 1,343 responses from students and faculty in the humanities and social sciences at the University of Maryland. These surveys posed questions to members of a target population to gauge their awareness of, use of, and attitudes about e-books of different types (i.e., scholarly monographs, edited collections, and reference works) vis-à-vis other kinds of written materials, especially print books. The surveys also collected demographic data from respondents as to their college, department, and status. This information allows potentially useful comparisons between subgroups in the population. For example, when the Maryland survey asked users to indicate what format they prefer for scholarly monographs (print, e-book, no preference, it depends), results showed that 41% of all respondents preferred print, including 44% of faculty and 40% of graduate student respondents. The next question asked their format preference for edited collections: faculty preferred print to e-books, 36% to 25%, but graduate students chose e-books over print, 37% to 31% (Corlett-Rivera & Hackman, 2014, p. 268). Although most questions in surveys are tied to multiple-choice answers, there are usually a few open-ended questions that allow respondents to elaborate on "it depends" and provide details about their experience with—and within—particular texts. For instance, regarding his preferred format for scholarly monographs, a Maryland respondent wrote that it "depends on the urgency that I am reading with and what my end goal is, i.e. research, paper writing, personal betterment" (Corlett-Rivera & Hackman, 2014, p. 270).

Diary-based studies, supported by interviews, can provide an even closer look at reading behaviors because subjects (often students) write down—or are supposed to write down—some details not only about what they read, but also about the context and purpose of their reading (i.e., preparing for classes, preparing for exams, reviewing texts for research, gaining specific information, or learning new topics). With knowledge of the students' assignments and the tasks they perform, the investigators are able to identify different reading practices or techniques applied to different tasks and subjects. In a diary-based study of 39 University of Washington Computer Science and Engineering graduate students attempting to use Kindle DX e-readers to accomplish their academic reading, Thayer and colleagues (2011) analyzed the meta-level relationship between reading tasks and associated reading techniques. Students recorded their academic and leisure reading activities, including specific tasks that proved difficult to perform on the Kindle DX, such as marking up texts, using references, using illustrations, and creating cognitive maps. Thayer and colleagues then associated each task with specific reading techniques, or "styles," defined by A. K. Pugh (1978, pp. 52–55):

- **Receptive reading**: reading sequentially from beginning to end with little variation in pace, to find out what an author has to say;
- **Responsive reading:** active engagement with arguments in the text, with frequent changes of pace, pauses, rereading;
- **Skimming:** a quick overview of the structure or content of a text to locate potentially useful information;
- **Searching:** looking in a general way for answers to a question;
- **Scanning:** searching for a specific word or phrase.

Nonacademic and leisure reading of novels and short articles indicated *receptive reading*; text markup indicated *responsive reading*; and using references and using illustrations indicated *skimming*. *Skimming* also was associated with creating cognitive maps, the way readers notice and remember the physical location of information within a text and its spatial relationship to other locations in the text as a whole (Thayer et al., 2011, pp. 2921–2924). The study concluded that electronic documents on the Kindle DX were well suited to *receptive reading, searching*, and *scanning*, but were not suited to *responsive reading* and *skimming*.

Before there were digital texts and computer logs, it was nearly impossible to study natural reading behavior over many pages of text. It was obtrusive and even "creepy" (Marshall, 2009, p. 96). It was also seldom done (McKay, 2011, p. 204). With user session logs, researchers are now able to collect reading pattern data unobtrusively from a large number of users as they interact naturally with e-books.

DESCRIPTION OF THIS STUDY

The idea for this log analysis project was inspired by 1) the recent availability of detailed EBL session logs of Purdue Libraries' users; 2) a research article by McKay (2011), who was probably the first to publish an analysis of reading patterns in EBL user logs; and 3) the authors' longstanding interest in comparative use of academic library collections in different subject areas.

EBL is a large aggregator that provides e-books to many academic libraries. In 2011, Purdue University Libraries chose EBL as the provider for the e-book patron-driven acquisitions (PDA) plan. Coordinated through the library's primary book vendor, YBP, the plan started with an initial pool of a little over 11,000 titles. Although librarians bought some EBL titles outside the PDA plan, most EBL e-books in Purdue's catalog arrived as part of the PDA plan (the library does not pay for PDA titles until patrons use them). The collection grew steadily and, by the end of February 2014, reached nearly 33,000 titles. Users have opened one-quarter of the titles at least briefly. To open a title, users link from the catalog record to the e-book and arrive at a summary page that features the book's cover, bibliographic information, and, often, an abstract—this webpage is not recorded in the user log. From here, users click "read online" and arrive at an introductory page in the EBL online reader that displays the e-book, starting with its cover, a scrollbar on the right, and, on the left, a hyperlinked navigation menu based on the table of contents. There are navigation keys and a jump-to-page feature above the e-book image, as well as a search function. There is also a download button that allows the reader to download a PDF or EPUB version of the title into Adobe Digital Editions.

In her article "A Jump to the Left (and Then a Step to the Right): Reading Practices within Academic Ebooks," McKay (2011), a librarian at Swinburne University of Technology in Melbourne, Australia, pioneered the use of EBL logs to gain insight into users' e-book reading patterns, specifically those patterns associated with in-book navigation and with document triage or book selecting, that is, when a user chooses to select or reject a book. She tracked sequential forward patterns and backward jumps, and verified that continuous sequential reading, the linear pattern associated with immersive reading of novels, seldom occurs for long in academic e-reading before readers jump forward or back to other sections of the e-book (pp. 207–208). Although the authors did not adopt McKay's quantitative methodology or units of measure, they were inspired by her description of three reading patterns comprising various degrees of linear forward movements and backward and forward jumps: *linear progression* for logs that proceed forward in a more or less orderly reading fashion; *contextual confirmation* for those instances in which the reader makes a large jump forward in the paging, then backs up a few pages to verify the context of the part, and then proceeds to read continuously for several pages; and *exploratory assessment* for when the reader makes large jumps forward and backward in the pages consulted, apparently in search of particular material.

In her 2011 study and in a follow-up article (McKay et al., 2012), McKay's focus was on patrons' e-book selection behavior. This is especially relevant to EBL users at Swinburne and other institutions where, after five minutes in an EBL "browse" session (with an unowned title) or ten minutes (with an owned title), a window pops up that requires anyone who wants to continue reading to click "yes" on a dialog box and thereby initiate a "loan" session. Separating browse-session from loan-session data, McKay found statistically significant differences in the reading patterns in each group. Browse sessions showed more instances of *exploratory assessment,* while loan sessions showed more patterns of *linear progression* and *contextual confirmation* (pp. 19–20).

Separating browse and loan sessions was not relevant to the log analysis at Purdue because EBL users at Purdue do not have to take any action.

The transition from browse to loan occurs seamlessly, and users remain unaware of the change. Nevertheless, the authors were inspired by McKay's idea of analyzing EBL log data to show reading patterns, and hoped to devise a method to use EBL log data to support the hypothesis that users read and navigate within a book differently depending on the type (i.e., monograph or edited collection) and subject area of the book.

This study reports on research analyzing data from EBL e-book user sessions at Purdue University to attempt to answer two questions:

1. How do users' reading practices differ when interacting with e-books that are authored monographs versus e-books that are edited collections of chapters by different authors?
2. How do users' reading practices differ when using e-books in different subject areas?

The authors expected the data to show significant differences, for example: that users would read authored monographs in a less jumpy and more continuous linear pattern than they read edited collections; that users of edited collections would proceed directly to one or two relevant chapters, rather than explore the whole book; or that users of animal science and technology e-books would do more searching and scanning than readers of history and literature e-books. The results of the log analysis, however, did not meet expectations. The similarities were more impressive than the differences, which were not as great as had been imagined.

METHODOLOGY

The analysis of logs of e-book use to describe reading behavior is still a new research venture. Consequently, the methodologies for this type of analysis are intuitive rather than based on any theoretical considerations or on the results of past research. Some of the most important questions, such as, what are the basic "units" of analysis or how does one distinguish reliable data from dirty data, are still to be answered. Therefore, the methods used here are driven by the questions asked rather than by any previously established measurements or methodologies. From this perspective, the results of this chapter are exploratory and descriptive, rather than conclusive as a comparative analysis. They are as much about the evolution of workable methodologies as they are about the results of the analysis.

For this study, the authors pulled data from the EBL use report for Purdue University for one year (July 1, 2013–June 30, 2014). The resulting data set covered 29,884 user sessions with 5,245 titles viewed by 4,579 users. The user or reader session logs are part of EBL use reports available to Purdue through LibCentral, EBL's administrative site, which collects detailed information on the use of EBL e-books. Although the data do not provide any personal details about each user, such as academic status or department, they do track each anonymized user's e-book activities across time. Session details essential to this study include:

- duration of each session;
- page numbers in the sequence in which they were viewed;
- anonymized user identification for each user;
- EBL identification number for each title;
- bibliographic details for each title including ISBN and e-ISBN; and
- Library of Congress class and a broad subject heading for each title.

The report also provides names of author(s) and editor(s), but combines them without distinction within an author field, making it difficult to separate authors from editors. This difference is important in this study to distinguish the type of e-book used. To overcome this difficulty, the research team extracted the e-ISBN from the EBL use report and then pulled matching title records from YBP's GOBI database that present author(s) and editor(s) in separate fields, and then merged these fields into the EBL use report.

EBL data come packaged as "user sessions" or "reader session logs." Each session log is a record of what transpires between the time the user opens the book and the time he or she stops reading. The same reader, however, may open and close the same e-book several times the same day or on immediately successive days. The authors decided that the best unit of analysis would be all of the reader session logs for the same reader while he or she was reading the same book. For simplicity, the authors called this unit of analysis a "Read." This group of activities by the same person in the same book tells more about reading habits than does a single reader session log. Also, nearly all session logs show the reader flipping through pages numbered 1–5 when first opening an e-book. Although there are variations between e-books, these first few pages are invariably front matter, some of them being advertisements for other books or even blank pages. They contribute little or nothing to the analysis, so they were eliminated from the log. However, if a log began on a page number higher than five, say page 15, then nothing would be eliminated.

It must be noted that the "page numbers" given in the log are *file page image numbers* rather than a book's *real* or *actual page numbers*. For example, page 1 in the log refers to the image of the book's cover, and page 15 in the log might refer to the image of the book's actual page xii, a page in the introduction. It proved difficult for the authors to use a page image number from the log to find the equivalent actual page in an EBL e-book because the EBL online reader does not display image numbers. Patrons using the EBL online reader only see actual page numbers. An automatic way to translate or convert log image numbers into actual page numbers would make it easier to do research that combines log analysis with examination of e-book content. Fortunately, when EBL e-books are downloaded, the Adobe Digital Reader displays both actual page numbers and file image numbers together. Because of the large number of reader logs, however, the authors did not include downloading e-books to the Adobe Digital Reader as part of the methodology.

Much of this log analysis focused on the sequence of page numbers for each Read. The objective was to find patterns that would indicate where the reader was going while looking at particular pages. Was the reader looking at consecutive pages, or was the reader jumping to later pages in the book or flipping back to earlier pages? Comparing sequences of page numbers between one Read in one title and another Read in another title is meaningless. So, in this study, to make comparisons possible, the sequence of page numbers was converted to a sequence of page changes (i.e., Did the reader turn one page or did he or she jump ahead?). The sequences of page changes were then partitioned into units of "reading passages" where the partitioning was based on evidence that the reader had skipped over some reading material or had jumped back to earlier material. The word "jump" was used as part of the nomenclature to name these passages. (See the Appendix A for an illustration of the partitioning of the page changes and naming them.) The "Passage" itself contains a sequence of page changes that show that the user has read consecutive pages or skipped only one page or gone back only a single page. The rationale behind allowing one page skipped forward or one page turned back to be considered consecutive reading is that in a normal reading one sometimes comes across blank pages that are numbered or pages with illustrations that are numbered, or sometimes one turns back a page to see where one left off. The authors created five Passage distinctions:

1. Forward (FOR): A reading Passage that begins with no jumps.
2. Small Jump Forward (SJF): A reading Passage that begins with a forward jump of more than two pages but less than nine pages.
3. Big Jump Forward (BJF): A reading Passage that begins with a forward jump of nine or more pages.
4. Small Jump Back (SJB): A reading Passage that begins with paging back more than one page but fewer than nine pages.
5. Big Jump Back (BJB): A reading Passage that begins with paging back nine or more pages.

The authors created small jumps and big jumps to distinguish between a pattern in which a reader examines pages that are near one another, probably within the same section of the book, and a pattern in which a reader examines pages that are far apart and probably in a different section or chapter. Nine pages, although somewhat arbitrary, seemed like a reasonable estimate of the average length of text that would fit within a section or chapter of a book.

For some analyses, it was useful to join successive Passages into pairs of Passages. Figure 1 shows how a sequence of Passages, SJB BJF SJF BJB, is combined into pairs of Passages.

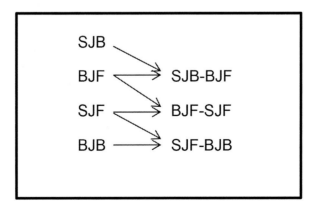

Figure 1. Transformation of a sequence of Passages into pairs.

These transition pairs of Passages provide another unit of analysis that allows us to see changes in the direction of turning pages; a simple count of Passage directions does not accomplish this. A sequence of Passages that jumped forward continuously and then backward continuously gives very different results than a sequence that is constantly alternating direction, even though the number of forward and backward jumps might be the same for both sequences. For a clearer understanding of these procedures, see Appendix A for an example.

RESULTS

The EBL use report for Purdue University contained 29,884 reader session logs. The reader session logs pertained to 5,245 e-books read by 4,579 readers. There was a broad range of use of the e-books. For example, one title, *Handbook of Human Factors and Ergonomics*, was opened 1,551 times by 277 readers. In another example, a single reader accounted for 1,664 reader session logs ranging over 703 e-books.

The 29,884 reader session logs reduced to 10,974 Reads. For in-depth analysis, the authors decided to select those Reads that had 11 or more pages and had one or more paired Passages. Those Reads with fewer pages or zero paired Passages did not provided sufficient data for in-depth analysis. As a result, 7,224 Reads were analyzed in depth and 3,750 received only a summary analysis. Table 1 shows the basic data for both groups of Reads.

The data for the 3,750 Reads only used for the summary analysis closely parallel the data for the 7,224 Reads in the in-depth analysis. Looking at the data for all 10,974 Reads, we see that when readers jumped around in the text, it was more likely to be a jump backward to earlier sections of the e-book. The number of times a reader turned pages back to an earlier section of the e-book (143,269) was greater than the number of times he or she jumped forward to a new section (97,571). This is confirmed by the number of Small Jump Back Passages (71,605) compared to the number of Small Jump Forward Passages (42,979), and by the number of Backward pairs (35,282) compared to the number of Forward pairs (14,797). Will these patterns repeat when subpopulations of the Reads are analyzed?

The raw sums of data, however, do not reveal all. If one were to create distribution graphs for these data, they would be highly skewed, with a high number of Reads having low values and a small number with very

Table 1. Sums across Reads for different measures of e-book reading.

	Sums across all 10,974 Reads	Sums across 7,224 Reads of 11 or more pages	Sums across 3,750 Reads of less than 11 pages
Minutes	305,024	292,987	12,037
Pages	457,764	439,918	17,846
Sessions	29,884	24,439	5,445
Passages	179,780	172,469	7,311
Paired Passages	170,167	165,245	4,922
Individual Page Turns			
Consecutive turns	219,785	211,693	8,092
Jump forward turns	97,571	94,727	2,844
Jump back turns	143,269	138,909	4,360
Passages			
Forward Passages	7,903	5,914	1,989
Small jump forward Passages	42,979	42,178	801
Big jump forward Passages	26,526	26,017	509
Small jump back Passages	71,605	69,636	1,969
Big jump back Passages	21,812	21,500	312
Paired Passages			
Forward pairs	14,797	14,470	327
Alternating pairs	120,088	116,166	3,922
Backward pairs	35,282	34,609	673

high values. The distributions would replicate typical power law distributions. The cause for this type of distribution is that a large number of Reads were of short duration, only a few pages in length, although some Reads were extremely long. Any distribution of measures relating to how readers navigate the text simply will be a function of the length of the Read; means and standard deviations will be uninterpretable. To compare Reads on the same scale, many of the measures for each Read were normalized by calculating ratios valued between 0 and 1 and then multiplying these ratios by 100. The result is a scale of 0 to 100 on which to compare data for individual Reads. In case the numerator and denominator are the same units, the result is a percent. The averages and standard deviations of normalized values will themselves be on the 0 to 100 scale. The length of the Read will have only a small effect on the normalized values.

Limiting the analysis to Reads having a minimum of 11 pages and one pair of Passages gives sufficient data points for reliable insights into the reading patterns of academic e-books. The restricted set of 7,224 Reads included 3,424 e-books read by 3,580 different readers. Most Reads consist of one patron reading one e-book, but at the other extreme, the data reveal that one patron read 405 e-books and that one e-book was read by 260 patrons. The statistical data for this set of Reads are presented as averages, medians, and standard deviations for the general characteristics of the data and for the three units of analysis: page turns or jumps, Passages of page turns or jumps, and paired Passages. See Appendix B for a complete set of the statistics. In the discussion and analysis that follow, the statistics in the tables are limited to those pertinent to the analysis.

Table 2 summarizes the principal features of patron reading habits for academic e-books. The average number of reader sessions for each Read was 3.4, and the average reading time spent on each Read was 40.6 minutes. The average number of pages read was 60.9 and the average number of Passages within those pages was 23.9. The medians for these three measures are lower than the averages, showing a skew toward the lower values in the series. On the other hand, the differences between average values and median values for the normalized variables are very small. The large number of Passages indicates a strong tendency to move about within the e-book. More striking was the high frequency of changing direction when going from one Passage to another: 72% of the paired Passages alternated between forward jumps and back jumps (e.g., BJF-SJB, SJB-SJF, etc.), while only 9.53% of such transitions maintained a steady forward reading direction, for example, BJF-SJF (see Table 2). This suggests that academic e-book users are more engaged in skimming, searching, and responsive reading than in receptive reading. Nevertheless, on average 45.21% of the pages turned in a Read were consecutive pages. Keep in mind that users probably still spent more time actually reading these pages than performing quick jumps.

Table 2. Measures of reading patterns for 7,224 Reads.

	Averages	Medians	Standard deviations
Duration of Reads in minutes	40.6	12.4	
Number of seconds to read a page	35.5		
Number of pages in a Read	60.9	37.0	
Number of sessions in a Read	3.4	2.0	
Number of consecutive pages turned	29.3	15.0	
Percent of consecutive pages turned	45.21%	43.50%	19.67%
Number of backward jumps in a Read	19.2	11.0	
Percent of backward jumps in a Read	32.77%	33.30%	13.25%
Number of Passages	23.9	14.0	
Number of paired Passages with forward jumps	2.0	1.0	
Percent of paired Passages with forward jumps	9.53%	7.10%	11.86%
Number of paired Passages with alternating jumps	16.1	9.0	
Percent of paired Passages with alternating jumps	72.00%	72.40%	16.19%
Ratio of # of Passages/# of pages in a Read	.409		.163

These broad statistical measures give a great deal of insight into the general patterns of patron reading behavior, but what might be the causes for such patterns? Do they come from different ways of constructing or formatting a text? Does the logical unfolding of concepts and explanations in different subject areas affect the way a book is read? Or are the causes basically determined by the different needs and objectives of the readers themselves? Given the data collected here, a random effects model would normally help answer such questions. It is doubtful, however, that the Reads are independent observations; in addition, the resulting model would have so many degrees of freedom as to minimalize its value. The less formal approach used here is to compare the averages of the normalized variables to understand any effects produced by e-book type and by different subjects, and to use the standard deviation of these variables as a surrogate measure for the effects of reader objectives.

One of the principal objectives of this study was to determine any differences in reading styles for authored monographic e-books and edited collection e-books. Table 3 shows that there are some small differences. Readers of edited collection e-books tended to read more pages per book and to divide their progress through the book into more Passages. Dividing the number of Passages by the number of pages indicates that the number of Passages is a function of the number of pages read. Overall there is great similarity in reading styles for both edited collections and authored monographs.

Another of this study's objectives was to determine whether or not there were significant differences between how books were read in different subject areas, or in different classes of the Library of Congress (LC) Classification. For this comparison, the authors chose to analyze Reads in three large categories—humanities, social sciences, and STEM—and selected three groups of LC classes that they thought would not only be representative of each category, but also would be different enough within each category that one would not replicate the other. As shown in Table 4, these LC classes, drawn from the 7,224 Reads used for in-depth analysis, formed a subset with a total of 3,907 Reads. Those Reads that fell into other LC classes were omitted.

The authors were concerned that the analysis for these subject areas might be skewed if some of the subject areas had a greater preponderance of very short Reads that would have been dropped from the analysis because they were part of the 3,750 Reads not analyzed in depth. To verify that this was not the case, the authors counted the number of Reads in each subject in both the analyzed and not analyzed groups. The 3,750 Reads not

Table 3. Comparative measures of reading patterns for authored and edited e-books.

Type	Authored	Edited
Number of Reads	4,338	2,886
	AVERAGES	
Duration of Reads in minutes	40.4	40.8
Number of seconds to read a page	35.9	35.0
Number of pages in a Read	59.7	67.1
Number of sessions in a Read	3.2	3.6
Number of consecutive pages turned	29.0	29.7
Percent of consecutive pages turned	46.27%	43.61%
Number of backward jumps in a Read	17.5	21.8
Percent of backward jumps in a Read	31.45%	33.50%
Number of Passages	22.1	26.6
Number of paired Passages with forward jumps	1.8	2.3
Percent of paired Passages with forward jumps	9.54%	9.50%
Number of paired Passages with alternating jumps	14.9	17.9
Percent of paired Passages with alternating jumps	72.27%	71.59%
Ratio of # of Passages/# of pages in a Read	.404	.418

analyzed represent 34% of the 10,974 Reads. Table 4 also shows the percentages of Reads not analyzed for each subject area were all reasonably close to that 34%, indicating very little skewing of the analytical results.

There are fairly large differences between subject areas in the average times spent reading in an e-book and in the number of pages read (see Tables 5, 6, and 7).[1] Readers in all three of the STEM areas read on average more pages in an e-book than did readers in any of the humanities or social science areas. They also returned to the same title for more reading sessions than did readers in any of the humanities or social science areas. On average, readers in the STEM areas also spent more time using an e-book than any group in the humanities and social sciences, except for historians.

Table 4. Number of Reads in each LC group for Reads used in analysis and Reads not used in analysis.

Categories	LC (Subject)	Reads used in analysis	Reads not used in analysis	TOTAL	% reads not counted
Humanities					
	D & E (History)	277	136	413	33%
	PR & PS (English & American Literature)	184	120	304	39%
	N (Art)	69	29	98	30%
Social Sciences					
	L (Education)	424	198	622	32%
	HD, HE, HF, HG (Business)	633	353	986	36%
	PE (English Linguistics)	48	30	78	38%
STEM					
	QA (Mathematics)	153	61	214	29%
	SF (Animal Science)	1608	538	2146	25%
	T (Technology)	511	175	686	26%
TOTAL		3907	1640	5547	30%

Looking at the number of Passages into which the pages are divided, one sees more or less the same pattern, the STEM subject areas exceeding the others. The same can be said for the number of paired Passages, both more with a forward direction and more with a back and forth direction. This could indicate that readers of STEM books did a lot of searching and scanning in pursuit of cross-references. One interesting difference, however, is between mathematics, with 15 paired Passages with alternating jumps, and technology, with 25.4 paired Passages with alternating jumps.

One must consider, however, the effect of the number of pages read on the number of Passages and direction pairs. The last line in Tables 5, 6, and 7 shows the ratio of the number of Passages divided by the number of pages read. Here we see that the ratios for mathematics and for technology are almost the same. Converting the other reading pattern measures to ratios or percentages also had the effect of reducing the differences between most subject areas, but it also highlighted the fact that the percent of continuously read pages is higher for mathematics, history, and art than it is for other areas. Although there are subject area differences, what is more striking is the degree to which they are all very similar, implying that readers' reading strategies of e-books differ to only a small degree for different subject areas.

On the other hand there appears to be a fairly large difference in reading patterns produced by the different objectives of the readers. Table 2 shows standard deviations for several variables used to measure the navigation of e-books. The standard deviations range in value from 11.86% to 19.67%. Given the very small effects for both book type and subject matter, and assuming there are no other factors producing a significant effect, the variance here is best explained by differences in reader objectives.

CONCLUSION

From a physical frame of reference, reading a book consists of eye movement and page turning. Within a mental frame, the reading of a book is the recognition of words, the absorption of meaning from the words, and reflection on the meaning. From a causal perspective, the mental frame drives the physical frame. The research problem is to connect the two frames.

Across disciplines and between differently formatted texts, such as edited collections and authored monographs, there exist small but perceptible differences in a few of the basic measures for turning pages and spending time on the text. Perhaps just as striking is the degree of similarity between readers of e-books in different disciplines or subject areas. Yet the data show that individual users are different from each other in large ways in their reading patterns. Thus, the inference from the physical act of turning pages to the mental actions of the reader is that personal objectives are of greater importance for determining the physical reading patterns than is the nature of the subject material being read.

Table 5. Comparative measures of reading patterns for three subject areas in the humanities.

	English & American Literature	Art	History
LC classes	PR & PS	N	D & E
Number of Reads	184	69	277
	AVERAGES		
Duration of Reads in minutes	34.3	32.0	49.1
Number of seconds to read a page	35.7	36.0	41.6
Number of pages in a Read	48.4	49.6	60.4
Number of sessions in a Read	3.1	2.5	3.3
Number of consecutive pages turned	21.1	25.6	29.5
Percent of consecutive pages turned	41.13%	48.37%	48.37%
Number of backward jumps in a Read	15.6	13.8	17.9
Percent of backward jumps in a Read	34.55%	30.47%	30.25%
Number of Passages	19.9	16.3	22.4
Number of paired Passages with forward jumps	1.5	1.1	1.9
Percent of paired Passages with forward jumps	8.40%	8.62%	9.35%
Number of paired Passages with alternating jumps	13.5	11.3	15.2
Percent of paired Passages with alternating jumps	72.63%	76.45%	72.51%
Ratio of # of Passages/# of pages in a Read	.441	.354	.395

Although the log data show that in general readers spend time engaged in continuous page-by-page reading—on average, over 45.21% of pages turned were consecutive—there was a surprisingly high percentage of transition pairs alternating between forward and backward jumps. This seems to indicate that

Table 6. Comparative measures of reading patterns for three subject areas in the social sciences.

	Business	Education	English Linguistics
LC classes	HD HE HF HG	L	PE
Number of Reads	633	424	48
	AVERAGES		
Duration of Reads in minutes	35.4	32.4	33.2
Number of seconds to read a page	35.0	34.2	41.5
Number of pages in a Read	59.7	54.1	45.5
Number of sessions in a Read	3.0	2.9	2.9
Number of consecutive pages turned	30.0	26.8	20.5
Percent of consecutive pages turned	38.34%	46.18%	43.36%
Number of backward jumps in a Read	16.9	15.6	14.0
Percent of backward jumps in a Read	30.08%	31.73%	31.49%
Number of Passages	21.8	20.0	18.9
Number of paired Passages with forward jumps	2.0	1.7	1.8
Percent of paired Passages with forward jumps	11.07%	9.54%	10.40%
Number of paired Passages with alternating jumps	14.4	13.4	13.0
Percent of paired Passages with alternating jumps	70.82%	71.79%	74.83%
Ratio of # of Passages/# of pages in a Read	.397	.405	.473

academic e-book users are more engaged in responsive reading, skimming, and searching than in receptive reading. The differences between reading patterns in different subject areas conform to our intuitive understanding of how

Table 7. Comparative measures of reading patterns for three STEM subject areas.

	Mathematics	Animal Science	Technology
LC classes	QA	SF	T
Number of Reads	153	1,008	511
	AVERAGES		
Duration of Reads in minutes	44.1	39.5	50.2
Number of seconds to read a page	37.3	31.9	32.2
Number of pages in a Read	68.4	69.5	91.7
Number of sessions in a Read	3.5	3.6	4.6
Number of consecutive pages turned	34.9	30.9	39.1
Percent of consecutive pages turned	48.94%	43.60%	43.08%
Number of backward jumps in a Read	19.5	22.5	31.1
Percent of backward jumps in a Read	29.74%	33.89%	33.82%
Number of Passages	22.9	27.2	37.6
Number of paired Passages with forward jumps	2.3	2.2	3.0
Percent of paired Passages with forward jumps	10.57%	8.17%	9.35%
Number of paired Passages with alternating jumps	15.0	18.6	25.4
Percent of paired Passages with alternating jumps	71.78%	73.14%	70.85%
Ratio of # of Passages/# of pages in a Read	.385	.412	.421

scholars absorb information and reflect on it. Historians, linguists, and mathematicians spend more time per page than do readers in the other disciplines. Traditionally, these are areas that require more concentration on textual details and reflection. The course requirements in different disciplines also certainly influence students' selection of particular texts and how they use those texts.

Many of the most heavily used e-books, such as *Handbook of Human Factors and Ergonomics*, were in the STEM disciplines and were undoubtedly assigned readings or essential reference works for one or more courses. These practical concerns probably explain why there were so many user sessions with these books and why the average time per page read was relatively short.

Although a powerful tool for revealing reader behavior patterns from many user sessions and large quantities of data, log analysis cannot provide insight into users' various circumstances and purposes. Future reading log analysis research should be informed by or done in tandem with the kind of survey or diary-based studies that gather information on readers' thoughts and intentions. Future e-book research also should be able to track or examine the specific content of e-book pages and connect the content to observed reading behaviors. Together these studies can lead to a more comprehensive understanding of reader behaviors.

ACKNOWLEDGMENTS

The authors thank Rebecca Richardson, Electronic Resources Librarian, Purdue University Libraries, for assistance in gathering data from EBL and YBP.

NOTE

1. Statistical hypothesis testing was not used. Given that the reader session logs are not independent of each other, the meaning of such tests would be problematic.

REFERENCES

Corlett-Rivera, K., & Hackman, T. (2014). E-book use and attitudes in the humanities, social sciences, and education. *portal: Libraries and the Academy 14*(2), 255–286. http://dx.doi.org/10.1353/pla.2014.0008

Levine-Clark, M. (2006). Electronic book usage: A survey at the University of Denver. *portal: Libraries and the Academy,6*(3), 285–299. http://dx.doi.org/10.1353/pla.2006.0041

Li, C., Poe, F., Potter, M., Quigley, B., & Wilson, J. (2011). UC Libraries academic e-book usage survey. Retrieved from http://www.escholarship.org/uc/item/4vr6n902

Liesaputra, V., & Witten, I. H. (2008). Seeking information in Realistic Books: A user study. In *Proceedings of the 8th ACM/IEEE-CS Joint Conference on Digital Libraries* (pp. 29–38). New York, NY: ACM Press. http://dx.doi.org/10.1145/1378889.1378896

Manguel, A. (1996). *A History of reading*. New York, NY: Viking.

Marshall, C. C. (2009). *Reading and writing the electronic book*. San Rafael, CA: Morgan & Claypool.

McKay, D. (2011, November 28–December 2). *A jump to the left (and then a step to the right): Reading practices within academic ebooks*. Paper presented at the OzCHI '11 Proceedings of the 23rd Australian Computer-Human Interaction Conference, Canberra, A.C.T., Australia (pp. 202–210). http://dx.doi.org /10.1145/2071536.2071569

McKay, D., Hinze, A., Heese, R., Vanderschantz, N., Timpany, C., & Cunningham, S. (2012). An exploration of ebook selection behavior in academic library collections. In P. Zaphiris, G. Buchanan, E. Rasmussen, & F. Loizides (Eds.), *Theory and practice of digital libraries* (pp. 13–24). Heidelberg, Germany: Springer. http://dx.doi.org/10.1007/978-3-642-33290-6_2

Nicholas, D., Rowlands, I., Clark, D., Huntington, P., Jamali, H. R., & Ollé, C. (2008). UK scholarly e-book usage: A landmark survey. *Aslib Proceedings: New Information Perspectives, 60*(4), 311–334. http://dx.doi.org /10.1108/00012530810887962

Pugh, A. K. (1977). Methods of studying silent reading behavior. *Research Intelligence, 3*(1), 42–43. http://dx.doi.org/10.1080/0141192770030115

Pugh, A. K. (1978). *Silent reading: An introduction to its study and teaching*. London, England: Heinemann.

Thayer, A., Lee, C. P., Hwang, L. H., Sales, H., Sen, P., & Dalal, N. (2011). The imposition and superimposition of digital reading technology: The academic potential of e-readers. In *Proceedings of the SIGCHI Conference on Human Factors in Computing Systems* (pp. 2917–26). Vancouver, British Columbia, Canada: Association for Computing Machinery. http://dx.doi.org /10.1145/1978942.1979375

APPENDIX A

Transforming Page Data for a Single Read

The sequences of page numbers for two reading log sessions of the same book by the same reader are:

Session one: 1,2,3,1,2,3,7,9,8,5,11,12,21,22,13,14,15

Session two: 16,17,18,19,20,23,24,44,45,33,34,35,31,32,49,50,48,47,5 1,52,46,3,4,5,1,2,1,3

The sequences of page numbers with beginning page numbers 1–5 removed:

Session one: 7,9,8,5,11,12,21,22,13,14,15

Session two: 16,17,18,19,20,23,24,44,45,33,34,35,31,32,49,50,48,47, 51,52,46,3,4,5,1,2,1,3

1. Concatenate page numbers into a single sequence or "Read":

7,9,8,5,11,12,21,22,13,14,15,16,17,18,19,20,23,24,44,45,33,34,35,31,32,49, 50,48,47,51,52,46,3,4,5,1,2,1,3

2. Convert page numbers to page changes:

2 -1 -3 6 1 9 1 -9 1 1 1 1 1 1 1 3 1 20 1 -12 1 1 -4 1 17 1 -2 -1 4 1 -6 -43 1 1 -4 1 -1 2

3. Partition page changes into "Passages":

{2 -1} {-3} {6 1} {9 1} {-9 1 1 1 1 1 1 1} {3 1} {20 1} {-12 1 1} {-4 1} {17 1} {-2 -1} {4 1} {-6} {-43 1 1} {-4 1 -1 2}

4. Add names to Passages. *Note.* The first number of each Passage is the number of pages jumped. The second is the number of continuous pages read after the jump.

FORWARD(2)(2) SMALL JUMP BACK(-3)(1) SMALL JUMP FORWARD(6) (2) BIG JUMP FORWARD(9)(2) BIG JUMP BACK(-9)(8) SMALL JUMP FORWARD(3)(2) BIG JUMP FORWARD(20)(2) BIG JUMP BACK(-12)(3) SMALL JUMP BACK(-4)(2) BIG JUMP FORWARD(17)(2) SMALL JUMP BACK(-2)(2) SMALL JUMP FORWARD(4)(2) SMALL JUMP BACK(-6)(1) BIG JUMP BACK(-43)(3) SMALL JUMP BACK(-4)(4)

5. Create a sequence of binary transitions or paired Passages:

FOR-SJB SJB-SJF SJF-BJF BJF-BJB BJB-SJF SJF-BJF BJF-BJB BJB-SJB SJB-BJF BJF-SJB SJB-SJF SJF-SJB SJB-BJB BJB-SJB

APPENDIX B

Averages, medians, and standard deviations for raw values and normalized values for 7,224 reads.

N = 7,224 Reads	AVERAGES		MEDIANS		STANDARD DEVIATIONS	
	Raw Values	Normalized Values	Raw Values	Normalized Values	Raw Values	Normalized Values
Minutes	40.55		12.38		85.57	
Pages	60.89		37.00		80.65	
Sessions	3.38		2.00		3.94	
Passages	23.87		14.00		31.92	
Paired Passages	22.87		13.00		31.92	
INDIVIDUAL PAGE TURNS						
Consecutive turns	29.30	45.90%	15.00	43.50%	43.87	21.50%
Jump forward turns	13.11	22.90%	8.00	22.20%	17.90	11.40%
Jump back turns	19.22	32.90%	11.00	33.30%	27.26	16.30%

APPENDIX B (CONTINUED)

N = 7,224 Reads	AVERAGES		MEDIANS		STANDARD DEVIATIONS	
	Raw Values	Normalized Values	Raw Values	Normalized Values	Raw Values	Normalized Values
PASSAGES						
Forward Passages	0.81	8.10%	1.00	5.50%	0.38	8.70%
Small jump forward Passages	5.83	21.00%	3.00	22.20%	8.93	10.80%
Big jump forward Passages	3.60	13.60%	2.00	13.90%	5.42	9.50%
Small jump back Passages	9.63	37.00%	5.00	38.20%	13.80	11.30%
Big jump back Passages	2.97	10.40%	1.00	10.50%	4.95	8.50%
PAIRED PASSAGES						
Forward pairs	2.00	9.50%	1.00	7.10%	3.23	11.80%
Alternating pairs	16.08	72.00%	9.00	72.40%	22.56	16.20%
Backward pairs	4.79	18.40%	2.00	18.10%	7.53	14.30%

15 | Library E-Book Platforms Are Broken: Let's Fix Them

Joelle Thomas and Galadriel Chilton

ABSTRACT

E-books promise users convenience and accessibility, but library e-book platforms contain so many barriers to use and access that patrons often turn away in frustration. In addition, aggregators' e-book platforms often include intrusive, onerous digital rights management (DRM) restrictions. The traditional solution of DRM-free e-books generally is available only in large and expensive publisher packages. One approach to solving these problems is to negotiate contracts directly with publishers for an evidence-based selection of e-books program, which not only offers access to hundreds of DRM-free, unlimited simultaneous-user e-books that are integrated with similar e-journal content, but also includes an agreement that libraries will only purchase titles with the highest use.

USER EXPECTATIONS AND THE E-BOOK REALITY

When scholars disseminated their ideas primarily through print, physical access and discovery were considerably challenging. In this environment, even the earliest, clumsiest iterations of electronic search and access were revolutionary, and users' information-seeking paths included either learning the intricacies of the few systems available or turning to a librarian for advice or mediation. Scarcity made even rudimentary electronic access valuable; any search method more efficient than paging through paper indexes was worth investing the time to master.

Today users are more likely to complain about finding too much information than not enough; we have come a long way from the finicky spearfishing of DIALOG to the massive trawl of Google. Once the prospect of watching a movie without leaving your home was an unthinkable luxury; now subscribers spend half the evening scrolling through their Netflix queues, paralyzed by choice. When it comes to accessing information, scarcity is no longer as compelling as convenience. Entire business models are built on the delivery of content, rather than on the content itself. It is not enough to offer access; a physical video rental shop with twice the inventory of Netflix is unlikely to siphon away many customers.

Libraries have failed to keep pace with their users' technical expectations. By 2000, online access to full-text journal articles was in and of itself impressive, a vast improvement over combing through physical indexes; now it is taken for granted. Universities would not expect to delight and astonish a new undergraduate with the prospect of being able to find and read an article without visiting the library. Yet libraries offer thousands of e-books via deeply flawed aggregator platforms as if users will put up with these inconveniences for the now-everyday experience of reading the text on a screen.

Users accustomed to buying e-books from Amazon and reading them on their iPads bring the expectations of that experience to library e-books. Once users buy an Amazon e-book, they can read it on any device with the Kindle app—an app available for nearly all devices and with an installation process already familiar from installing dozens of other apps. After buying the Amazon e-book with a single click, the user can highlight, annotate, and customize the text display, and can easily send the book to other devices. Aggregator e-book platforms seldom meet a single one of these expectations (although publisher platforms often do).

A user attempting to check out an e-book through an academic library will likely first be required to download software, usually either Adobe Digital Editions or something similarly specialized and proprietary, and then create one or two accounts separate from the institutional account with which he has already authenticated. Once he has jumped through several minutes' worth of hoops (even a best-case scenario, in which the user already has software and accounts squared away, takes longer than a minute—a small eternity in Internet time), the features he expected to find may or may not be available. Printing, highlighting, and copying are seldom available in any consistent, predictable fashion. If the user is allowed to transfer the book to additional devices, the process is convoluted and multistep, nothing like the seamless Amazon experience. A user who masters the complexities of downloading one e-book will quickly discover that the thicket of rules varies by publisher, platform, and even by title—and that e-books downloaded via an academic library do not have any value-added features that make the long, complicated download process worthwhile.

This is not to say that e-books marketed to end users are trouble-free; famously, Amazon retroactively removed purchased copies of *1984* from customers' Kindles (Stone, 2009) and the Kindle edition of J. K. Rowling's *The Casual Vacancy* was initially unreadable (Owen, 2012). Such incidents are, however, acknowledged problems, and users who encounter them can expect a refund or a solution when they complain. The problems plaguing aggregator e-book platforms exist largely by design and as direct consequences of the digital rights management (DRM) with which third-party provider platforms and some publishers encase their e-books.

Additionally, this is not simply a case of a product marketed to individuals being superior to one marketed to institutions. Library e-journal article platforms offer a much smoother user experience; in almost all cases, a user simply downloads a fully searchable PDF. For e-journal articles, users do not need special software or additional accounts, there are rarely user limits, and downloaded articles can be read on any device. A heavy user of library e-journal platforms brings these expectations to library e-book platforms. For instance, instructors accustomed to pointing their students to online journal articles sometimes assign e-books as course readings without noticing that the e-books in question are limited to one user at a time. Even an instructor who notices the user limit on the book is unlikely to realize that it allows one user to lock the rest of the class out of the book for two weeks at a time. No other online resource behaves like this.

Even users who are not well-versed in the use of online journal articles or nonlibrary e-books find library platforms disappointing. In Berg, Hoffmann, and Dawson's (2010) study of undergraduates' interactions with e-books, "Participants articulated a set of expectations for e-books, even though few of them had extensive experience with the format" (p. 522). Instead, they expected e-books to follow the same general conventions of websites, easily searchable and thoroughly cross-referenced with hyperlinks, like Google Books. Participants complained that chapter titles and page numbers in library e-books were "not clickable" and expressed frustration with the search functionality. Furthermore, in a study of undergraduate preferences for electronic or print textbooks, Woody, Daniel, and Baker (2010) found that "previous experience with e-books does not increase preference for e-books" (p. 947). Glackin, Rodenhiser, and Herzog's (2014) study of students accessing e-books on mobile devices found that the primary complaint participants had about e-books was usability, followed by functionality, with specific complaints about the inability to highlight content. Although participants in Glackin's study were generally more positive about their e-book experiences, they also were having those experiences on mobile devices given to them by their university.

Even without the solicitation of a formal study, our users communicate their frustrations to University of Connecticut (UConn) librarians. When users receive rejected interlibrary loan requests for books available locally in electronic format, they sometimes reply that the e-book version is unsuited to their needs, often because the e-book prohibits copying lines of text or printing even a handful of pages. For scholars seeking to engage with a text, such restrictions are seldom acceptable. As Schomisch, Zens, and Mayr (2013) put it, "'Read only' appears insufficient in a scholarly context; additional features for printing, marking, annotating, and excerpting are crucial for textual work in academia" (p. 389). Librarians also routinely field questions from users who want a print copy of an e-book, particularly tech-related titles such as programming textbooks. For these users, the prospect of flipping between tabs or browser windows while completing exercises on a computer is less appealing than having a book open beside the computer screen; in cases where printing is disallowed or severely restricted, the e-book is deemed too inconvenient to be useful. Additionally, some e-books are missing images, tables, graphs, and even sections of text, either because of formatting difficulties or because publishers lack the rights to include them; in either case, their absence diminishes the usefulness of the book. For many users, the e-books that libraries offer simply are not acceptable substitutes for print books, let alone the feature-rich, value-added improvements they have the potential to be. Frustrated users would probably be appeased with the ability to print the e-book in whole or in part, but very few platforms allow this. A user who has just printed 80 pages' worth of journal articles without incident suddenly discovers that a 10-page e-book chapter is off-limits, a realization that is likely to dawn only after the user has downloaded software, signed up for an account, and jumped through a series of hoops.

The DRM protections attached to many e-books resemble those of earlier generations of other electronic products and are quite unlike anything a tech-savvy user would expect—and are completely overwhelming to those uncomfortable with technology. As most other industries are coming to acknowledge, onerous DRM discourages use of the legitimate purchased product in favor of the more convenient pirated product and, under the right conditions, eliminating DRM restrictions increases sales (Vernik, Purohit, & Desai, 2011, p. 1022). Reasonably unobtrusive DRM that adds value in some way has proven more popular with consumers; for example, end-user-marketed e-books that use DRM in exchange for personalized features can give users the ability to store their library virtually and remember the point at which they left off reading across multiple devices. The nature of temporary library checkouts does not allow this sort of per-user long-term personalization, so librarians can offer users only the irritating parts of DRM with none of the benefits.

By and large, publishers created e-books to mimic physical books and thus try to treat them the same way. Platforms are saddled with analogues such as "checking out" items that are inherently not finite. Anyone who has ever explained to an irritated user that an e-book cannot be viewed online because someone else has "checked it out" is likely aware of how absurd this sounds. The current model for electronic resources familiar to most users is one in which any number of users can view the resources simultaneously, although access may be limited by geography (such as when YouTube videos are restricted to certain countries' IP ranges) or to paying customers (such as paying a monthly fee for Netflix). With each new wave of undergraduates, users increasingly bring with them expectations formed in this digital world.

Interviews with UConn Students on Research Process

In spring 2014, librarians at UConn conducted a series of interviews with undergraduates, asking them to walk through the process of their research for a recent assignment. Use of multiple devices was common; students routinely accessed articles they had found from personal laptops, library workstations, and tablets. One senior's workflow involved searching for and downloading articles on her laptop, reading and highlighting articles on her iPad, and then printing relevant pages from library workstations so they would be handy while she wrote. She had never used library-offered e-books in her research and likely would have been profoundly frustrated had she tried. Another student became so frustrated trying to find and access e-books through the catalog that he settled for reading only the preview pages available on Google Books. Another student explained that she has no preference for print or electronic when she reads, but her instructor required a physical book for the assignment. (Although very few of our faculty direct students to print journals over e-journals, requiring print books and forbidding e-books is still somewhat common.) All of the students interviewed made extensive use of online journal articles; several of them used print books; none of them used library e-books successfully.

Librarians might ask why any patrons put up with dysfunctional e-book platforms, and why e-books show substantial use statistics despite all the impediments. The most likely explanation is that users cannot afford to purchase expensive academic e-books individually. Patrons dissatisfied with the library's streaming video options can try YouTube, Netflix, Hulu, and other low-cost services; users dissatisfied with library study spaces can go elsewhere on campus. "Never mind, I'll just buy it" is a frequent remark heard at the reference desk when it becomes clear that an affordable commercial alternative exists to an inconvenient library offering. Users dissatisfied with library e-books are limited to looking for a print alternative, (which many do), paying steep prices for individual access with fewer restrictions to the content, or attempting to make the best of a bad situation. Hoping that users will be desperate enough to put up with frustrating products is not fair, appropriate, or a winning strategy for academic libraries. Worse, offering substandard access through the library puts lower-income students, who already face a digital divide from their peers, at an even greater disadvantage from those able to afford a functional alternative (Hargittai, 2010, p. 108).

Academic libraries can offer better access to e-books, just as they already do for online journal articles; even streaming video options are improving. There is nothing inherent to e-books that precludes a better user experience. As Norman (2010) puts it in *Living with Complexity*, "The major cause of complicated, confusing, frustrating systems is not complexity: It is poor design" (p. 8).

It is past time that librarians stop accepting poorly designed e-book platforms and start offering users better access, while at the same time working within finite budgets and paying only for what our user communities need for their learning, teaching, and research. Although many libraries develop patron-driven acquisitions or demand-driven acquisitions profiles to acquire only those e-books that their patrons use, academic libraries still need to work with e-book publishers and providers to create models that also meet users' access expectations. UConn Libraries is attempting to do so by working with publishers to create "Evidence-Based Selection of E-Books" programs.

UCONN LIBRARIES AND PATRON-DRIVEN ACQUISITION OF E-BOOKS

Between July 2011 and August 2014, UConn Libraries had patron-driven acquisition (PDA) e-book profiles with EBL and ebrary. Although librarians adjusted the profiles throughout this period, the most recent and long-standing settings were from February 2012 through August 2014:

- Books over $100 for EBL,
- Books up to $99.99 for ebrary,
- Imprints from three years ago to present,
- Textbooks excluded, and
- Three short-term loans (STLs), with the fourth use triggering a purchase.

In one sense, UConn Libraries' PDA program was successful in that numerous e-books were available to users, some of which were only available as individual titles via EBL and ebrary, and because use statistics suggest a demand for the content. PDA allows user discovery of content that libraries may not have purchased via other means of library-initiated collection development. Additionally, "in many cases, user selections have, not surprisingly, been ahead of the librarian selections because the users are the ones doing research, working in labs, conducting fieldwork, and studying the latest disciplinary trends. . . . Individual readers know what is in their own interest better than librarians do" (Dillon, 2011, p. 193).

Additionally, PDA meant paying only for content that patrons used, which, from an acquisitions perspective, was PDA's primary benefit. For example, although patrons had access to approximately 50,000 e-books via

UConn Libraries' EBL profile from July 2011 through January 2013, they used just under 3,000 unique e-book titles. Use triggered 4,597 short-term loans; patrons used only 100 e-books enough to trigger purchases. If all 2,894 titles used had been purchased outright, they would have cost more than $450,000. Instead, UConn Libraries spent just over $100,000 for 4,579 short-term loans and 100 purchases.

However, the user experience for PDA e-books was less than ideal. In addition to a faculty member wondering "Why is the library buying things that are nearly impossible to use?" (user comment [name removed for privacy], personal communication, March 12, 2013), patrons placed interlibrary loan requests despite e-book availability. When asked about why an interlibrary loan request was placed for a book with online access, one user indicated via an e-mail correspondence that it was not easy to capture the minimal text needed for a citation; typing quotes from a print text would be easier (user comment [name removed for privacy], personal communication, September 10, 2014). Specific feedback from one faculty member indicated that he preferred e-book access directly via the publisher's platform because of the better user experience:

> Thanks very much for these links. However, I must share my feedback that this e-reader format is quite possibly the worst publication format that I have yet come across. In printing off the full chapters I wanted, some suddenly were truncated and every one had many page duplications, probably a result of subsections being defined part way through the page. I'm sure that this affected the number of pages I was allowed to print off too. The normal SpringerLink format would have been a thousand times better. I take what I can get, of course. (J. Klassen, personal communication, February 21, 2014)

It should be noted that, although UConn Libraries did not proactively and systematically conduct usability tests of EBL and ebrary platforms, librarians received over 110 technical support requests for e-book access between December 2013 and November 2014. Anecdotal comments such as those above were frequent enough—at least once a week—to warrant posting extensive how-to guides on accessing and using e-books. Yet low use statistics of the e-book guides suggest that patrons did not use these guides regularly. Perhaps this is because "in the current environment, most people do not have time to spend searching for information or learning how to use a new information source or access method. In order to be one of the first choices for information, library systems and interfaces need to look familiar to people by resembling popular Web interfaces, and library services need to be easily accessible and require little or no training to use" (Connaway, Dickey, & Radford, 2011, p. 188).

What is convenient and familiar to academic library users is the one-click download of an e-journal article—an access experience that is far less complicated than e-book access via DRM-restricted aggregator platforms such as EBL, ebrary, and EBSCO.

In addition to the less-than-ideal user experience of DRM-encased PDA e-books, UConn librarians encountered poor profile integrity in which there was use, and over $30,000 in charges, for content that was not supposed to be in the EBL PDA profile. Although librarians can report PDA profile integrity issues or e-book functionality and missing content problems to vendors, the bottom line is that the vendors should deliver what the libraries paid for. However, with the volume of online content increasing and the number of staff managing online content remaining flat or decreasing, it is harder to track, report, and monitor e-books for such issues.

Adobe's unencrypted collection of e-book user data also caused great concern. In October 2014, Nate Hoffelder (2014) wrote on *The Digital Reader* blog that Adobe Digital Editions 4 gathers "data on the e-books that have been opened, which pages were read, and in what order. All of this data, including the title, publisher, and other metadata for the book is being sent to Adobe's server in clear text" (para. 6). According to Hoffelder, "Adobe is not only logging what users are doing, they're also sending those logs to their servers in such a way that anyone running one of the servers in between can listen in and know everything" (para. 7). For people using Adobe Digital Editions on an e-reader, Adobe is scanning and gathering metadata for all e-books on the device, not just for the e-books opened in Adobe Digital Editions 4, but also all EPUB e-books and e-books stored in calibre, the e-book collection management software.

Profile integrity issues coupled with such an egregious breach of privacy when accessing and using UConn Libraries' e-books culminated in discontinuing the EBL and ebrary PDA programs in October 2014.

LET'S FIX IT

How can libraries capture the acquisitions benefit of PDA but make e-book access and use a pleasant, easy, and confidential experience for users? Knowing what users need, UConn librarians strive for DRM-free, unlimited simultaneous, e-journal article-like, and title-by-title access to e-books, while only paying for what the scholarly community needs. With continuing flat or reduced budgets and increased need to justify spending, librarians can neither afford nor justify buying packages of e-books to access select titles.

Analysis of UConn's EBL PDA use data showed that of the 294 publishers with titles that patrons used, 75% of the funds were spent for e-books from just seven publishers. ebrary PDA use data showed that of the 492 publishers with use, 48% of the funds were spent for books from seven publishers, many of them the same as the EBL high-use publishers. Such data became the germ for an idea: UConn Libraries pays a small deposit to an e-book publisher for 12 months of access to all their DRM-free e-books via the publisher's platform. At the end of the 12 months, a predetermined amount spent would be applied to the perpetual access purchase of those e-books with the highest use and that best matched the university's curricular needs. The goal of this evidence-based selection (EBS) of e-books model would be to purchase DRM-free, in-demand e-books with access analogous to e-journal articles. Depending on the publisher, the guaranteed amount spent may be similar to an e-book package price and would help show that title-by-title purchasing is a viable and needed model.

Thus, in fall 2012 UConn librarians began talks with select publishers about a trial to explore this new model of acquiring e-books. During these conversations, it became clear that—regardless of the term used to describe the model—some publishers (e.g., Elsevier and Wiley) were also beginning to offer alternatives to publisher-provided e-book packages and aggregate PDA programs. By November 2014, UConn Libraries had active EBS e-book pilots with Wiley (Wiley's Usage Based Collection Management Model), Taylor & Francis, and Digitalia. Librarians also set up a similar model for Gale's Archives Unbound primary source collections. Elsevier and SAGE also offer variations on EBS e-book programs and Alexander Street Press offers an evidence-based acquisitions model for their streaming video collection.

EVIDENCE-BASED SELECTION OF E-BOOKS: BENEFITS AND CHALLENGES

Based on UConn's experience thus far with evidence-based selection of e-books, there are notable advantages, including DRM-free e-book access similar to, and integrated with, e-journal access for similar publisher content. Additionally, the data gathered during the access year can be applied not only to purchase decisions at the end of the 12-month period, but also can be used to make data-informed collection allocations for the following year or as hard evidence when submitting funding requests. Although it is not yet known whether EBS will also result in higher use of e-journal content on publisher platforms, there is reason to be optimistic given cross-linking and integrated search on some publisher sites.

However, there are downsides to such models. Not all e-books are available directly from the publisher, nor do all publishers have their own website for accessing their e-books. For example, librarians found that an undetermined number of Wiley e-books are only available as separate purchases (e.g., Wiley reference titles) or via aggregator platforms such as EBL and ebrary, rather than as part of the evidence-based selection of e-books pilot via Wiley Online. Thus EBS is not an all-encompassing solution for academic libraries to provide e-book access to their communities, but it is one of many approaches to collecting e-books. Additionally, the disappearance of those e-books that a library decides not to purchase after a set amount of time will likely frustrate users, though the case of disappearing e-book access seems to be commonplace regardless of platform and acquisition model. Another downside of evidence-based selection of e-books is that DRM enables most PDA profiles to use technology in an attempt to differentiate between "real" and "casual" use so that no use is triggered for views of the front or back matter, or for fewer than 15 minutes of browsing; longer use of core content, printing, and downloading all trigger use. Use reports of non-DRM e-books show raw downloads only; there is no way of knowing from COUNTER reports how a patron used a downloaded book.

A further challenge of evidence-based selection models is that they add yet another multilayered and unique e-resource management workflow to an acquisitions "aquarium" that is already quite full of exotic fish in need of ongoing care. However, when a model helps provide unfettered access to needed information that it is librarians' responsibility to provide, allocating the resources to implement and monitor it is a far better use of a library's staff time than activities such as constantly troubleshooting lost e-book access, developing user guides for unintuitive and hard-to-use e-book platforms, monitoring the integrity of a PDA profile, or ordering print copies of a book when it is discovered that the key diagrams, images, and tables are not available in the electronic edition.

RECOMMENDATIONS

When developing a plan for evidence-based selection of e-books, the following points may be helpful to determine which publishers to approach, to avoid duplicate e-book purchases, and to estimate budget allocations per publisher. Analyze:

1. Aggregator PDA reports for spending and use by publisher,
2. COUNTER turnaway and denied-access/unlicensed content reports,
3. Publisher e-book price lists (title by title and packages),
4. Faculty feedback and requests for e-book access via publisher platforms,
5. Library-owned e-book title lists by publisher to help prioritize which publishers to approach about an evidence-based selection program and to avoid duplicate e-book purchases.

Models for evidence-based selection of e-books are just one means of providing access to e-books, addressing the issues of user experience, and paying only for what is in demand and used by an academic community.

CONCLUSION

Academic librarians need to know their users' expectations for accessing information and what users do with that information; this understanding is vital to informing not only what collections to acquire, but also the access methods. Additionally, with continued strains on library collection budgets and calls for justifying spending, data-rich models for acquiring e-books should be the norm. Academic libraries are well positioned to shape collection models. Librarians need not wait to see what information providers offer to them; instead, they should proactively propose models to publishers that work from financial, user experience/expectation, and information access perspectives, such as buying only DRM-free e-books and adopting evidence-based selection models to buy only what patrons use.

Although developing new models of e-book acquisition and access is slow and time-consuming, it is important to acknowledge, celebrate, and continuously evaluate the effectiveness of small changes so that library resources are both relevant *and* accessible. With the multitude of platforms, interfaces, and devices that are now part of the information access equation, it is fundamentally unacceptable for libraries to provide relevant information to their academic communities without also making sure that the user experience accessing those collections meets or exceeds the users' expectations. Library collections become irrelevant if users cannot easily access them.

Just as the academy is responsible for supporting freedom of speech, so too is the academic library responsible for mitigating the impediments so that there is also freedom of access. When libraries purchase content encased in poor interfaces and behind artificial barriers, it is a form of censorship—a situation that the library community should challenge in the "fulfillment of [our] responsibility to provide information and enlightenment" (American Library Association, 1939, para. 4). As the primary buyers of academic publishers' content, academic libraries are uniquely situated to change the way that scholarly content is packaged and delivered. Librarians have a duty to advocate for what users need, to practice good fiscal stewardship, and to refuse to support business models that deliver substandard access at unreasonable costs. Let's explore creative options for access to scholarly material such as e-books, refuse to support broken business models, and advocate for something better.

REFERENCES

American Library Association. (1939). *The Library Bill of Rights*. Retrieved from http://www.ala.org/advocacy/intfreedom/librarybill

Berg, S. A., Hoffmann, K., & Dawson, D. (2010). Not on the same page: Undergraduates' information retrieval in electronic and print books. *The Journal of Academic Librarianship, 36*(6), 518–525. http://dx.doi.org/10.1016/j.acalib.2010.08.008

Connaway, L. S., Dickey, T. J., & Radford, M. L. (2011). "If it is too inconvenient I'm not going after it": Convenience as a critical factor in information seeking behaviors. *Library & Information Science Research, 33*(3), 179–190. http://dx.doi.org/10.1016/j.lisr.2010.12.002

Dillon, D. (2011). PDA and libraries today and tomorrow. In D. A. Swords (Ed.), *Patron-driven acquisitions* (pp. 191–195). Berlin/Boston: Walter de Gruyter. http://dx.doi.org/10.1515/9783110253030.191

Glackin, B. C., Rodenhiser, R. W., & Herzog, B. (2014). A library and the disciplines: A collaborative project assessing the impact of ebooks and mobile devices on student learning. *The Journal of Academic Librarianship, 40*(3–4), 299–306. http://dx.doi.org/10.1016/j.acalib.2014.04.007

Hargittai, E. (2010). Digital Na(t)ives? Variation in Internet skills and uses among members of the "Net Generation." *Sociological Inquiry, 80*(1), 92–113. http://dx.doi.org/10.1111/j.1475-682X.2009.00317.x

Hoffelder, N. (2014, October 6). Adobe is spying on users, collecting data on their ebook libraries. *The Digital Reader*. Retrieved from http://the-digital-reader.com/2014/10/06/adobe-spying-users-collecting-data-ebook-libraries/

Norman, D. A. (2010). *Living with complexity*. Cambridge, MA: MIT Press.

Owen, L. H. (2012, September 27). *J. K. Rowling's new ebook: Literally unreadable*. Retrieved from https://gigaom.com/2012/09/27/j-k-rowlings-new-book-on-kindle-literally-unreadable/

Schomisch, S., Zens, M., & Mayr, P. (2013). Are e-readers suitable tools for scholarly work? Results from a user test. *Online Information Review, 37*(3), 388–404. Retrieved from http://dx.doi.org/10.1108/OIR-12-2011-0221

Stone, B. (2009, July 18). Amazon erases Orwell books from Kindle. *New York Times*. Retrieved from http://www.nytimes.com/2009/07/18/technology/companies/18amazon.html

Vernik, D. A., Purohit, D., & Desai, P. S. (2011). Music downloads and the flip side of digital rights management. *Marketing Science, 30*(6), 1011–1027. http://dx.doi.org/10.1287/mksc.1110.0668

Woody, W. D., Daniel, D. B., & Baker, C. A. (2010). E-books or textbooks: Students prefer textbooks. *Computers & Education, 55*(3), 945–948. http://dx.doi.org/10.1016/j.compedu.2010.04.005

Case Studies

16 | A Balancing Act: Promoting Canadian Scholarly E-Books While Controlling User Access

Ravit H. David

ABSTRACT

In 2013, the Ontario Council of University Libraries (OCUL) and 12 members of the Association of Canadian University Presses/Association Des Presses Universitaires Canadiennes (ACUP/APUC), in conjunction with eBOUND Canada, partnered to provide access to a comprehensive collection of over 3,000 e-books via OCUL's Scholars Portal (SP) book platform. Although the agreement was a major step toward ensuring that the wealth of Canadian scholarship is readily accessible and preserved in digital format for the benefit of the OCUL community, the license agreement included a section on Digital Rights Management (DRM) that asked SP to provide access control technologies limiting the use of content and devices in both online and offline environments. This case study outlines the challenges and lessons learned from making Canadian scholarship in e-book format available to the OCUL community while assuring presses that SP could enforce restricted use of their e-books. It concludes that the agreement as it stands works well for both partners, as well as for users, since the overall use of the collection is high. Perhaps the best outcome of the move, however, has been the building of trust between libraries, publishers, and an aggregator. Indeed, the overall response of the OCUL community to the loading of the Canadian scholarly collection may testify to the shift in favor of e-books by academic libraries.

BACKGROUND

In January 2013, the Ontario Council of University Libraries (OCUL) reached an agreement with 12 members of the Association of Canadian University Presses (ACUP/APUC), in conjunction with eBOUND Canada, to offer 10 universities in Ontario access to a full range of ACUP e-books. OCUL Chair and University Librarian at Carleton University Margaret Haines commented that in a time when "academic libraries everywhere are being challenged to stretch their budgets to acquire all the appropriate resources for their universities . . ." this agreement would provide users with a "signature collection of Canadian academic scholarship" (as cited in Ervin-Ward, 2013). Indeed, the agreement was a major step toward ensuring that the wealth of Canadian scholarship would be accessible and preserved in e-book format for the benefit of the OCUL community. As a consortium, OCUL could use its combined power when negotiating with publishers and not only secure better pricing than would be possible for a single institute, but also negotiate perpetual local hosting on the Scholars Portal (SP) e-book platform and access rights based on purchase agreements (Horava, 2013). The agreement to provide OCUL with local hosting rights and perpetual ownership is significant because otherwise, as is often the case with subscription access to e-book collections, content can be withdrawn without notice (Ludbrook, 2013).

Scholars Portal is a locally built platform for loading, accessing, and preserving scholarly content to support teaching, research, and learning. At its base is ebrary software, purchased in 2009. When ebrary moved to cloud technology, the SP e-book team developed services that communicated with the software to migrate the content to MarkLogic Ejournal technology. The bilingual interface (English–French) of SP allows various search facets and presents basic metadata for each title. Access to the full content of each e-book is managed through an entitlement system that reflects the license agreement and makes sure that the agreement is enforced at the title, collection, or school level, depending on the agreement signed between the publisher/aggregator and OCUL. The platform features allow PDF downloads at the chapter level, highlights or bookmarks, and the exporting of citations to the RefWorks, EndNote, and Zotero citation management systems.

The agreement with ACUP was notable for SP in that it not only provides perpetual access to the collection, but also includes digital rights management (DRM) restrictions that required new technological deployment on the SP e-book platform using a third-party server.

DRM TECHNOLOGY

Within the scholarly market, publishers are still experimenting with different business models for selling patron-driven acquisitions (PDA) title lists or full collections to academic libraries. In a recent report, Amy Kirchhoff and Sheila Morrissey (2014) defined DRM as "a set of technologies employed to protect commercial intellectual property rights in digital content. . . . It enforces the use of digital licenses, which restrict a customer's access to a digital object in certain ways, including frequency and duration of access to the object, as well as restrictions of rights of transfer, or the ability to copy the object" (p. 10). This definition depicts DRM as a restrictive technology, one that corresponds with business models that control e-books in a manner that some librarians consider conflicting with their libraries' collection development policies. This control is ostensibly aimed at preventing e-book piracy by creating file-locking protection, but it also is used for locking customers into a specific retail platform (Maxwell, 2013).

For the ACUP/OCUL deal, the parties agreed on Adobe's DRM system, Adobe Digital Editions Protection Technology (ADEPT), with Adobe Content Server (ACS) 3 managing the DRM of e-book files from a server.[1] This DRM model includes three levels of restrictions:

- MUPO: Multiple users with no restrictions. Users may download, print, and digitally copy no more than 20% or a single chapter of individual work.
- SUPO: Single user access (one concurrent view). Authorized users may download, digitally copy, save, and print no more than 20% or a single chapter of individual work.
- SUPO PLUS: Single user access (one concurrent view) with view-only rights. Users may not download, digitally copy, save, or print any of the work (Ontario Council of University Libraries, 2013).

Figure 1 shows the breakdown of the levels of access by consortium members. It is not the case that the SP platform was free of DRM locks before the agreement with ACUP or that this was the first time SP had dealt with a new DRM model. The difference here is that, although the locks that SP previously had accepted from publishers were minimal, and the kind that the regular e-book platform could enforce with little user involvement, the new restrictions would force users to log in to the e-book platform. The need for a login not only brought with it privacy issues, but the creation of user accounts did not coincide with SP's approach of allowing schools to manage their user accounts while SP managed access at the school level only.

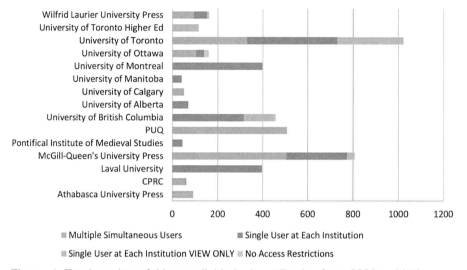

Figure 1. Total number of titles available in the collection from 2009 to 2013 (Maidenberg, 2014).

Since MARC is the main metadata format used by the SP platform, the e-book service coordinator, in discussion with OCUL catalogers, decided that the different e-book access levels (MUPO, SUPO, and SUPO PLUS) would be tagged for each book in the 956 field of each MARC record. This tag lets the e-book team know which e-books to load onto the regular e-book database (MUPO) and which ones to pack into Adobe Content Service (SUPO) and (SUPO PLUS). Although this tag is not intended for DRM statements, the catalogers wanted to know the level of restriction when loading the records onto their local discovery systems.

Choosing the Adobe model to restrict access meant purchasing ACS and training the OCUL staff and community. OCUL was fortunate to have strong community support for the deal, since librarians sometimes will relinquish a plan to purchase e-books if the titles cannot be easily integrated into their acquisitions workflow (Slater, 2010). Purchasing and managing e-books on a consortial level means that central staff develop technical solutions so that each member library does not need to devote staff to solving common problems

The loading process began by adding each e-book and its corresponding metadata onto the Scholars Portal regular e-book database. Then, depending on the metadata in the records, they were packaged with the proper DRM to go into ACS. When users search the SP e-book platform, they encounter two types of books: those in the regular database and those that require the user to download the file and open it using the Adobe Digital Edition software. The layout for the cover icons for ACS books is slightly different from those for MUPO books, as can be seen in Figure 2.

Figure 2. Comparison of the layout for ACS books and MUPO books. "Read this book" indicates users will not need any special software. "Borrow this E-Book" indicates users will need to use Adobe Content Edition or similar software.

For DRM e-books, users can see if the book is available (it is available for only one user at a time, and each school has only one copy per title) and they then need to open the token in Adobe Digital Editions if they are using their desktops, or, for instance, Bluefire Reader for Android or Kobo Reader for Apple iOS. The token communicates with the server, which then presents the title according to the DRM restrictions. The token has an Adobe ID, which enables each title to open on six different devices.

OCUL scheduled webinars to train librarians to support users in their efforts to access the DRM books on the ACS. Although e-books from the ACUP collection were loaded as early as May 2013, the new service was not announced until September, the beginning of the school year, in order to attract the most attention from students and faculty members. To support and encourage readers to use the DRM titles, Scholars Portal added an FAQ that includes a download link to Adobe Digital Editions, instructions for signing up for an Adobe ID, and answers to common questions about borrowing books via ACS on the SP e-book platform (Scholars Portal, 2014).

The process for using DRM books on the SP platform is subject to changes as staff analyze use logs in order to look for ways to improve service. For instance, the SUPO and SUPO PLUS books on ACS are available for three-day loans; the use logs indicate that most readers let the loans expire rather than actively returning the book. This behavior suggests that SP could launch an e-mail notification option for readers who wish to know when a specific DRM title becomes available. SP staff also will review the three-day loan policy in light of new data on the use of DRM titles to decide if this is the optimal loan period for some or all titles.

THE PUBLISHER'S PROMISE: UNIVERSITY OF BRITISH COLUMBIA PRESS

The license agreement between OCUL and ACUP includes a commitment by publishers to review DRM restrictions on an annual basis and gradually limit them.[2] The reason for this review is that when a title changes to MUPO, it can be loaded onto the SP platform with only the most basic restrictions (as is the case with most OCUL e-book collections), thus allowing easier user access.

In early 2014, Scholars Portal sent all the ACUP publishers a title use report covering September 2013 to January 2014. The SP use report included numbers of non-DRM "viewdocs," meaning that every time a user landed on or was referred to the first page of an e-book, it was recorded as one event. Also included were numbers of DRM "downloads," meaning that every time an ACS token was used, it was counted as one download of a title. The use report also showed publishers' use breakdown by school, since each school has only one copy of each SUPO and SUPO PLUS title. The first publisher that delivered a DRM-change list was the University of British Columbia Press (UBCP). UBCP was one of the Canadian presses that had no MUPO titles in its original list, but in the spirit of relaxing copyright restrictions, it changed about 60 titles from SUPO or SUPO PLUS to MUPO. In other words, it switched these books from DRM to non-DRM titles. Only four titles changed from SUPO to SUPO PLUS.

Use reports always carry the danger that such data will encourage publishers to raise prices on specific, extremely popular titles or to exclude highly popular titles from the following year's package. However, the growing market of e-books and the slow but consistent increase in e-book use among scholarly communities require mutual trust. In this case, ACUP had faith that SP was the proper sole hosting platform with the ability to enforce DRM for their e-books, and the OCUL schools trusted ACUP publishers to keep their word regarding the gradual removal of DRM from their titles.

Of particular interest to Scholars Portal was the fact that UBCP's changes did not correlate with SP's use report. For instance, two titles that changed from SUPO to SUPO PLUS were *First Nations Education in Canada* (1995) and *Oral History on Trial* (2011). When checking for total "view-docs" and "downloads" on the SP platform, the first title had 105 hits and the latter had only 42 hits. Both titles are older works in aboriginal studies, but the two were used very differently on the SP platform. According to UBCP, the reason for adding restrictions was that both titles were doing very well in print sales. In fact, these titles were among the few titles that did not "die off" as soon as they were published, and so the publisher may have wanted to maintain the titles' perennial use by restricting the e-book format. Likewise, declining print sales were the deciding factor in opening up other titles to MUPO. These titles were not recent ones, so it could be said that publication year was a factor in the decision. In both cases, e-book format sales, either on the SP platform or through other channels, did not carry as much weight as print sales in the publisher's decision. This lack of correspondence between use and DRM changes as detected by SP makes the point that publishers still count on print sales to determine how to sell titles in e-format.

Another interesting finding is that readers often viewed a specific title from the UBCP collection, but would not open it in Adobe Digital Editions (see Table 1). One possible explanation might be that users were unwilling to download software to read the book (for analysis of the SP use report, see also Jacobs, Maidenberg, & Schmidt, 2014). Another explanation may be that glancing at the book's metadata satisfied most readers. Still, if academic librarians wish to foster an "e-book culture" among their users, the discrepancy between the number of views and the number of downloads may call for further investigation. For instance, it would be worthwhile measuring use for UBCP titles that were moved out of the ACS and put onto the SP regular platform. If use increased after this change, it might imply that DRM e-books do not encourage e-reading. In looking at this issue, however, one would need to be aware that UBCP sells their books through many digital channels and packages. It might be difficult to determine the cross-platform impact that some of those channels have on the use of these titles through Scholars Portal.[3]

DISCUSSION OF THE PROCESS

No DRM model is perfect, but in the case of the ACUP deal, it is significant that OCUL did not compromise perpetual access rights for the ACUP e-books. It is worth noting that the DRM restrictions requested by ACUP were not aimed at locking the readers' loyalty onto a specific device or platform. Thus, although the agreement restricts the use of some titles to one user at a time, it conforms to the OCUL e-book strategic plan, which is to have local access to all e-books. Furthermore, by deciding to choose the Adobe Digital Editions server to enforce the ACUP DRM restrictions, OCUL did not compromise the privacy of its users. Members of the OCUL community can go on the SP e-book platform without having to identify themselves beyond their school login information.

Implementing novel technology to build a new e-book service, as was needed in the case of DRM books, and then integrating this service into an existing e-book platform, turned out to be an expensive and time-consuming project that could not have been undertaken by a single institution. The existing SP infrastructure made it possible for the OCUL consortium to commit to this technological and strategic endeavor. Even so, use of the ACUP collection did not happen immediately. It was first important to offer training and to create a support system to back up the absorption of the new DRM collection into the existing SP services. Further, the current workflow will probably need revision should use patterns suggest changes to improve access to e-books and to make technological barriers as transparent as possible. The strength of the partnership between OCUL and ACUP, and the heart of the deal, come from OCUL's commitment to maximizing access to e-books for its community. In other

Table 1. Sample UBC titles for which the press updated the DRM at the beginning of 2014 and showing the corresponding use on the Scholars Portal E-Book Platform.

Titles	Original DRM	Change to DRM	View docs	Downloads	Total (views + downloads)
Administering the colonizer: Manchuria's Russians under Chinese rule, 1918–29	ACUP_SUPO	M	4	0	4
Against orthodoxy: Studies in nationalism	ACUP-SUPOPLUS	S	27	6	33
American missionaries, Christian Oyatoi, and Japan, 1859–73	ACUP_SUPO	M	2	0	2
Arming the Chinese: The Western armaments trade in warlord China, 1920–28, Second Ed.	ACUP_SUPO	M	6	0	6
Beyond mothering earth: Ecological citizenship and the politics of care	ACUP_SUPO	M	9	0	9
Biotechnology unglued: Science, society, and social cohesion	ACUP_SUPO	M	0	0	0
Captain Alex MacLean: Jack London's sea wolf	ACUP_SUPO	M	2	0	2
Child and youth care: Critical perspectives on pedagogy, practice, and policy	ACUP_SUPOPLUS	S	7	0	7
First nations education in Canada: The circle unfolds	ACUP_SUPO	S+	97	8	105
Indigenous legal traditions	ACUP_SUPO	M	24	6	30
Oral history on trial: Recognizing the aboriginal narratives in the courts	ACUP_SUPO	S+	37	5	42
A Perilous imbalance: The globalization of Canadian law and governance	ACUP_SUPO	M	80	0	80

words, the detailed license agreement under which publishers committed to grow the DRM–free collections on the SP platform has made this agreement unique and successful.

There are, of course, outstanding concerns. There is some indication that DRM restrictions may drive away users who show interest in DRM titles but are not ready or able to overcome the technological barrier (i.e., getting an Adobe ID and installing software). Another concern is that DRM books do not have access to tools that are available on the general SP platform, such as the ability to save annotations and references, create bookmarks, and export references to citation management tools such as Zotero. This lack of access may compromise the use of e-books among the OCUL community. A final concern is the need for a greater understanding of how publishers make decisions about DRM books, since it seems that print and other sales channels drive some decisions about e-books.

CONCLUSIONS

The current agreement works well for both partners, but the real question is whether this collection works for users. Preliminary data suggest that it does, since the overall use of the collection is high. Of the first 2,000 most-used titles on the Scholars Portal platform, 24% (480) belong to the ACUP collection. This is impressive given that the SP e-book platform currently has 227,609 commercial titles (as of November 2014), of which only 2.25% (about 5,000 titles) belong to ACUP. It would seem, then, that OCUL's investment in the ACUP collection has been worth the effort.

Perhaps the best outcome of the move, however, has been building trust between libraries, publishers, and an aggregator. Both publishers and libraries have come to appreciate the advantage of local loading as a way to sustain academic collections. Indeed, the overall response of the OCUL community to the loading of the Canadian scholarly collection may testify to academic libraries' shift in favor of e-books.

ACKNOWLEDGMENTS

The author extends a special thank-you to e-book programmer Sadia Khwaja for her work on the data analysis that was the foundation of this case study. Thank you also to Murray Tong, UBC Press's digital projects manager, who kindly reviewed the use data of the DRM-change title list.

NOTES

1. Although privacy and security issues associated with e-books are beyond the scope of this case study, they may have a negative impact on DRM e-books in the future. Recently, the OCUL community raised concerns about price and security for the newly released Adobe Digital Editions 4 reader. OCUL replies were published on October 9, 2014, and are available at http://www.ocul.on.ca/node/3325.

2. The "Ontario Council of University Libraries Ebook License Agreement" (available for OCUL members at http://www.ocul.on.ca/products) notes that "DRM will be reviewed at least annually in January of all subsequent years. The terms and conditions for DRM will be consistent for the Licensors but may be applied to varying types of Licensed Materials and for varying length of time based on updates and changes made by the Licensors. When DRM is removed or changed for Licensed Materials, the Licensee and the Local Hosting and Archiving Service Provider, when appropriate, will be notified no later than 10 days after this change. More restrictive DRM will not be applied to Licensed Materials unless agreed to by both parties. DRM terms and conditions governing any additional purchase of Licensed Materials in the future will be discussed and agreed to by both parties at the time."

3. While publishers and aggregators rush to digitize—offering a variety of licensing opportunities and many new delivery channels—there is still much to learn about how academic communities use e-books in order to improve library services and enhance use.

REFERENCES

Horava, T. (2013). Today and in perpetuity: A Canadian consortial strategy for owning and hosting e-books. *The Journal of Academic Librarianship, 39*(5), 423–428. http://dx.doi.org/10.1016/j.acalib.2013.04.001

Jacobs, P., Maidenberg, K., & Schmidt, J. (2014). The stories we can tell: eBook usage in academic libraries [slideshow]. Retrieved from http://www.slideshare.net/janeschmidt/the-stories-we-can-tell-ebook-usage-in-academic-libraries-jacobs-schmidt-maidenberg-32545586

Kirchhoff, A., & Morrissey, S. (2014). *Preserving eBooks.* http://dx.doi.org/10.7207/twr14-01

Ludbrook, A. (2013). Canada's e-book withdrawal: Digital rights management and the Canadian electronic library. *Feliciter, 59*(1), 18–20.

Maidenberg, K. (2014). Analysis of the usage of the Association of Canadian University Presses eBook package. Internal report and presentation to OCUL-Information Resources Committee, Toronto, Canada.

Maxwell, J. (2013). E-book logic: We can do better. *Papers of the Bibliographical Society of Canada, 51*(1), 29–47.

Ontario Council of University Libraries. (2013, January 24). Ontario Council of University Libraries Ebook License Agreement between the participating Canadian University Press and OCUL [available for OCUL members only]. Retrieved from http://www.ocul.on.ca/products

Ontario Council of University Libraries, submitted by Anika [Ervin-Ward]. (2013, February 13). OCUL, ACUP/APUC and eBOUND partner to promote Canadian ebook scholarship. *OCUL*. Retrieved from http://www.ocul.on.ca/node/1650

Scholars Portal. (2014). FAQ. Retrieved from http://answers.scholarsportal.info/browse.php?tid=27764

Slater, R. (2010). Why aren't e-books gaining more ground in academic libraries? E-book use and perceptions: A review of published literature and research. *Journal of Web Librarianship, 4*(4), 305–331. http://dx.doi.org/10.1080/19322909.2010.525419

17 | Of Euripides and E-Books: The Digital Future and Our Hybrid Present

Lidia Uziel, Laureen Esser, and Matthew Connor Sullivan

ABSTRACT

Although the future of information may be digital, its present is clearly hybrid. Harvard's strategy looks to the digital future while remaining rooted in the hybrid present. For the Western Languages Division of Widener Library, the strategy involves the acquisition of both print and e-books, acquiring the same content in both formats where there is a demonstrable benefit. As an initial step in this process, in spring 2014, the head of the Western Languages Division initiated a six-month e-book pilot with Brill. Over 1,200 titles were made available and advertised to the community. This pilot afforded a unique opportunity to investigate the intersections between the use of print and e-books at this time of *both/and* rather than *either/or* collection development. This case study discusses some of the findings after six months of data and responses. Initial use of the e-books was high, but it flattened after the first month. The researchers also surveyed users on their preferences and report these results.

INTRODUCTION: E-BOOKS IN ACADEMIA

Although the future of information may be digital, its present is clearly hybrid. This is true not only in the obvious sense that the majority of the world's cultural, literary, and intellectual heritage remains undigitized, and that a tremendous amount of global information output is not yet available electronically. It is also true in the sense that much of contemporary scholarly practice, from the production of knowledge to its consumption,

277

remains embedded in print. There, is of course, a range of practices across the academic spectrum, with notable differences between and within disciplines, but the fact is that, despite clear gains in e-reading outside of the academy, the role of e-books in academic life has changed little over the past decade.

Although this paper is not the place for a comprehensive survey of the relevant literature, three general points about e-book use in academic libraries warrant mentioning. 1) Despite increasing reliance on e-resources in general, academic e-books have not been adopted as widely as was anticipated in the past or is assumed in the present. 2) Even where e-books are used, this often has to do less with preference for the format, which remains low, and more with availability and convenience. Given that many institutions cannot extensively duplicate holdings, users sometimes have no choice but to access the electronic version of a title—a fact that has sometimes been overlooked when accounting for the growth in e-book use (e.g., Shelburne, 2009). 3) Even if print and e-books were equally available and equally preferable, users would still discriminate between them based on how—and how much—they planned to use the work. Time and again, surveys of e-book use reveal a persistent preference for browsing or reading chapters as opposed to entire works.

These findings are thought to be particularly relevant for researchers in the humanities, whose scholarship has not migrated from print to digital as much as in other disciplines. This is due not to lack of awareness but rather a) to the ongoing importance of monographs, which remain an important career benchmark; b) to a disinclination, shared by members of nearly all disciplines, to use e-books for extensive reading; and c) to poorer representation in e-book packages of older works that remain relevant for humanities research.

The challenge for academic libraries, then, is determining not only how to navigate from the hybrid present to the digital future, but also how to balance the many and varying needs of user communities at present. This is particularly difficult when deciding how to enhance collections with a format that has not been widely adopted by the community those collections are intended to serve. If librarians are able to gauge what users across disciplines prefer, how do they define parameters for print and electronic collections, and establish ecosystems in which those formats coexist?

HYBRID COLLECTION MANAGEMENT

Harvard's current collections and content development strategy look to the digital future while remaining rooted in the hybrid present. For the Western Languages Division of Widener Library, the long-term collection development strategy involves the strategic acquisition of both print and e-books, acquiring the same content in both formats where there is a demonstrable benefit. This "access acquisition" model is thus not collection building so much as collection management, where the library grants users an alternative means of access. E-books will be acquired alone where necessitated by evolving publishing models and where there is a clear preference for this format, accompanied by a demonstrable decline in print use. This strategy will be evaluated on field-by-field and publisher-by-publisher bases to refine short- and long-term strategies.

E-BOOK PILOT PROJECT

As an initial step in this process, in spring 2014, the head of the Western Languages Division initiated a six-month e-book pilot with the scholarly publisher Brill. Brill was a natural choice for a number of reasons, including the high quality of its publications, its longstanding presence on the publishing market, its rapidly expanding e-book offerings, its experience working with academic libraries on licensing agreements, its technological capability to implement the pilot, and its adoption of certain digital best practices, such as using COUNTER statistics and archiving its electronic collections.

Over 1,200 titles from two of Brill's collections, Classical Studies (CS) and European History and Culture (EHC), were made available and advertised to the community. Since Harvard owned over 90% of these titles before the start of the pilot, and acquired the rest soon after, this pilot afforded a unique opportunity to investigate the intersections between the use of print and e-books at this time of *both/and* rather than *either/or* collection development.

Four overlapping goals drove the project. 1) The authors aimed to assess, both quantitatively and qualitatively, the print and e-book preferences and practices among a portion of the humanities community. 2) Given the inherent difficulties of comparing print and e-book use, the authors sought not to compare the use of each format directly, but rather to analyze whether access to digital versions of books would impact the use of print. 3) Through trial and error, the authors attempted to develop strategies for promoting e-book collections. 4) The authors hoped to use the results of the pilot to articulate ground rules for guiding future collection activities and refining business models for e-book acquisitions.

The present case study, only a small part of larger evaluation activities at Harvard, discusses some of the findings after six months of data and responses. After describing some of the project's successes and failures, the authors consider the implications for collection development at Harvard and beyond.

Pilot Setup

In February 2014, the authors downloaded lists of e-books available in CS (236 titles) and EHC (994 titles), combining them into one list for each discipline, covering the years 2007 to January 2014. On the basis of the individual ISBN numbers in each list, the authors used IBM's Cognos software to extract acquisitions information about the university's print holdings, and then matched the resulting lists to the original Excel lists to identify and fill any gaps in the university's holdings. In the end, 1,206 items were selected as available and appropriate for analysis.

Next, metadata staff added the e-book links via batch load directly to the print records. This was done, first, because Harvard adheres to a single record standard, and second, because adding e-book records to the catalog not only enhances discovery (Connaway, Densch, & Gibbons, 2002), but also presents users with a choice at the point of discovery. Would users be satisfied with the link to the e-book, or would they forego this easy access and seek out the physical volume?

To collect and compare data, the authors set up Excel tables illustrating use at the collection and title levels. Circulation data for regular loans, excluding reserves, could be pulled via Cognos at any point, for any period of time, but Brill only provided COUNTER 4 statistics on a monthly basis. The authors also created a dynamic survey with Qualtrics that featured up to 30 questions, depending on user responses (e.g., faculty, student, staff, e-book user, nonuser).

Pilot Promotion

From the outset, the authors knew that promoting the pilot and the survey would be important. Throughout the literature, one of the most frequently cited reasons for not using e-books is lack of awareness. As Shen (2011) writes,

"Students who would be happy to use e-books often did not realize such titles were available through their university libraries" (p. 187). Unfortunately, even if librarians are generally aware of the basic tools available for marketing e-books, few libraries have established a strategic approach (Vasileiou & Rowley, 2010). As a result, the authors took several steps to promote the e-book collections and the survey following the official start of the pilot on March 17.

March

- Announcement on the library's homepage.
- E-mail to faculty in relevant departments, with title lists and links to collections.
- Departmental liaisons from reference and collection development enlisted in promotion.
- Pilot included in weekly e-resource trial announcements.

April

- Survey promoted via link on Brill's website.

May

- Flyer posted on bulletin boards on campus and in relevant departments, each including tear-off tabs with TinyURL links to collections and survey.

Late in the spring, the authors requested and were granted a three-month extension of the pilot, through December 2014. Since the pilot began nearly two months into the spring semester, this extension accommodated a full semester in the fall. Over the summer, then, the authors devised new strategies for promoting the collections.

October

- E-mail from research librarian promoting e-books, featuring pilot and soliciting feedback.
- Displays in classics and history departments featuring flyer and free bookmarks advertising pilot, and two print-on-demand (POD) copies of popular titles. The displayed POD titles were part of Brill's MyBook program, which allows researchers to purchase an affordable, $25 paperback copy of a title if the library owns the relevant e-book collection (currently available for about two-thirds of the titles).

RESULTS AND DISCUSSION

Use Data

The initial results of the pilot were unsurprising. E-book use in the second half of March was more than 21 times the number of print circulations (38), and nearly 8 times the monthly print record within the previous year. In fact, e-book use for this half-month exceeded the annual circulation figures for all but one of the preceding seven years. This indicates that the initial promotion was successful in encouraging users to investigate the collections; over 200 titles in both CS and EHC were accessed in two weeks, constituting 87% and 22% of the respective collections.

What was surprising, however, was how quickly the e-book figures fell off. Between March and May, the numbers dropped by an average of 50% each month before flatlining for the next four months (see Figure 1).

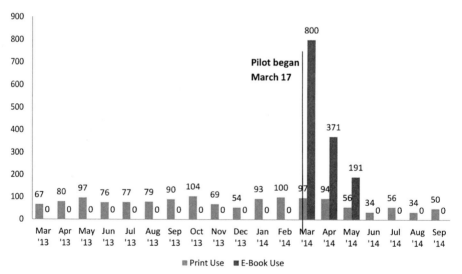

Figure 1. Print and e-book use during pilot, with previous year of print.

Print circulation of both volumes and titles declined within the second month of the pilot, after which the numbers were lower both than the average of the preceding year and the equivalent months in 2013. A few of these months saw less than half of the 2013 use, which is significant since, on average, total use has been increasing each year. However, it is difficult to identify access to e-books as the cause of this decline since this was (a) the start of summer session and (b) the same period when e-book use was flatlining.

One important observation so far is that there appear to be differences in the number and percentage of titles accessed in each format, for each collection. As Table 1 shows, users explored a far greater percentage of e-books in CS than in EHC (93% and 37%, respectively), despite similar percentages in print use (20% and 22%). There is a similar disparity in the titles accessed only as e-book (74% and 27%). This difference is most likely due to the relative size of the collections, which makes it easier to browse the CS offerings thoroughly.

Table 1. Comparison of print and e-book use for two Brill collections, Classical Studies (CS) and European History and Culture (EHC).

	CS		EHC		Total	
Titles available	234	19.40%	972	80.60%	1206	100.00%
E-book titles used	218	93.16%	358	36.83%	576	47.76%
Print titles used	46	19.66%	209	21.50%	255	21.14%
Titles used only as e-books	174	74.36%	264	27.16%	438	36.32%
Titles used only in print	2	00.85%	115	11.83%	117	09.70%
Titles used in both formats	44	18.80%	94	09.67%	138	11.44%
Titles not used in either format	14	05.98%	499	51.34%	513	42.54%

Survey

At the time of writing, survey participation has been modest: 39 total responses from faculty (11), graduate students (16), undergraduate students (2), and staff (10), with an unfortunate 44% completion rate, meaning that there are questions for which a maximum of 17 responses are available. These low response and completion rates are due to what is called *survey fatigue*, engendered by the barrage of survey requests received by these groups at the beginning and end of each year, particularly the latter. Last spring saw the lowest participation, which has increased in the fall with renewed promotional efforts.

Most respondents consider themselves to be "somewhat familiar" (59%) with Harvard's e-book offerings. Half use e-books "occasionally," with all but one of the rest selecting "frequently" and "rarely" evenly. When using an e-book, respondents were most likely to read a chapter or section, followed by browsing or searching for content. When faced with the choice of print or e-book, responses ranged across the spectrum, with "Sometimes print" and "It depends" sharing the top spot.

Reasons for preferring print are familiar: ease of reading and interacting with the text. Researchers feel more comfortable working with multiple articles, books, and other print resources than with their electronic counterparts. Most expressed a desire to write on a text or, as one respondent phrased it, "scribble on them."

Suspecting (hoping!) that respondents were not writing in the library copies of books, the authors updated the survey in June to ask respondents about the likelihood that they would purchase their own copy of a book and, if so, how much they would typically spend. Only a handful answered this question so far, but those responses are "often" or "very often," with all willing to spend over the $25 Brill MyBook price. Since, according to one survey, 40% of faculty considered their personal collections or subscriptions "very important" (Housewright, Schonfeld, & Wulfson, 2013, p. 36), the authors suspect that POD options will prove popular among researchers, possibly increasing their enthusiasm for e-book collections. Early feedback from faculty and staff reaffirms this suspicion.

Reasons for preferring e-books ranged from access and portability to cost and environmental concerns. Significantly, responses here illustrate how print and e-book preferences can overlap depending on a user's research activities, and how e-book collections can supplement rather than supplant print ones. This is particularly important for traveling scholars and institutions with research centers or libraries elsewhere.

Harvard's Center for Hellenic Studies (CHS) in Greece serves as an example. In the current recession, universities are unable to renew digital and sometimes even print subscriptions. As a result, the CHS Digital Library has been met by researchers with great enthusiasm, as indicated by the following survey response:

> For every researcher who visits the Center's Library in Greece
> the e-collection is priceless because it provides access to content

they could find nowhere in Greece but here. We all wish this
pilot project to last forever and we would like to thank you for
all your efforts to enrich the collection and provide access to it.

Among those respondents who report using the Brill collections, all
found it at least "somewhat useful," with most "very useful." Faculty mostly
found it "somewhat useful," with some of the ambivalence resulting from
difficulties with discovering books or navigating the publisher's website.
When asked what Harvard's strategy for collecting print and e-books
should be, most answered that Harvard should collect both print books and
e-books, depending on the subject matter, with a strategy prioritizing print
beating one prioritizing e-books by one vote.

PROBLEMS AND PROSPECTS

Six months into the pilot, the biggest problem facing the researchers is the
limited data. At the time of writing, e-book data from only one month in
the fall semester are available. Will use increase as faculty and students,
now exposed to the collections, settle into the semester?[1] It is also too soon
to tell whether the most recent round of promotional activities will pay off.
Even though the pilot was extended for three months, the authors recommend at least a full year for a pilot, if not more—ideally synced with the
academic calendar.

The project has also suffered from survey fatigue. Does this mean that
future surveys need to be shorter, or perhaps more enticing, to encourage
participation and discourage falloff? Can the importance of this input be
better communicated? Should alternate forms of feedback be promoted? If
so, how can these be aligned and compared?

Other challenges arise from the information itself. As mentioned previously, comparing e-book and print use has historically been intractable due
to the tendency to overcount e-book "use" online (compared to the likelihood of undercounting print use). In the case of the Brill pilot, the authors
face the opposite problem. Since users can download PDF files of chapters
or entire books, it is impossible to know whether users have continued
to take advantage of these resources offline (whereas a print copy would
at least need to be renewed periodically). In the case of CS, where 218 of
the 234 titles (93%) have been accessed 736 times, it is uncertain to what
extent, or whether, any of these users will return to the collections online.

With Harvard's recent adoption of Ex Libris' discovery tool Primo, branded HOLLIS+, e-book collections now have an additional site for discovery and access. What impact will this have on e-book use in general? Further, will it be possible to compare any new data arising from this discovery layer to varying forms of data provided by vendors?

Of course, the most pressing challenge is determining how to meet the diverse needs of the hybrid present. Considered holistically, the current strategy of the Western Languages Division is decidedly print-preferred, even if, in accordance with the strategic plan of the Harvard Library, it is charting paths toward trustworthy electronic resources. Pilots such as the one presented in this case study, shortcomings notwithstanding, can inform that process by providing important data about the preferences and practices of a subset of the user community, but this is only one part of an elaborate picture. However that picture looks in the end, it will undoubtedly be a heterogeneous and dynamic one that will evolve over time.

NOTES

1. After submitting this case study, the authors learned that e-book use did in fact resume in October, returning to and slightly surpassing the pre-lull level in May, in terms of both volumes and titles used.

REFERENCES

Connaway, L. S., Densch, K. L., & Gibbons, S. (2002). The integration and usage of electronic books (eBooks) in the digital library. In C. Nixon (Ed.), *17th Annual Computers in Libraries 2002: Collected presentations, 2002* (pp. 18–25). Medford, NJ: Information Today.

Housewright, R., Schonfeld, R. C., & Wulfson, K. (2013, April 8). *US Faculty Survey 2012*. New York, NY: Ithaka S + R. Retrieved from http://www.sr.ithaka.org/research-publications/us-faculty-survey-2012

Shelburne, W. A. (2009). E-book usage in an academic library: User attitudes and behaviors. *Library Collections, Acquisitions, & Technical Services, 33*(2–3), 59–72. http://dx.doi.org/10.1016/j.lcats.2009.04.002

Shen, J. (2011). The e-book lifestyle: An academic library perspective. *Reference Librarian, 52*(1–2), 181–189.

Vasileiou, M., & Rowley, J. (2010). Marketing and promotion of e-books in academic libraries. *Journal of Documentation, 67*(4), 624–643. http://dx.doi.org/10.1108/00220411111145025

18 | Transitioning to E-Books at a Medium-Sized Academic Library: Challenges and Opportunities— A Feasibility Study of a Psychology Collection

Aiping Chen-Gaffey

ABSTRACT

Slippery Rock University of Pennsylvania Library, a medium-sized academic library, is transforming its building space to support creative learning and collaborations. One of the projects related to this goal involved mass weeding of the library's print collections to free space for new types of user services. In embracing the new library service model and space utilization plan, one of the major collection development questions was "Can e-books serve as an effective alternative for the future library monographic collections?" This paper explores the feasibility of transitioning a print psychology collection to electronic format, using the library resources requirement for a new undergraduate psychology course as an example. This case study evaluates the library's current print and electronic books relevant to the course topics, and then investigates whether and to what degree e-books can fulfill the course requirements. Based on the findings, it recommends a gradual transition from print to e-books; for the immediate future both print and electronic books will be needed to support this course.

BACKGROUND

Like many academic libraries, Slippery Rock University of Pennsylvania Library, the library in this case study, has been implementing a new service model to support teaching, learning, and career development. One of the strategic goals was to redesign the Library space, that is, change the current collection-centered building space to a multifunction, multipurpose facility.

This goal included a significant reduction of the library's print collections, thus clearing space for study and collaboration, and in particular, creating space for new types of services, such as a technology learning center, a writing center, and a mathematics laboratory. Under this plan, the library has undertaken a series of collection rearrangement projects since 2011. The librarians have weeded about 25% of the print collections, which included books, bound journals, and government documents.

In embracing the new library service model and space utilization, one of the psychology librarian's major questions was "Can e-books serve as an effective alternative for the library's print monographic collections in the future?" This case study explores the feasibility of transitioning the library's psychology collection from print to electronic format.

LIBRARY'S PSYCHOLOGY COLLECTION

The library's psychology collections encompass both print and electronic formats. The psychology monographs are mostly classified under Library of Congress (LC) Classification in these areas: BF (psychology), RA790-790.95 (mental health), RC49-53 (psychosomatic medicine), RC321-571 (biological psychiatry and neuropsychiatry), and RJ499-507 (mental disorder and child psychology). Books with psychology-interdisciplinary content may be found in other LC classes. For example, books dealing with both psychology and sociology are often classified under H (social science), and books on psychology and physiology can be found under QP (physiology).

Print Books

Before the massive weeding project described in the introduction, the library held about 10,000 volumes of print books in psychology. According to the circulation statistics, patrons rarely or never checked out over 50% of the library's print books. Taking the psychology books in BF and RC classes as examples, 47% and 48% of them, respectively, had never circulated during the last 15 years. The collection's age was one of several factors contributing to the low use. Over 65% of the books in the print collection had been published between 1960 and 1990. Table 1 shows the steady decline in circulation statistics over a five-year period for psychology books correlated to publication date.

Table 1. Use of psychology print books by publication decade during a five-year circulation period (2009–2014).

Decade of publications	Total number of titles under RC	Number of circulated titles	Percentage of titles circulated
Pre-60s	244	9	3.6%
60s	690	39	5.6%
70s	906	72	7.9%
80s	676	111	16.4%
90s	409	120	29.3%
00s	291	152	52.2%

Aside from the weeding mandated by the library's space remodeling project, this investigation identified the even more urgent need to update the collection from a content standpoint. For example, if the psychology librarian removed all books published before 1990, the psychology print collection in certain subject areas would be starkly depleted. The accelerating age of the collection was not only a direct result of the generally shrinking library materials budget, but also due to inadequate collection weeding in the past. So although the primary goal of the current weeding project was to free space, the weeding also made the subject librarians aware of the critical need to renew the collection with more recent publications. The challenge is that under the new library service model, future space will be allocated more to study and research activities and less to the physical collections. One solution would be to replace print books with e-books when possible.

E-Books

The library currently provides access to 250,000 e-books, mostly acquired through packaged subscriptions, although there are a small number of single-title purchases. With steady growth in the library electronic collections over the last decade and their availability in the online catalog, patrons have had opportunities to use e-books. The use statistics and user feedback suggest that e-books have gained increasing popularity among students and faculty. According to the latest use report from ebrary (one of the library's major e-books vendors), library users viewed 2,286 unique e-books between January 2013 and January 2014; this was 2.6% of the entire ebrary collection accessible via the library catalog. Under the category of psychology, users viewed 137 unique e-books, or 4% of the total psychology e-books available from ebrary. (This statistic includes only titles from which at least five pages were viewed.) Compared with print, the use of psychology e-books was considerably higher: only 2.7% of the print books in BF class circulated during the same time period. To the psychology librarian, both print and e-books use statistics support the future transition of the library's psychology collection to electronic format.

This significant percentage of use of psychology e-books led to two important questions. First, to what extent could psychology print books be replenished with more current e-books? And, second, will it be feasible to acquire new psychology publications exclusively in electronic format?

AVAILABILITY OF PSYCHOLOGY E-BOOKS

Studies indicate that only a small portion of scholarly titles are available in electronic format. According to Anderson and Pham (2013), who checked a sample of their library's current print collection against electronic sources, the overlap between print and e-books was no more than 33%. The percentage of e-editions falls when it comes to useful academic books, such as titles on specific subjects that match a library's collection profile or titles that have been heavily used by students in the past. Pomerantz (2010) compared the print monographs that her library acquired in nursing and business to equivalent electronic editions available from aggregators and found that only 31% of the library-profiled books in these subjects had electronic counterparts. Link, Tosaka, and Weng (2012) concluded that fewer than 25% of locally checked out or interlibrary loan-requested print books were also available in e-format.

This paper approached the assessment of the print vs. electronic collection differently. The author used a new psychology course proposal to investigate the availability of psychology e-books, not by matching print books with their equivalent electronic editions, but by finding relevant e-books on specific topics covered by the course.

Library Resources for New Course Proposal

This study investigated book resources to support one course, Lifespan Development, in which students learn about infant, child, adolescent, and adult development and aging in the social, emotional, cognitive, and biological realms of human development.

The library resources relevant to the major subjects of this course fell into various LC classes: BF710 to BF724.85 (developmental psychology), HQ and QP (physiological and sociological aspects of development), and RJ (child development). The author matched the material that the library already held on topics related to this course by LC subject headings and LC classification numbers or number ranges. (See Table 2 for print books by LC subject and classification for the Lifespan Development course.) All existing monographs, print and electronic, were identified through the Voyager (the library's integrated library system) Access Reports through subject heading and call number matches, then sorted by classification number and publication date. The report identified 1,573 print books as relevant resources for the course.

However, a significant portion of these books were dated. For example, after filtering out the pre-1990 publications, the total number of print books relevant to the course dropped to 335—that is, reduced by 79%. The reduction of the titles in certain other subjects is even more alarming. For example, the number of potentially useful titles in child psychology (BF721-723) fell 90%, from 583 to 60 titles. These dramatic figures helped the psychology librarian realize the need to update the collection by purchasing more recently published books. By contrast, Table 3 shows that the psychology e-books to which the library already had access were much more current; of the 473 titles identified for the course, 384 (81%) had been published between 2000 and 2014.

Lifespan Development E-Books Available at YBP

The author's ultimate goals were, first, to update the library's print psychology collection and fill the gaps with e-books and, second, to transition the print collection to electronic in the future. Although the library will retain ebrary's Academic Complete, this collection alone does not satisfy the needs of the psychology program, since only a very small percentage of the titles are psychology books, and many of those titles do not fit the local curriculum

Table 2. The library's print books identified for the lifespan development course, by LC subject and classification.*

LC subject heading	LC classification	Total print books	Post-1989 publications
Maturation (psychology)	BF710	5	1
Developmental psychology	BF712-713	66	10
Child development	HQ767.8-777	163	49
	RJ131-137	98	36
Psychology of play	BF717	16	3
Infant psychology	BF719-720	14	6
Child psychology	BF721-723	583	60
Adolescent psychology	BF724-724.3	60	11
	HQ796	80	15
Adulthood	BF724.5-724.85	68	20
	HQ799.95	8	3
Middle age	HQ1059.4-HQ1059.5 (BF724.6-BF724.65)	10 (2)	5
Older people	HQ1060-1064 (BF724.8)	276 (14)	83
Gerontology	HQ1060-1064	(276)	(83)
Life cycle, human	(HQ799.95) (BF713)	(8) (58)	(3)
Human growth	QP84	34	4
Longevity	QP85	12	4
Aging	QP86 (QH1061) (BF724.55.A35)	80 (110) (11)	25
Total		1573	335

*For statistical purpose, the numbers of books already counted once are in parentheses.

Table 3. The library's e-books identified for the lifespan development course, by LC subject and classification.*

LC subject heading	LC classification	Total e-books	Post-1999 publications
Maturation (psychology)	BF710	1	1
Developmental psychology	BF712-713	10	8
Child development	HQ767.8-777	80	68
	RJ131-137	12	10
Psychology of play	BF717	9	7
Infant psychology	BF719-720	14	11
Child psychology	BF721-723	126	99
Adolescent psychology	BF724-724.3	23	17
	HQ796	32	28
Adulthood	BF724.5-724.85	23	21
	HQ799.95	5	3
Middle age	HQ1059.4-HQ1059.5 (BF724.6-BF724.65)	4 (2)	3
Older people	HQ1060-1064 (BF724.8)	112 (11)	91
Gerontology	HQ1060-1064	(112)	(91)
Life cycle, human	(HQ799.95) (BF713)	(5) (10)	(3)
Human growth	QP84	5	4
Longevity	QP85	5	4
Aging	QP86 (QH1061)	12 (44)	9 (35)
Total		473	384

*For statistical purpose, the numbers of books already counted once are in parentheses.

needs. The library collection needed titles on very specific subjects to fill the gaps left by weeding outdated print books. The author chose YBP Library Services, the library's main book vendor, for the future e-books acquisition investigation, because YBP supplies e-books from most major aggregators as well as from individual publishers. First, the author searched e-book titles in GOBI3, YBP's online bibliographic database, between August and October 2014, using the following parameters and varying the query only by LC classification range:

- Query: [A specific LC classification range, e.g. "BF712-BF713"]
- Content Level: General Academic
- Date: > = 2000
- Binding: eBook only

Then, to compare the availability of e-books with the print counterparts, the author conducted separate searches with the same parameters, altering only the binding preference. The author organized the results into five categories for each LC classification range:

- total number of books found
- number of books available in electronic format
- number of books available in print
- number of books exclusively in electronic format
- number of books exclusively in print

The searches yielded a total of 730 books under the selected classification ranges regardless of format and binding; 229 (31%) were available in electronic format. Of these 229 e-books, 41 were available only as e-books. All major aggregators, such as EBL, ebrary, EBSCO, and JSTOR, could supply the majority of the e-books. Nevertheless, a fairly significant number of titles were only available from particular aggregators or individual publishers. About 8% of the electronic titles were not available from the library's contracted aggregators. (Currently the library's contracted e-book aggregators are ebrary and EBSCOhost.) By comparison, the author identified 501 books in print (paper and/or cloth binding). Of these 501 books, 273 (55%) were only available in print. Table 4 summarizes the results of the searches in YBP's database to identify recently published psychology books.

Table 4. Availability of subject e-books at YBP as identified for the lifespan development course, 2000–2014: GOBI results A (as of October 2014).

LC classification	Total books	E-books	Print books	E-books only	Print only	% available as print only
BF710	2	1	1	0	0	0.0%
BF712-713	80	14	66	0	46	57.5%
BF717	6	3	3	1	1	16.7%
BF719-720	10	3	7	1	5	50.0%
BF721-723	113	33	80	4	43	38.1%
BF724-724.3	13	5	8	2	4	30.8%
BF724.5-724.85	29	12	17	3	8	27.6%
HQ767.8-777	202	63	139	13	74	36.6%
HQ796	82	27	55	2	26	31.7%
HQ799.95	5	1	4	0	2	40.0%
HQ1059.4-1059.5	13	6	7	3	4	30.7%
HQ1060-1064	123	44	79	7	38	30.9%
QP84	5	3	2	3	0	0.0%
QP85	8	4	4	2	2	25.0%
QP86	10	4	6	0	2	20.0%
RJ131-137	29	6	23	0	18	62.1%
Total	730	229	501	41	273	37.4%

To identify potential future acquisitions, the author searched GOBI for more recent publications by altering the date from "> = 2000" to "> = 2010." The percentage of e-books of the total retrieval fell from 31.4% to 30% (see Table 5). One explanation for the lower percentage of electronic editions among newer academic titles is the delay of electronic release of academic books in general. According to Walters (2013), the delay of the electronic release, which varies between three to 18 months, maximizes the publishers' print profits (p. 191).

Based on the GOBI search results, if the library only acquires electronic copies at YBP, more than 40% of the publications relevant to the course subjects would be excluded from the selection process because e-versions are not available. In certain subject areas, in which the print collection will be

Table 5. Availability of subject e-books at YBP as identified for the lifespan development course, 2010–2014: GOBI results B (as of October 2014).

LC classification	Total books	E-books	Print books	E-books only	Print only	% available as print only
BF710	0	-	-	-	-	-
BF712-713	33	4	29	0	23	69.7
BF717	2	1	1	0	0	0
BF719-720	0	-	-	-	-	-
BF721-723	38	10	27	0	15	39.5
BF724-724.3	4	2	2	2	2	50.0
BF724.5-724.85	19	9	10	3	5	26.3
HQ767.8-777	69	15	54	1	35	50.7
HQ796	32	12	20	0	10	31.2
HQ799.95	6	3	3	3	0	0
HQ1059.4-1059.5	2	0	2	0	2	100.0
HQ1060-1064	42	18	24	2	8	19.0
QP84	2	1	1	0	0	0
QP85	2	1	1	0	0	0
QP86	0	-	-	-	-	-
RJ131-137	16	4	12	0	9	56.3
Total	267	80	186	11	109	40.8

more heavily affected by the continuing weeding (e.g., child development, child psychology, adolescent psychology, and developmental psychology in general), acquiring e-books will be more challenging due to the even lower percentage of available e-books.

To investigate further whether the YBP print-only titles are available in electronic format outside the GOBI database, the author checked a sample of the YBP print-only titles against the Amazon and OCLC databases. About 14% of the titles were available in a Kindle edition at Amazon. About 40% of the titles had bibliographic records for e-editions in OCLC database, but only 20% of these led to the actual e-book sites.

RECOMMENDATIONS

Based on the current findings on the availability of e-books on lifespan development, it is not realistic to replace the psychology print collection completely with e-books in the near future. A combination of print and e-books will be needed. Even if the library's acquisitions budget allowed the maximum purchase of e-books, the transition from print to electronic will be gradual, since it is anticipated that over time publishers slowly will make a larger percentage of scholarly books available in e-book format closer to the print edition release dates. For current collection development, one approach to take advantage of as many books in e-format as possible is to set the YBP profile to prefer electronic format. In other words, if a desired title is available both in print and electronic at YBP, librarians should order the e-edition. The psychology librarian will need to continue buying print books for those titles where a print copy is the only choice—because even if an electronic version may be available elsewhere, the licensing and platform restrictions often prohibit the library from purchasing e-books outside YBP (Polanka, 2011).

FUTURE RESEARCH

In light of emerging e-book acquisition models, librarians should diversify acquisition methods and select the best options for developing subject e-book collections. To investigate and refine collection development of e-books further, a cost/value study of various acquisitions models will inform the acquisition strategies. For example, while title-by-title selections might match the library's profile more closely, purchasing backlist packages often results in a lower per-title price (Walters, 2013). Special subject packages can leverage the increasing cost of individual purchases. Besides the major vendors, librarians also can identify publishers or aggregators that specialize in certain subjects and therefore offer e-books relevant to specific academic disciplines, either as single titles or as packages. For an example in the field of psychology, *APA PsycBOOKS* (http://www.apa.org/pubs/data bases/psycbooks/index.aspx) is a full-text database of nearly 4,000 books and 50,000 individual chapters (as of October 2014) and is updated monthly.

REFERENCES

Anderson, C., & Pham, J. (2013). Practical overlap: The possibility of replacing print books with e-books. *Australian Academic & Research Libraries, 44*(1), 40–49. http://dx.doi.org/10.1080/00048623.2013.773866

Link, F., Tosaka, Y., & Weng, C. (2012). Employing usage data to plan for e-books collection: Strategies and considerations. *Library Resources & Technical Services, 56*(4), 254–265. http://dx.doi.org/10.5860/lrts.56n4.254

Polanka, S. (2011). Purchasing e-books in libraries: A maze of opportunities and challenges. *Library Technology Reports, 47*(8), 4–7.

Pomerantz, S. (2010). The availability of e-books: Examples of nursing and business. *Collection Building, 29*(1), 11–14. http://dx.doi.org /10.1108/01604951011015240

Walters, W. H. (2013). E-books in academic libraries: Challenges for acquisition and collection management. *portal: Libraries and the Academy, 13*(2), 187–211. http://dx.doi.org/10.1353/pla.2013.0012

19 | E-Books and a Distance Education Program: A Library's Failure Rate in Supplying Course Readings for One Program

Judith M. Nixon

ABSTRACT

When Purdue University's College of Education decided to offer its first fully online master's program in Learning Design and Technology, the education librarian volunteered to find and organize all the course readings by creating a LibGuide webpage with links to the readings for each course. This paper analyzes these course readings, delivered to distance education students through links to the library's electronic holdings, between January 2012 and June 2014. It categorizes the readings as journal articles, books (or chapters in books), and other openly available scholarly resources on the web. Since this volume is primarily about e-books, the analysis focuses on chapters and books used for these courses. Approximately half the required readings are journal articles, about one-third are books or book chapters, and about one-fifth are freely available reports or webpages. The journal articles are readily available via library subscriptions; however, approximately 60% of the books needed are not available for purchase in electronic format *at any price*. The analysis concludes that the library cannot meet the e-book demand for distance education students because many of the required books are not available for library purchase in digital format.

CASE STUDY QUESTION

In a distance education program, students do not have physical access to the library's printed books and journals. In many cases these students live miles from campus and cannot come to the library even occasionally.

Therefore, librarians need to deliver the course readings in electronic format. This can be done successfully for journal articles since electronic journal subscriptions have been available for some time; however, access to book content is more limited. This case study of one online master's program at Purdue University analyzes the library's ability to supply the book content needed for course readings in 16 courses in the program between January 2012 and June 2014.

PROGRAM BACKGROUND

In May 2011, Purdue's College of Education announced that a two-year master's program in Learning Design and Technology (LDT) would be offered by the Department of Curriculum and Instruction. Tim Newby, the educational technology area convener at Purdue, stated that one motivation for the fully online program was the drop in enrollment for the face-to-face master's program (Hunter, 2011). An asynchronistic distance-education master's program would meet the needs of individuals employed full time; it would be more convenient and less expensive. The College of Education was correct in anticipating a successful program and, in fact, underestimated the demand. During its first term in fall 2011, the program enrolled 39 students. By spring semester, enrollment increased to 69 students and continued to grow rapidly so that by spring 2014, there were 201 students.

PLANNING ACCESS TO THE COURSE READING

The education faculty members adapted the curriculum, course design, and course readings for distance education; like its on-campus counterpart, the program requires 33 credit hours. They planned 16 courses and sent the bibliography of course readings to the education librarian, who coordinated the gathering of links. After discussion with Tim Newby, the author organized the course links on a LibGuide website, with each course having its own page (or tab). LibGuide, produced by Springshare, is a content management software system used by Purdue and many other libraries to create guides to library material and websites. With the links gathered onto a single website, students can look at all the readings for their present courses, as well as for courses that they plan to take in the future and courses that they have already taken. The LibGuide gives them a convenient resource to find articles and books that they recall from earlier courses so that they also can use them in further research. The LibGuide is "private"; only students in the program have access to the link. This privacy is an option in LibGuide software and is the choice of the teaching faculty members, since they are interested in protecting their course development efforts.

The LibGuide has course-reading links to 14 of the 16 courses; two courses have no readings. There are a total of 176 assigned readings. Nearly half the readings (n = 84, 48%) are journal articles. This comparatively large percentage of journal articles is expected for the social sciences, since the article is the first place of publication for research and the preferred source for scholars. Books, either for one chapter or for the full book, constitute 32% of the readings (n = 57). This indicates relatively heavy dependence on the book literature by these courses. Faculty members select chapters, instead of articles, because they generally provide a good summary of a conceptual aspect of the model or theory being studied, give comprehensive coverage, and can be easier to read. Adding the six assigned government reports and ERIC documents, which are more similar to books than to articles or webpages, brings the reliance on book-type material to 35%. Open access webpages constitute 16% of the total assigned readings (see Figure 1).

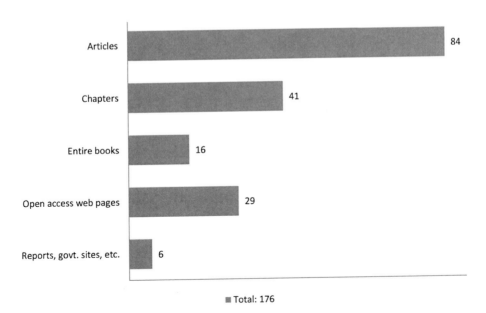

Figure 1. Number of course readings listed on LibGuide, January 2012–June 2014.

LIBRARY'S ABILITY TO SUPPLY COURSE READINGS IN ELECTRONIC FORMAT

Overall, the library could supply 79%, or 139, of the 176 course readings in electronic format. This figure includes 81 of the 85 articles needed, but only 23 of the 57 books needed. Only 40% of the book material needed was available in electronic format. The rate of success for books from which one or two chapters are assigned is worse than the rate for books assigned in their entirety. This finding is contrary to what the author expected, since assigning a whole book suggests that it is being used as a textbook or supplemental textbook, and textbook publishers usually are reluctant to sell electronic access to libraries (see Figure 2).

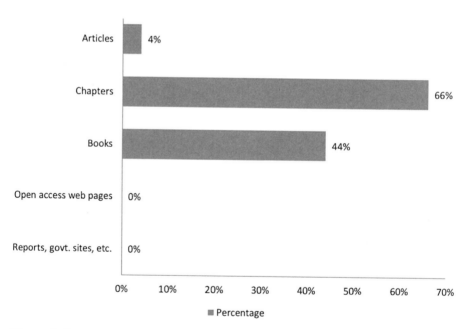

Figure 2. Percentage of course readings not available in electronic format, January 2012–June 2014.

In sum, 34 (60%) of the 57 books needed for this master's program are not available in electronic format despite the library's willingness to pay any price or to purchase the book from any source for e-access. The library, the teaching faculty, and the students are left with a dilemma. The solutions include students buying the books directly, buying faculty-prepared course packets with paid copyright clearance, or faculty scanning and posting the material for a short term on the course management pages. This last option, although providing a digital copy, places these readings in a different place than the rest of the links to the course readings and so inconveniences both the faculty member, who has to scan the chapter, as well as the students. In addition, scanning and posting entire books is not a legal option.

AVAILABILITY OF COURSE-READING E-BOOKS WITH CAMPUS-WIDE NEED FOR E-BOOKS

The author thought that perhaps because these data represent a rather small sampling of campus needs, they present an unusually dismal outlook of the library's ability to purchase required e-books. However, comparing this project for a single online program with Purdue's system-wide ability to provide e-books reveals an even lower rate of availability. Purdue does not routinely collect statistics on the total number of books needed for course readings system-wide, but in spring 2014, as part of a project to reduce the cost of a Purdue education, the administration issued a call to faculty members to identify books needed for all course readings. Faculty submitted a total of 5,735 titles; of these, only 3,212 had ISBNs. After removing titles without an ISBN and eliminating duplicates, 2,341 books remained. Library staff matched these books' ISBNs against the holdings of YBP Library Services, the library's major supplier of e-books, on a title-by-title basis. Only 603 books (26%) were available in e-book format, a much lower percentage than the 40% of books available in e-format for the Learning Design and Technology program. So the 40% figure may, in fact, be deceptively high. This reinforces the point that librarians cannot meet users' demand for e-books because publishers do not offer libraries all the titles they need in electronic format.

CONCLUSION AND RECOMMENDATION

It has long been a responsibility of libraries to supply course readings to students. As in the past, library staff still place physical copies of the readings on reserve in the library for short-term loans. Students consult the books and photocopy these articles while remaining in the library. Distance education programs are now expanding rapidly at many campuses, but the students enrolled in them usually cannot come to campus to use library material. The most convenient and obvious method for librarians to meet distance education students' needs for course readings is to provide electronic copies. Libraries are in a good position to meet this need for journal articles. However, this study has shown that a library could not meet even 50% of the need for electronic copies of books or chapters in books because many titles were simply not available for purchase in e-format.

This dilemma represents an opportunity for publishers and librarians to work together. Libraries are ready and willing to pay for e-access to material needed for their students in both distance education and on-campus courses. Developing a satisfactory model for providing e-access to these high-use titles will be a win-win situation, resulting in revenue for publishers and satisfaction for the librarians as well as for the students and faculty they serve.

ACKNOWLEDGMENTS

The author thanks Rebecca A. Richardson for the data on books needed across campus for course readings.

REFERENCE

Hunter, C. (2011, May 25). Purdue now offers fully online degree. *Exponent Online.* Retrieved from http://www.purdueexponent.org/campus/article_26ee152c-8673-11e0-8f2d-0019bb30f31a.html

20 | Mobile Access to Academic E-Book Content: A Ryerson Investigation

Naomi Eichenlaub and Josephine Choi

ABSTRACT

In 2014, the authors conducted two series of tests using four different mobile devices to ascertain how well the e-book collections at Ryerson University met their users' mobile information needs. They developed criteria based on factors such as ease of access, online viewing, offline reading, download icon, and necessity of using special apps. Then they scored each of 25 e-book collections and, based on the total scores, grouped the collections into three categories (high, medium, low). Most collections scored five (out of 10) or higher. The authors passed on feedback for the lowest scoring e-book collections to the vendors and urge other librarians to do the same.

INTRODUCTION

Ryerson University is an urban commuter campus in the heart of downtown Toronto, Canada's largest city, with a population of approximately 30,000 full-time students as well as a very large continuing education contingent. Library collections include approximately 500,000 e-books, 500,000 print volumes, and 80,000 e-journals and other online resources, as well as subscriptions to almost 400 databases. E-book use reports show that Ryerson University Library e-book collections are well used. These reports, together with the global increase in mobile devices—"more smartphones purchased than PCs in the United States" (Mobile Future, 2011)—motivated the electronic resources staff at Ryerson Library to determine how effectively the e-book collections met their users' mobile information needs. In fall 2013, a project team consisting of an electronic resources librarian and an electronic resources technician set out to investigate mobile access to Ryerson e-book collections. In January 2014, the project team completed the first phase of testing using a first-generation iPad and a Samsung Galaxy Note 2, and presented the results as a poster at the Ontario Library Association Super Conference. The project team completed a second phase of testing in July 2014, this time using an iPad Mini and an iPhone 4S.

BACKGROUND

Wilson and McCarthy's (2010) article, "The Mobile University: From the Library to the Campus," predicted that by 2013 Ryerson student mobile device use could reach as high as 80% (p. 214). Moreover, with regards to the status of mobile access to e-books described, Wilson and McCarthy lamented that "the provision of mobile versions of eBooks represents a large challenge to academic libraries" (p. 224).

Ryerson library directs e-mails reporting problems accessing electronic resources to erm@ryerson.ca, a mailbox monitored by the electronic resources technician with backup from electronic resources librarians. From 2010 through 2013, this mailbox received an average of approximately 600 queries annually. Although the library had not received many questions from students, faculty, and staff about accessing e-book content on mobile devices, the authors certainly fielded challenging questions on this topic from time to time. One incident in particular was a catalyst for this project. In August 2013, an engineering faculty member, attempting to view Safari e-books on his iPad, contacted erm@ryerson.ca. He indicated he was being asked for an organizational ID and wondered what it was so that he could access content. After many e-mails back and forth with Safari's technical support team and many weeks of follow up, the authors finally learned that, instead of an organizational ID, a personal account was required to download content for offline viewing in the Safari To Go app that is available for both IOS and Android devices. After passing this information along to the faculty member nearly seven weeks after his initial query, the authors resolved to become more proactive when dealing with requirements for mobile access to e-books and offline viewing.

The January 2014 call to propose a poster session for the Ontario Library Association Super Conference offered a good opportunity for the authors to start mobile e-book testing. After their poster proposal was accepted, the project team set to work with the following four objectives:

- test mobile access to Ryerson library e-book collections using different devices;
- evaluate the ease with which a user can access e-book content for online viewing, offline reading, and downloading using a set of criteria;
- rank e-book platforms on a scale of 0–10 based on performance on each device; and
- group results into an overall measure based on each platform's score.

PHASE 1

Methodology

The project team employed the following methodology:

Step 1. Compiled a list of the 25 largest and most popular e-book collections and platforms from 60 available collections.

Step 2. Decided to test two devices in the first phase of testing. (Originally the team intended to test access on up to five different devices: Android, Apple iPhone, iPad, Kobo, and Kindle; however, due to time constraints and the limited availability of devices, the authors limited the study to two devices.):

- Samsung Galaxy Note 2 Android Jelly Bean 4.3
- Apple iPad iOS 5.1.1

Step 3. Selected the following criteria (see Table 1 footnotes for scoring criteria for each category):

- Is there an option to download for offline reading?
- Does the user have to create an account to access or work with content?
- Maximum range of content users are allowed to download (whole book, one chapter, range of pages)?
- How easy is it to locate the icon to download content?
- Does the user have to download a special app to view content?

- How does the overall user experience on each device rate (including, for example, online viewing experience, how many steps were involved to access content, etc.)?

Step 4. Assigned a score of 1–10 to each e-book collection based on the above criteria. Scores for subjective user experience for each device were largely dependent on whether downloading was available. The authors presumed that a user would find it useful to be able to access content offline without using a mobile data plan; therefore, a score of "0" was automatically given to those platforms that did not allow downloading. Each author used one of the devices to test all the collections, and each author worked independently of the other.

Step 5. Ranked each e-book collection into one of three categories: 8–10 (high); 5–7 (medium); 0–4 (low).

Findings

Using the criteria described above, the team evaluated 25 e-book collections on two mobile devices: a Samsung Galaxy Note 2 and an Apple iPad. Ten collections (40%) scored at least 8 points and received a ranking of "high" (see Table 1). Nine collections (36%) scored between 5 and 7 points and were assigned a ranking of "medium." Only six collections (24%) scored between 0 and 4 points, and these were ranked "low." A total of 19 out of 25 collections scored at least a 5 or higher, meaning that 76% of Ryerson e-book collections scored either at a "medium" or "high" in terms of mobile access to their content. Only 24% performed below this level.

Overall, the authors were pleasantly surprised by the general accessibility of e-book content in Ryerson Library e-book collections on the Samsung Galaxy and the Apple iPad. For the most part, e-book collections were easily accessible for online viewing and did not require additional steps that can restrict access to content and frustrate users (for example, the need to download a special app to view content, or to create an account to view content, or to enter special identifiers such as access codes). They did, however, encounter some challenges with mobile access to library e-book collections, including the following:

- Online viewing of content sometimes required manual resizing of text before it displayed properly or in full on the smaller of the two devices, the Android Samsung Galaxy Note 2.

- Download speed experiences sometimes varied greatly between the Samsung Galaxy and the iPad. This was likely due in part to the differences in the age and operating systems of the two devices.
- A handful of platforms had barriers such as the need for access codes, personal accounts, installation of readers or apps, and so forth, or other limitations such as having to switch to the full site to view content or being unable to view content on the mobile site.
- Although automatically redirecting to the mobile site may enhance online user experience, in some cases the mobile site makes it harder to download. For example, on one of the platforms, the option of unchecking "Preview Only" disappears when using the smaller-screened Samsung Galaxy Note 2. Consequently, users are unaware that in these cases they are not searching the full text access.

The team decided to contact the vendors of the platforms that scored on the lower end and share suggestions for enhancing access to their content on mobile devices.

PHASE 2

At this point, the team determined that future work in this area should include retesting on a smaller-screened mobile device such as an iPhone. This was partially based on Julie Shen's (2011) observations in 2011, "a recent usability test showed that, although most e-books in Cal Poly Pomona's current collection were next to unreadable on smaller mobile devices such as the iPad Touch, all of our titles worked well on larger mobile devices such as Apple iPad" (p. 187).

Methodology

Based on the findings from the first phase of testing in January 2014, the project team introduced a second phase that would incorporate retesting the same e-book collections on two additional devices. Notably, one of these devices was smaller-screened than the mobile devices used in the first phase of testing. The authors conducted the second phase in July 2014 on the following two devices:

- iPhone 4S iOS 7.1.2i
- iPad mini iOS 6.1.3

The team used methodology similar to the first phase of testing, but they made a few small changes to the spreadsheet criteria (see Tables 1 and 2 footnotes for scoring criteria for each category):

Table 1. Scores from Phase 1 (Samsung Galaxy Note 2 with Android Jelly Bean 4.2 OS & Apple iPad iOs 5.1.1).

Name of the package	Option for download[1]	Do you have to create an account to download?[2]	Maximum range that can download each time[3]	Icon visibility for download on mobile device[4]	Does it require an special app[5] for viewing download?[6]	User experience on iPad[7]	User experience on Android phone[8]	Total score
18th Century Collections Online (ECCO)	1	2	2	1	1	0	1	●8
19th Century Collections Online (NCCO)	1	2	2	1	1	0	0	○7
ACLS Humanities e-books (HEB)	0	0	0	0	0	0	1	○1
Adam Matthew Collection (5 collections)	1	2	2	1	1	1	1	●9
Cambridge Collections Online	1	2	1	1	1	1	1	●8
Classical Scores Library	1	2	1	0	1	0	0	○5
Cognet	1	2	1	1	1	1	1	●8
CRCnetBase	1	2	1	0	0	0	0	○4
EBL	2	1	2	1	0	0	1	○7
ebrary	2	1	2	1	0	1	1	●8
IEEE / Wiley e-books	1	2	1	1	1	1	1	●8
InteLex Past Masters via Gibson LC	0	0	0	0	0	0	1	○1

	[1]	[2]	[3]	[4]	[5]	[6]	[7]	[8]
Knovel library	1	2	1	1	1	1	1	● 8
Latino Literature	0	0	0	0	0	0	1	○ 1
LWW/Ovid E-books (Books @Ovid)	1	2	0	0	1	0	1	● 5
MyiLibrary	2	2	1	1	1	0	0	● 7
NetLibrary Collection 1 (EBSCO)	1	2	0	1	0	0	0	○ 4
North American Indian drama	1	2	1	0	1	1	1	● 7
OECD iLibrary (formerly SourceOECD)	1	2	1	1	1	1	1	● 8
PsycBOOKS (on ProQuest Platform)	1	2	1	1	1	0	1	● 7
Safari Tech Books Online	1	1	0	0	0	0	0	○ 2
Scholars Portal Books	1	2	1	1	1	1	1	● 8
Springer	1	2	1	1	1	0	0	● 6
Synthesis Digital Library(Morgan/Claypool)	1	2	2	1	1	1	1	● 9
University Press Scholarship Online	1	2	1	0	1	0	1	● 6

[1]No Download = 0; PDF = 1; PDF + EPUB = 2; [2]No = 2; Yes = 1; No Download = 0; [3]Whole book = 2; Chapter = 1; Smaller than Chapter or no download = 0; [4]Icon/Link = 1; Without or No Download = 0; [5]Including Bluefire but exclude PDF Reader; [6]No = 1; Yes or No Download = 0; [7]1 = Pass; 0 = Fail; [8]1 = Pass; 0 = Fail

- Modified the download scoring criteria (Footnotes 1 and 9 on Table 1 and Table 2) from pdf = 1 to pdf or other = 1
- Modified the maximum download scoring criteria (Footnotes 3 and 11 on Table 1 and Table 2) from "chapter" = 1 to "chapter or 10+ pages" = 1

In addition, during the second phase of testing, the authors resolved to reach consensus about the ratings by conducting the testing together, thereby increasing the interrater agreement. Like the first phase, each author was responsible for testing one of the devices; however, during Phase 2 they discussed the mobile experience before giving the ratings for the user experience. One of the platforms, Cambridge Collection Online, had to be dropped out of the testing for Phase 2, since the library had cancelled the subscription in mid-2014. Table 2 shows the results of Phase 2 testing.

Findings

Overall, the authors found that the platforms scored better in this phase of testing. Only four platforms were assigned to the ranking of "low," and that was because none of them allowed downloading of content. Only six collections fell in the mid-range score. The number of platforms that scored in the "high" zone increased from 10 to 15 (63%), with five platforms (21%) achieving a high score of 9 out of 10. Although there were two platforms (8%) that scored significantly worse in the second phase with smaller-screened devices, the team saw more improvements overall in the performance of the e-book collections. The most dramatic improvement was the American Council of Learned Societies (ACLS) Humanities E-Books (HEB). During Phase 1, HEB received a score of 1 out of 10 (low) mainly because of the limitation of downloading only three pages at a time. During the second phase of testing, the maximum range that could be downloaded had increased to 10 pages; as a result, both authors agreed that the user experience had improved significantly.

FURTHER INVESTIGATION

The team also observed some differences between Phase 1 and Phase 2 that prompted further investigation. For instance, in the second phase, both authors had difficulty reading books offline through the Safari To Go, the app from Safari Tech Books Online that sparked this project. The team wondered if the vendor changed the policy during the six-month period between the two tests, or if the "Offline Bookbag," the folder in which offline readings should be placed, had not been available earlier. After following up with the vendor, the authors found out that this feature is not available for Safari's Academic or Library account.

Another difference in Phase 2 occurred with NetLibrary Collection 1 from EBSCO. This collection scored poorly during the first phase of testing because it only allowed downloading one page at a time. When the team tested the same titles in the second test, both iPhone and iPad mini provided options to "Download (Offline)." This option was not visible when using a desktop, so the authors will have to conduct further testing to see if it is available on an Android or other tablet.

CONCLUSION

In summary, the majority of Ryerson Library's e-book collections tested for mobile access usability received favorable scores. During the first phase of testing on an iPad and a Note 2 (January 2014), a total of 19 out of 25 collections scored at least a 5 or higher, meaning that 76% of the e-book collections scored either at the 5–7 (medium) or the 8–10 (high) range. During the second phase of testing on an iPad mini and an iPhone (July 2014), six collections fell in the mid-range score, while the number of platforms that scored in the "high" zone increased from 10 to 14, meaning that 20 out of 24 collections (83%) scored at least a 5 or higher, an increase from 76% in Phase 1. Table 3 compares the scores between the two tests.

It is indeed an accurate proclamation that "the challenges and opportunities presented to libraries, librarians, and library users by the mobile revolution are massive, exciting, and sometimes daunting" (Bell & Peters, 2013, p. ix). Librarians have an important role to play in ensuring that vendors receive feedback to encourage improving mobile access to their resources. The authors passed along feedback for the lowest scoring e-book collections and received varying responses from most of the vendors; however, only one provider indicated that they would take any action based on the feedback. Vendors would be wise to place priority on improving access to their content through mobile devices. As Brynko (2013) reports in "What's Trending in Ebooks," a Library Resource Guide study found that "the greatest demand in libraries will be delivering ebooks to mobile devices, whether those are iPads, tablets, or smartphones" (p. 34). In conclusion, sustained

Table 2. Scores from Phase 2 (iPhone 4S iOS 7.1.2i and iPad Mini iOS 6.1.3).

Name of the package	Option for download[9]	Do you have to create an account to download?[10]	Maximum range that can download each time[11]	Icon visibility for download on mobile device[12]	Does it require an special app[13] for viewing download?[14]	User experience on iPad mini[15]	User experience on iPhone phone[16]	Total score
18th Century Collections Online (ECCO)	1	2	2	1	1	1	1	● 9
19th Century Collections Online (NCCO)	1	2	2	1	1	0	0	◑ 7
ACLS Humanities e-books (HEB)	1	2	1	1	1	1	1	● 8
Adam Matthew Collection (5 collections)	1	2	2	1	1	1	1	● 9
Classical Scores Library	1	2	1	0	1	0	0	◑ 5
Cognet	1	2	1	1	1	1	1	● 8
CRCnetBase	1	2	1	1	1	1	1	● 8
EBL	2	2	2	1	0	1	1	● 9
ebrary	2	1	2	1	0	1	1	● 8
IEEE / Wiley e-books	1	2	1	1	1	1	1	● 8
InteLex Past Masters via Gibson LC	0	0	0	0	0	0	0	○ 0
Knovel library	1	2	1	1	1	1	1	● 8
Latino Literature	0	0	0	0	0	0	0	○ 0

Platform								Total
LWW/Ovid E-books (Books @Ovid)	1	2	1	1	1	1	1	●8
MyiLibrary[17]	2	2	1	1	1	1	1	●9
NetLibrary Collection 1 (EBSCO)	1	1	2	1	0	1	1	○7
North American Indian drama	0	0	0	0	0	0	0	○0
OECD iLibrary (formerly SourceOECD)	1	2	1	1	1	1	1	●8
PsycBOOKS (on ProQuest Platform)	1	2	1	1	1	1	1	●8
Safari Tech Books Online	0	0	0	0	0	0	0	○0
Scholars Portal Books	1	2	1	1	1	1	1	●8
Springer	1	2	2	1	1	1	1	●9
Synthesis Digital Library (Morgan/Claypool)	1	2	2	1	1	1	1	●9
University Press Scholarship Online	1	2	1	0	1	0	0	○5

[9](No Download = 0; PDF or HTML = 1; PDF + EPUB = 2); [10](No = 2; Yes = 1; No Download = 0); [11](Whole book = 2; Chapter or 10 pages = 1; Smaller than 10 pages or no download = 0); [12](Icon/Link = 1; Without or No Download = 0); [13](including Bluefire but exclude PDF Reader); [14](No = 1; Yes or No Download = 0); [15](1 = Pass; 0 = Fail); [16](1 = Pass; 0 = Fail); [17]The maximum number of pages varies for MyiLibrary and Scholars Portal. The authors thus decide to score this option as "1," as it seems to be the norm for most of the books

Table 3. Comparison of scores from Phase 1 and Phase 2.

Name of the package	Score for Phase 1	Score for Phase 2	Phase 2 minus Phase 1	
18th Century Collections Online (ECCO)	● 8	● 9	→	1
19th Century Collections Online (NCCO)	◑ 7	◑ 7	→	0
ACLS Humanities e-books (HEB)	○ 1	● 8	↑	7
Adam Matthew Collection (5 collections)	● 9	● 9	→	0
Cambridge Collection Online	● 8	N/A		N/A
Classical Scores Library	◑ 5	◑ 5	→	0
Cognet	● 8	● 8	→	0
CRCnetBase	○ 4	● 8	↑	4
EBL	◑ 7	● 9	→	2
ebrary	● 8	● 8	→	0
IEEE / Wiley e-books	● 8	● 8	→	0
InteLex Past Masters via Gibson LC	○ 1	○ 0	→	-1
Knovel library	● 8	● 8	→	0
Latino Literature	○ 1	○ 0	→	-1
LWW/Ovid E-books (Books @Ovid)	◑ 5	● 8	↑	3
MyiLibrary	◑ 7	◑ 7	→	0
NetLibrary Collection 1 (EBSCO)	○ 4	◑ 7	↑	3
North American Indian drama	◑ 7	○ 0	↓	-7
OECD iLibrary (formerly SourceOECD)	● 8	● 8	→	0
PsycBOOKS (on ProQuest Platform)	◑ 7	● 8	→	1
Safari Tech Books Online	○ 2	○ 0	→	-2
Scholars Portal Books	● 8	◑ 7	→	-1
Springer	◑ 6	● 9	↑	3
Synthesis Digital Library (Morgan/Claypool)	● 9	● 9	→	0
University Press Scholarship Online	◑ 6	◑ 5	→	-1

focus on the mobile user experience both at the library level and the resource provider level should be a priority so that libraries can seamlessly deliver content to users no matter what devices they use.

REFERENCES

Bell, L., & Peters, T. (2013). *The handheld library: Mobile technology and the librarian*. Santa Barbara, CA: Libraries Unlimited.

Brynko, B. (2013). What's trending in ebooks. *Information Today, 30*(9), 1.

Mobile Future. (2011, December 15) Mobile year in review 2011. Retrieved from: http://mobilefuture.org/resources/mobile-year-in-review-2011-paper/

Shen, J. (2011). The e-book lifestyle: An academic library perspective. *Reference Librarian, 52*(1–2), 181–189.

Wilson, S., & McCarthy, G. (2010). The mobile university: From the library to the campus. *Reference Services Review, 38*(2), 214–232. http://dx.doi.org/10.1108/00907321011044990

21 | E-Reader Checkout Program

Vincci Kwong and Susan Thomas

ABSTRACT

In 2013, the Franklin D. Schurz Library at Indiana University South Bend was awarded a Library Services and Technology Act (LSTA) grant from the Indiana State Library to launch an E-Reader Checkout Program to provide students with the opportunity to enhance digital literacy and technology skills and to encourage reading. With the grant, the library purchased 10 electronic reading devices and a selection of leisure reading e-books. The authors describe the processes involved in implementing and assessing the E-Reader Checkout Program, as well as some of the challenges they encountered and how they addressed each challenge.

BACKGROUND

The Franklin D. Schurz Library is an academic library serving the faculty, staff, and students of Indiana University South Bend (IU South Bend). IU South Bend is a comprehensive public university in north central Indiana with an enrollment of 7,860 undergraduate and 630 graduate students. The library's mission is to advance excellence in teaching, learning, and research by providing access to, and facilitating the use of, a quality collection of comprehensive information resources.

In spring 2013, the authors (the head of Library Web Services and the director of Collection Services, respectively) applied for an Institute of Museum and Library Services (IMLS) Library Services and Technology Act grant administered through the Indiana State Library. The grant proposal outlined how the library wanted to purchase various e-readers to achieve three main objectives through an E-Reader Checkout Program.

PROGRAM OBJECTIVES

There were three main objectives to the implementation of the E-Reader Checkout Program at the Library. The first objective was to increase the digital literacy of students at IU South Bend. At IU South Bend, 48% of students receive financial aid. To finance their college educations, 75% of IU South Bend students work. Among those students who work, 25% of them work full time. With limited financial resources, most students at IU South Bend are not able to afford new technologies. As a result, many students become victims of the digital divide. The grant provided the library with the means to provide electronic readers so students could increase their knowledge and skills with digital devices.

Second, librarians wanted to encourage leisure reading by providing popular e-books. The library's primary collection development focus is to build a collection that supports academic programs. With a limited budget, acquisitions focus on academic and scholarly material. Popular material for leisure reading is added primarily through gift donations or at the request of faculty for instruction purposes. The grant provided the library with the funds to add nearly 400 leisure reading electronic books.

Lastly, the E-Reader Checkout Program offered a third indirect goal that supported the first goal of increasing digital literacy. The e-readers provided IU South Bend faculty and students with the opportunity to explore the use of e-readers with electronic textbooks as a new tool for teaching and learning. In August 2009, Indiana University initiated an eTexts initiative that includes digital versions of textbooks and other educational resources. Contents of the eTexts are available in multiple electronic formats through computer browsers and e-readers such as the Kindle, Nook, or iPad.

PROGRAM IMPLEMENTATION

Funding Sources

In July 2013, the Schurz Library was awarded the LSTA grant in the amount of $5,764 from the Indiana State Library. The grant enabled the library to purchase several e-readers, equipment for the e-readers, and e-books for the E-Reader Checkout Program. The library also contributed $1,000 to purchase e-books for the program.

Purchase of Equipment and E-Books

Librarians bought 10 e-readers for the program: two iPad Minis, three Kindle Fires, three Nook HD+s, and two Kindle Paperwhite 3Gs. To protect the e-readers from damage, protective covers and carrying cases also were purchased. Power kits/adapters enabled patrons to recharge the e-reader as needed. To keep the screens clean, cleaning pads were added. Shortly after launching the E-Reader Checkout Program, program administrators realized that screen protectors also were needed. In addition, a plastic tag attached to each carrying case enabled circulation staff to identify the corresponding device in each bag quickly and easily.

Librarians consulted standard lists of popular books to select titles to load on the devices: Goodreads College Book Lists, the *New York Times* fiction best sellers, and Amazon Kindle e-book best sellers. Since the launch of the E-Reader Checkout Program, librarians bought e-books from Amazon (351 titles), ebrary (40), and EBSCOhost (50). In addition, they downloaded 98 additional free titles from Amazon. Although the majority of the e-book titles were fiction, some nonfiction titles including cookbooks, graphic novels, and DIY books were included. Patrons can discover the Amazon e-book titles by consulting the E-Reader Checkout Program LibGuide at http://libguides.iusb.edu/ereader. E-book titles purchased from ebrary and EBSCOhost can be found using the library catalog.

Staff Collaboration

Launching the E-Reader Checkout Program required collaboration among different library departments. The business operations manager bought all the equipment and Amazon e-books, as well as tracked all of the program's financial transactions. The head of Public Relations and Outreach created marketing materials and then promoted of the E-Reader Checkout Program through different communication portals. Acquisitions staff ordered the ebrary and EBSCOhost e-books; cataloging staff cataloged the e-books and equipment. The circulation supervisor established the circulation policy for the e-readers and trained student assistants in the circulation procedures for the devices. In addition to checking out the e-readers, the student assistants also reminded and encouraged patrons to fill out a paper survey about their experience when they returned the e-readers.

Circulation Policy and Checkout Kit

E-readers circulate from the library's circulation desk. The loan period for all e-readers is two weeks, without renewal. The library charges patrons a late fee of $10 per day if devices become overdue. To protect the e-readers from damage, e-readers must be returned at the circulation desk rather than through library book drops.

When patrons check out an e-reader, they receive an e-reader checkout kit that contains the following:

- E-reader with protective cover
- Charger
- Cleaning pad
- Instructions on how to connect to IUSecure (the wireless network at IU South Bend)
- User experience survey
- Checklist of all components in the checkout kit
- Carrying case with plastic tag

Marketing and Promotion

Librarians used several different avenues to promote the E-Reader Checkout Program. In September 2013, they initiated a prelaunch marketing campaign during GameOn, a campus-wide IT event. The prelaunch marketing campaign not only raised awareness of the upcoming E-Reader Checkout Program among a large number of faculty, staff, and students, but also generated continued inquiries about the program after the GameOn event. In addition to this prelaunch campaign, a display in the library lobby showcased the different types of e-readers and e-book titles.

Librarians placed table tents, flyers, and a large poster throughout the library to inform patrons of the new service. To reach campus constituents who were not frequent visitors of the library, information about the E-Reader Checkout Program appeared on the library's website, Facebook page, Twitter feed, library blog, library newsletter, the *Daily Titan* (the official e-mail communication tool of IU South Bend), and on a number of digital signs across the campus. The head of Public Relations and Outreach also promoted the program directly to students through the Student Government Association. Since using e-readers for eText was an indirect goal, all promotional materials and activities focused on e-readers and the leisure reading collection. None of the promotional material contained information related to eText.

CHALLENGES ENCOUNTERED

Librarians encountered five major challenges while implementing the E-Reader Checkout Program. An early challenge was the need for protective screen covers as previously mentioned. Although not every issue was so easily resolved as this one, the librarians also were able to address some of the other issues they encountered.

In launching the E-Reader Checkout Program, librarians discovered that not only did the faculty, staff, and students show interest in checking out e-readers, but also many community members inquired about checking out the devices. As a public institution, the library is open to Indiana residents. However, because the intent of the LSTA grant was to buy the devices for IU South Bend students, staff, and faculty, circulation was restricted to that population.

The third challenge involved product registration of the Nooks. To register a Nook and ensure that it functions properly, Barnes & Noble requires a default credit card on file. To prevent users from buying additional material through the Nook, librarians used a reloadable credit card as the default credit card on file. Using the child profile feature also established a customized (restrictive) profile for patrons.

The fourth issue concerned the e-books' licensing restrictions. Each Amazon Kindle e-book can only be shared among six devices at once. Librarians needed a way to make the e-books available to all 10 devices without making the titles device-specific. The solution was to place the e-books in the Amazon cloud. From the cloud, all e-books are available for download and can be browsed on all the devices. Since the Kindle readers already have access to these e-books, the Kindle App was installed on the Nook and iPad mini readers, so users can browse the e-books in the cloud. Selected e-books can be downloaded as long as they are within the six-user limit. Current use patterns indicate that it is unlikely that more than six patrons will attempt to download the same e-book simultaneously.

The e-readers and Kindle e-books are registered to one Amazon account. To confirm that the library was not violating the Kindle e-book user agreement, the authors contacted Amazon first by e-mail and then by telephone to discuss concerns and ensure library compliance. According to both the e-mail and telephone conversations with a Kindle customer service representative, lending e-readers with Kindle e-books to multiple users in a library setting is no different than an individual customer letting a friend borrow a Kindle. Because the purchased e-readers all are tied to a single Amazon account, sharing the purchased Kindle e-books among those e-readers connected with that account is also an acceptable practice. However, if the library were to make the library-purchased Kindle e-books available to users on their personal Kindles, it would be a violation of the user agreement. The Kindle service representative also saw no violation in adding catalog records for the Kindle e-books to the online catalog to enhance discovery as long as the Kindle e-books remain accessible only on the e-reader devices registered to the Amazon account used to purchase the e-books (Amazon Customer Service, personal communications, January 23, 2015).

The final challenge related to the university's tax-exempt status. As a public institution, Indiana University is not allowed to pay sales tax on any purchase. When buying e-books from the Nook store, there is no option for waiving the sales tax during the checkout process. The Library Business Operations manager had extra work requesting refunds of the sales tax from Barnes & Noble. The initial intention was to buy e-books from both Barnes & Noble and Amazon, but because of the sales tax difficulty with Barnes & Noble, librarians eventually decided to buy e-books only through Amazon because that website allows tax-exempt purchases.

PROGRAM ASSESSMENT

Since the E-Reader Checkout Program launched in November 2013, patrons checked out the e-readers 116 times over the course of nearly a year. Table 1 provides the circulation statistics for each type of e-reader through mid-October 2014.

By June 22, 2014, 20 patrons had completed the user experience survey for the E-Reader Checkout Program. Most patrons (83%) used the e-readers to read books, and of these 72% read fiction. When asked about

Table 1. Device checkout, November 2013–October 2014.

Type of device	Total number of checkouts
Kindle Paperwhite	12
Nook HD+ Tablet	29
Kindle Fire HD	38
iPad Mini	37

the e-book leisure collection provided by the Schurz Library, almost 70% of respondents indicated that they either were satisfied or very satisfied. In addition, 86% indicated they either were likely or very likely to recommend the E-Reader Checkout Program to others. The survey data also indicated that the *Daily Titan* was the most successful marketing channel for the E-Reader Checkout Program. Over 50% of users indicated learning about the E-Reader Checkout Program primarily through the *Daily Titan,* followed by word of mouth (28%) and the library newsletter (17%).

Staff notified the head of Library Web Services each time a device was returned; using the Amazon app, she recorded the titles and reading progress for each downloaded e-book. Because circulation student assistants sometimes failed to notify the librarian when the e-readers were returned, detailed use data from only 68 of 97 checkouts (70%) were recorded. During these the 68 checkouts, patrons downloaded 230 e-books and read 161 of them. Table 2 shows the breakdown of how much or how far patrons read when they used e-books through the Amazon app. The data show that most users read less than 30% of a particular e-book; however, it is interesting to note that 12% of patrons read over 90% of an e-book.

Table 2. E-book use, November 2013–October 2014.

Portion of book read	Percentage
Read < 90%	12%
60% < Read < 89%	4%
30% < Read < 59%	9%
30% < Read	75%

The recorded data reveal that 134 unique titles were downloaded to e-readers. The most frequently downloaded titles were:

1. *A Thousand Splendid Suns*
2. *The Hunger Games*
3. *Catching Fire*
4. *Mockingjay*
5. *Artemis Fowl*
6. *Easy Vegetarian Recipes*
7. *Fifty Shades of Grey*
8. *The Perks of Being a Wallflower*
9. *The Yiddish Policemen's Union: A Novel*
10. *Twilight*
11. *Water for Elephants: A Novel*

ebrary use data show that patrons viewed 4,732 e-book pages and downloaded 29 chapters over the course of a year. The ebrary use data do not indicate how users accessed the titles. Librarians have not yet reviewed the EBSCOhost use data.

Patrons accessed the E-Reader Checkout Program LibGuide 240 times during the program's first year. LibGuide use data indicate that 52% of users searched for information about the program, for the device user guide, how to connect to IUSecure, and how to access the leisure reading collection. In searching the collection, 27% looked for information related to fiction titles, 9% looked for information related to nonfiction titles, and 5% looked for information related to graphic novels. The data show that fiction is more popular among users than nonfiction and graphic novels, suggesting that future purchases should focus on adding more fiction e-books.

PROGRAM OUTCOMES

To determine user satisfaction with the E-Reader Checkout Program, librarians included a paper survey in each e-reader checkout kit. When users returned e-reader checkout kits, circulation student assistants reminded and encouraged them to fill out the user experience survey.

Survey responses demonstrate that the program succeeded in achieving the stated objectives. Specifically, some responses indicate that the e-readers were being used to access apps (28%) and browse the Internet

(66%). These activities indicate success in meeting the goal of increasing students' digital literacy. Survey responses also indicate interest in the program's exploration of the various e-readers on the market in order to make informed purchase decisions. Selected comments regarding the reasons users checked out a specific type of e-reader include:

- Just to try out the iPad.
- Wanted to try each kind.
- It was the last e-reader available.
- The other types were all checked out.
- To see which e-reader I liked the most for apps and reading.
- Looking to buy. Trying different options. Have an older Kindle [and] liked it.
- Because I have never used one before.
- Wanted to see how one works—I read a lot.
- Have a Nook, lower version, and wanted to compare/contrast.
- To try out prior to purchase.
- I heard good things about it and I wanted to try it.
- So that I could see if I'd like to purchase one for myself.
- To compare devices.

One of the indirect objectives for the E-Reader Checkout Program is enabling faculty and students to explore the use of e-readers and e-Texts as a new tool for teaching and learning. According to the survey, 17% of patrons used the e-readers to read eTexts. This use also supports the goal of increasing digital literacy. Since there was no promotional activity targeted for e-reader use for eTexts, the authors found it encouraging that patrons did use the devices to read eTexts.

FUTURE PLANS

Although the grant program officially concluded in June 2014, the library continues to check out e-readers to IU South Bend faculty, staff, and students. Using the information gathered from the user experience survey, librarians plan to implement the following measures to promote further use of the E-Reader Checkout Program. First, implementing additional marketing campaigns will increase awareness of the E-Reader Checkout Program. Second, librarians will add records for all titles purchased from Amazon to the library's catalog, Indiana University Online Catalog (IUCAT), to increase the discoverability of leisure materials available for the e-readers. Third, librarians will continue buying electronic leisure reading materials to sustain the leisure/recreational collection.

CONCLUSION

More than 10 years of reductions to the monograph budget have made it increasingly difficult to support the purchase of academic/scholarly materials as well as leisure materials to encourage reading. With support from the LSTA fund, the faculty, staff, and students at IU South Bend now have access to an e-book leisure/recreational collection to meet their leisure reading needs. User comments confirm that the E-Reader Checkout Program is a welcome addition to the library's services.

22 | Out With the Print and in With the E-Book: A Case Study in Mass Replacement of a Print Collection

Stephen Maher and Neil Romanosky

ABSTRACT

In this case study, the authors describe how one academic health sciences library, the New York University (NYU) Health Sciences Library at the NYU Langone Medical Center, is replacing the bulk of its print collection with e-books. Although the circumstances surrounding the replacement are unique—damage from a storm surge during Hurricane Sandy—the lessons learned from the case study, including appraising the collection, working with vendors, and articulating strategy and rationale to key stakeholders, could be used to advocate for a similar mass replacement in many library contexts.

HURRICANE SANDY AND NYU HEALTH SCIENCES LIBRARY

When Hurricane Sandy came ashore in the northeastern United States on October 29, 2012, the New York University (NYU) Langone Medical Center sustained $2 billion of damage as a result of the powerful storm surge that hit its main facility. NYU Health Sciences Library, the main library for the medical center and NYU School of Medicine, occupied three floors in the university building that was hardest hit by the storm. The extent of the damage to the library was substantial, resulting in its closure until a new facility could be built (Romanosky & Dement, 2014).

Even before the storm, the library experienced a period of rapid change, much of which was indicative of changes in most health sciences libraries in the era of electronic resources (Miller, 2011). The library's print collection had decreased 42% between 2008 and 2012. The demand for and ubiquity of electronic journals and e-books had resulted in fewer print purchases in the decade preceding Sandy. Demand for more student study space resulted in considerable weeding efforts. Although much of the library's print collection had been moved to offsite storage, that collection also had been reduced considerably to eliminate duplication with electronic content. Thus, at the time Sandy hit, the library's on-site print collection consisted of approximately 12,000 items, most of which were reference materials and recent biomedical monographs, in addition to some bound periodicals. The bulk of these collections was stored in compact shelving in the basement of the library, which was completely destroyed. The remainder was in the main reading room, one floor above the basement. Although the flooding in that room was not as severe, humidity and heat rendered most of that collection unsalvageable. Thus, days after the storm, library administration declared the bulk of the library's remaining print collection a total loss.[1]

FEDERAL EMERGENCY MANAGEMENT ASSOCIATION (FEMA)

In early 2013, library administration met with representatives from the FEMA and the medical center's finance department to discuss the library's losses as a result of Sandy.[2] FEMA provided the library with guidelines for determining collection and object eligibility for FEMA assistance (Federal Emergency Management Agency, 2008). FEMA outlined that the library would need to compile a list of all of the lost books, noting the value of each item. If FEMA funding was granted, the library would replace each item on a one-to-one, print-for-print basis. The rule of thumb would be to attempt to replace lost items with exact equivalents.

Given the changes in user behavior and decreased library acquisitions of print materials in recent years, and the uncertainty of whether the newly rebuilt library would contain space for a print collection, library administration decided to advocate for a 100% electronic replacement of the lost print collection. The library had to estimate the value of the lost collection, demonstrate to FEMA the rationale for this bulk replacement, and present viable options for electronic content that the library could purchase and own, not license indefinitely, given the temporary availability of FEMA funding.

METHODOLOGY

The first challenge the library addressed was assessing the value of the lost print collection. Prior to Hurricane Sandy, the library undertook two migrations of its integrated library system (ILS) in less than four years. These migrations greatly compromised the quality of the library's catalog records, most notably in terms of acquisitions data. In 2008, the library migrated its ILS from Innovative Interfaces' Millennium product to the open-source ILS Koha. During this migration the price information for print monographs and journals did not transfer successfully from Millennium to Koha. In early 2012 the library commenced its migration from Koha to Ex Libris's Aleph. Although the cost information from Millennium had been saved and could have been included in the second migration, this information was lost on the library servers that were damaged during Hurricane Sandy.

Given these difficulties, the library took several approaches to appraise its collection.[3] First, the library contacted its book vendors, Majors/YBP Library Services and Rittenhouse Book Distributors (www.rittenhouse.com) for records on its purchases. However, this would only capture a small segment of the collection, namely recent acquisitions. Also, the book vendors' records could only tell the library what it had paid, not the current value of those items, which is what FEMA required. Next, the library compiled a list of the print monographs sorted by ISBN and shared it with the library's book vendors to provide cost estimates for one-to-one print replacement (see Tables 1 and 2). Before providing the quote, the book vendors were given the following caveats:

- If a title was out of print but superseded by a newer edition, the book vendors were instructed to use the cost of the latest edition in the estimate.
- If a title was out of print and had no newer edition available, the book vendors were instructed to provide a quote for what it would cost to acquire the title in the estimate.[4]

Finally, the library ran the same list of ISBNs through Readerware (www.readware.com), a commercial software that retrieves bibliographic and cost information based on ISBN (or UPCs for CDs or videos) from various websites, including Amazon. With Readerware the library retrieved price quotes from Amazon and the various booksellers who sell on the website, providing a unique perspective of current marketplace value (see Table 3).

Table 1. Quote from Rittenhouse Book Distributors.

Rittenhouse Book Distributors	Quantity	Total
Items in stock	4,790	$741,864.86
Items out of stock	1,205	$194,504.44
Other	5,836	N/A
Total Estimate	**11,831**	**$936,369.30**

Table 2. Quote from YBP.

YBP	Quantity	Total cost
Items in stock	5,444	$753,992.04
Items out of stock	2,795	$377,039.04
Other	3,592	$47,885.63
Total Estimate	**11,831**	**$1,178,916.71**

Table 3. Quote from Readerware/Amazon.com.

Amazon.com	Quantity	Total cost
Items in stock	7,253	$696,072.87
Average price per item	N/A	$95.97
Items out of stock (based on avg. price per item)	4,578	$439,350.66
Total Estimate	**11,831**	**$1,135,423.53**

The estimates from YBP, Rittenhouse Book Distributors, and Reader-ware were not only useful in calculating the value of the print collection, but they also illustrated the challenge of finding an exact one-to-one replacement for each item. Moreover, upon reviewing the collection budget from 2009 to 2013, the library had evidence of a steady decrease in print collection purchasing and an increase in spending on e-books (see Tables 4 and 5). These data reflected the prevailing trend among academic libraries to offer e-books. To explain the merits of this trend, the following quote from Michael Heyd's (2010) article in *Journal of Electronic Resources in Medical Libraries* was included in the library's proposal to FEMA:

> The advantages of online electronic books over their printed counterparts include the ability to search in greater depth than traditional tables of contents and indexes; hyperlinking to related information in the text, citations, or full-text references; access from multiple locations within the institution or from other locations; access by multiple users at one time (depending on the platform and the license terms); updating of text between printed editions; and features such as news updates, dictionaries, atlases, calculators, videos, and other content that add value beyond the original printed text. (p. 14)

These points were essential in creating a case to FEMA for the mass replacement of a print collection with e-books.

Table 4. NYUHSL print book purchases, 2009–2013.

Fiscal year	Total Amount	Year to year	Total budget	% of total budget
2009	$80,238	--	$1,424,521	5.63%
2010	$42,405	-47%	$1,259,166	3.37%
2011	$23,704	-44%	$2,747,645	0.86%
2012	$3,598	-85%	$2,967,576	0.12%
2013	$2,955	-18%	$2,903,480	0.10%

Table 5. NYUHSL e-book purchases, 2009–2013.

Fiscal year	Total amount	Year to year	Total budget	% of total budget
2009	$98,853	--	$1,424,521	6.94%
2010	$47,845	-48%	$1,259,166	3.80%
2011	$288,933	608%	$2,747,645	10.52%
2012	$118,437	-41%	$2,967,576	3.99%
2013	$171,224	145%	$2,903,480	5.90%

These findings also reflected a prevailing trend among academic libraries to offer e-books to their users (see Figure 1).

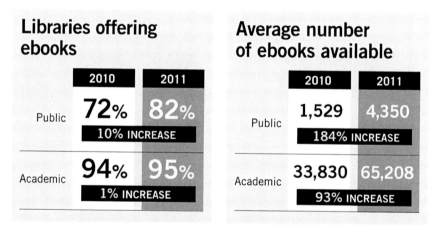

Figure 1. From "Dramatic Growth: *LJ*'s [*Library Journal*'s] Second Annual Ebook Survey" (Miller, 2011).

With this evidence in hand, the library drafted its proposal for the mass replacement of print with e-books. The proposal offered a two-tiered approach for the replacement. First, where it was applicable, the library would attempt to purchase one-to-one replacements of print books with e-book versions. To do this, third-party aggregators like STAT!Ref, ebrary, and Rittenhouse Book Distributors' R2 Digital Library would receive a list of the ISBNs for the lost print items. They then would provide a quote for items they could match with an e-book version on their respective platforms. Next, for items for which publishers did not have an e-book available, the library would use Library of Congress (LC) Classification to analyze the items according to LC's classes and sub-classes. The library would compare the classifications of the lost print items against those in a publisher's backfile collection and make e-book purchases in the same subject areas as the lost print books. Although in most cases the e-books would not be exact replacements of the lost print, the library valued acquisition of subject content over replacing specific titles. In all cases, the library would purchase perpetual access to the e-books.[5] Subscription content or collections requiring maintenance fees would not be considered for purchase given the temporary availability of FEMA funding.

CONCLUSION

Over the course of 2013 and early 2014, the librarians held several meetings with FEMA staff and medical center finance personnel to present the evidence and rationale outlined in the preceding section. FEMA ultimately approved the mass replacement program as presented, awarding the library $1.5 million in funds to be spent over a three- to five-year timeframe. The library was positioned to start purchasing immediately, as it already had identified two e-book backfiles and one journal backfile. The awarded amount was slightly higher than the library's estimate of $1.1 million for the print collection, but it also built capacity for conservation of storm-damaged archival materials and other affected library programs.

The approval of this plan also was fortuitous since the plans for the rebuilt library facility, which had been unfolding over the same time period, ultimately contained very little book shelving in favor of more program space for technology, group and individual study, and special collections display. Thus, the mass replacement of the print collection with e-books aligned with the library's strategic vision going forward.

DISCUSSION

Although the circumstances prompting the mass replacement program outlined in this case study were unique to the NYU Health Sciences Library, the experience yielded several valuable lessons for any library contemplating a mass replacement of print with e-books:

- Know the market value of the collection: The loss of acquisitions data through multiple ILS migrations and a natural disaster proved a considerable stumbling block for NYU at the outset. Maintaining and backing up these data so that they can be easily resurrected, compiled, and analyzed is essential to this type of replacement program. Readerware proved to be an excellent tool for determining current market value of the collection.

- Maintain strong vendor relationships: Vendors proved to be invaluable partners throughout this process, assisting with both appraisal and content-matching aspects of the library's proposal development. Although the value proposition for the vendors was clear in this scenario, the circumstances demanded that the library articulate a focused program for e-book purchasing with specific stipulations attached.

- Be able to tell your library's story to nonlibrary audiences: Federal government agencies and institutional finance departments are usually not a medical library's core audience. The same could be said of university finance offices, boards of trustees, and other groups to which libraries are held accountable. Therefore, it was critical for the library to explain the rationale for a mass replacement program in terms that these groups could easily understand. Focusing on the cost and value associated with e-books proved successful in this case, but offering evidence of changing library business practices based on shifting patron behaviors and needs largely contributed to the approval of this replacement program. Although not used in this case study, other types of data, such as circulation and use statistics, could also be beneficial in communicating the library's story and vision—especially to data-centric audiences.

NOTES

1. Some rare and historic collections were shelved on a floor that experienced no flooding and were saved.

2. The library's damaged archival and special collections also were a focus of this meeting, but this case study focuses strictly on the library's general print collection.

3. The value of the lost bound periodicals was not included in the appraisal. Because there is no market for replacement copies of bound periodicals, a "one-to-one" replacement would not be possible. Therefore no value would be assigned to those items.

4. Rittenhouse Book Distributors chose not to observe the second caveat.

5. The library also would purchase some journal backfiles with perpetual access.

REFERENCES

Federal Emergency Management Agency. (2008). FEMA Disaster Assistance Policy DAP9524.6, Collection and individual object eligibility. Retrieved from http://www.fema.gov/pdf/government/grant/pa/9524_6.pdf

Heyd, M. (2010). Three e-book aggregators for medical libraries: NetLibrary, Rittenhouse R2 Digital Library, and STAT!Ref. *Journal of Electronic Resources in Medical Libraries, 7*(1), 13–41. http://dx.doi.org/10.1080/15424060903585693

Miller, R. (2011, October 12). Dramatic growth: *LJ*'s second annual ebook survey. *The Digital Shift*. Retrieved from http://www.thedigitalshift.com/2011/10/ebooks/dramatic-growth-ljs-second-annual-ebook-survey/

Romanosky, N., & Dement, F. (2014). A year after Sandy: One library's experience. *Library Leadership & Management, 28*(2), 1–6. Retrieved from https://journals.tdl.org/llm/index.php/llm/article/view/7060/6274

Epilogue

Michael Levine-Clark

The University of Denver has been working with e-books in academic libraries since 1999, when it participated in a proto-demand-driven acquisition project with NetLibrary through the Colorado Alliance of Research Libraries. At the time, Colorado Alliance librarians grumbled about the digital rights management (though without yet using that term), complained about poor selection of content, protested the high prices relative to print, and speculated that no one would ever want to use these things for immersive reading. The Colorado Alliance and the University of Denver went ahead with NetLibrary because they were convinced that e-books offered enormous potential benefits to their users, and they wanted both to learn about that potential and to help shape it. Sixteen years later, the University of Denver has over half a million e-books available, and use data show that it was wise to invest so heavily in this collection. Yet many of those same problems still exist, and librarians continue to complain about the unrealized potential of e-books.

In 1999, there were few choices for e-books for academic libraries. NetLibrary was founded in 1998, ebrary was founded in 1999, and EBL, founded in 1997, did not begin selling to libraries until 2000–2001 (Machovec, 2003; ebrary, n.d.; Paulson, 2011). Many publishers were wary of e-books, so their participation with these early aggregators was limited at best. It was impossible to purchase e-books through traditional academic library sales channels, so for most libraries e-books were something extra, something librarians thought of as marginal to their main collecting practices. As late as 2007, e-books had still not caught on in academic libraries.

A special issue of *Against the Grain* that year explored some of the reasons why that might have been the case, but Horava's (2007) lead article, "The Renaissance of the eBook," took a generally optimistic view, referring to "the newfound acceptance of eBooks" (p. 1). He then laid out the many challenges libraries faced in integrating e-books into their collections. In that same issue, I argued that e-books needed to be better integrated into approval plans for academic libraries to adopt them readily (Levine-Clark, 2007). Three years later, Slater (2010) made a similar point: "Ideally, the choice to acquire a print or electronic copy of a book should be as simple as a single choice (print, electronic, or both) integrated into the same acquisition systems libraries already use for print books" (p. 238). Although e-books have proven difficult for academic libraries, today they are a key component of our collections. At the University of Denver, as at many academic libraries, there are e-books from multiple vendors, delivered through multiple access models. In some ways, this is because libraries have been able to build e-books into traditional workflows—managing demand-driven acquisition (DDA) pools through approval vendors, for instance—but in others, it is because they have compromised. Librarians now accept access models and restrictions that seemed unacceptable early on and juggle acquisition across multiple platforms in sometimes inefficient ways. E-books are clearly here to stay, but just as clearly, there is room for improvement. What follow are a few thoughts on the current state of e-books in academic libraries, and some suggestions for how e-book access and use models might be improved.

TENSIONS

There are a number of tensions at play in the academic library e-book landscape. E-books have been widely adopted in the consumer space, yet have been less successful in academic libraries. Sometimes librarians want e-books to behave more like print, but in other ways want to take advantage of the benefits the technology can offer. Librarians often are uncomfortable with access restrictions to e-books, yet accept those restrictions to get content to their users. And, perhaps fundamentally, the ability to understand use patterns and user behaviors is forcing librarians to change the way they build collections and is forcing publishers to reconsider what to publish. The chapters in this book hint at some of these tensions, while also exploring many of the possibilities that e-books offer.

PLATFORMS

When academic libraries began offering e-books to their users, they were leading the game, but in 2007, with the introduction of the Kindle, libraries were suddenly very much behind the consumer market (Amazon Kindle, n.d.). Academic library e-books, which already seemed cumbersome, became comparatively even harder to use, and they have only improved a little since then. Loading academic library e-books onto an e-reader is a multistep process and is sometimes impossible. This inability to use the devices that patrons expect means that some forms of reading are extremely unlikely for these e-books, but may mean that other types of use are more likely. Vassallo's (2016) observation that immersive reading has been immensely successful on devices like the Kindle, while nonimmersive reference-like use of materials such as cookbooks has been almost nonexistent, is fascinating, given that the experience in academic libraries has been the opposite. Academic librarians hear from their users that they prefer print books for longer periods of immersive reading, while accepting or even preferring e-books for brief forays into the book to look up information or check citations. This suggests that academic libraries need to do a better job getting users to the device they need for a given task: a dedicated e-book reader for immersive reading or the web interface for shorter tasks, combined with the ability to provide local print-on-demand services for any e-book in the collection. Further, librarians and their vendors should consider whether these interfaces—which are designed for both immersive and short reading—might be better designed with only shorter reading and accompanying behaviors in mind, with easy capability to transfer an e-book to a reader when needed.

SOMETIMES LIBRARIANS WANT TO REPLICATE PRINT, SOMETIMES THEY DON'T

Academic librarians often express frustration that e-books do not yet allow users to do things that were impossible in the print world, but should be easy in the e-world. E-books, according to these arguments, should be accessible to many users at once, should be easily searchable, should be "chunk-able" into chapters or other logical parts, and should be easy to read online. In short, e-books should be better versions of their print antecedents. Solutions to some of these problems involve better digital rights management (DRM), others involve better platform and interface development by vendors, and still others involve better integration into library discovery services.

A slight variation on this theme is that e-books should allow publishers to build something better than a digital version of a print book. Why are they still publishing long-form scholarship in the way it was a generation ago when e-books should allow users to experiment with hypertext, embedded media, and other creative forms of content? So far, the publisher and vendor platforms that libraries use have been built to provide nothing more than digital versions of print books. Experiments with enhanced e-books are relatively rare, because as Costanzo (2014) points out, "the market as it currently exists doesn't allow publishers to deliver the same enhanced product across all current digital platforms" (para. 3). So academic libraries are stuck with digital versions of print books instead of something new and improved. This is a tricky problem to solve, in that any solution involving a purpose-built platform exacerbates the existing problem of titles being unevenly available across publisher and vendor platforms.

Somewhat contradictorily, librarians also ask why e-books cannot behave more like print, because there are some features of print books that work very well. Perhaps most significantly, one copy of a print book is the same as all other copies of that print book. Libraries can get a print book from their preferred vendor, and if a copy of that book ends up in the collection from some other source, it is fully compatible with the existing collection. Not so with an e-book, which may only be available on selected platforms from particular vendors and will have slightly different functionality on each platform. It is completely reasonable for librarians to expect e-book purchasing to be as easy as print book purchasing.

In some ways, the basic structure of the print book is so effective that librarians wish to replicate it in e-books. Despite the wish for better searching in e-books, the traditional index is in many ways still a better entry point to the text than keyword searching. Reporting on important studies by Abdullah and Gibb (2008), Zhang and Niu (2016) observe that the index can sometimes still be the most effective way to access content within a monograph of any sort. This is a good reminder that there are aspects of the traditional print monograph that work very well and should be retained, and even highlighted in the designs of e-book platforms.

In other cases academic librarians use a print mindset to manage e-book collections. One simple way in which they do this is assigning a single call number to each book (as a shelf location) instead of many (as subject access points). Another is trying to replicate interlibrary loan (ILL), a function of the print world, instead of inventing something new. Interestingly, Litsey, Ketner, Blake, and McKee (2016) are explicit about having adopted a print model to create an e-book ILL system. ILL is fundamentally about providing a user with temporary access to an item not in that user's home collection. ILL is one way of providing that access, but is probably more labor intensive and costly than simply carrying out a short-term loan (STL) of an e-book from a vendor. This seems to be a case where inventing something entirely new might be more effective. For an expansion of this point, see Levine-Clark (2011).

DIGITAL RIGHTS MANAGEMENT

Librarians, rightly, are concerned about DRM of e-books. Providing access to content that has limitations on use is frustrating for the user and ultimately will make it harder for e-books to succeed. It may be useful to think of DRM as falling into two very broad categories, the second of which should concern librarians much more than the first. The first category of DRM has to do with controlling access to the library; it has a financial intent and involves mostly differential pricing for single vs. multiple user models. Libraries can choose to spend more to get broader access or less for narrower access. In reality, most books have low enough use that a single user license will suffice, and a model that would allow unmediated buy-up to add additional users at the point of need would solve most problems caused by this limitation. In some cases, such as course adoption titles, these limits on simultaneous use allow libraries to have access to titles that economic pressures otherwise would keep out of libraries entirely. This sort of limitation may be a necessary compromise, but, as Thomas and Chilton (2016) note, it is not reasonable for a user to be told that an e-book is "checked out" and therefore unavailable. Limited user models must allow some flexibility to increase access so as not to inconvenience the user.

The second category of DRM involves restraints placed directly on the user—such as limiting the number of pages that can be copied or printed and preventing the e-book from being loaded onto an e-reader. These barriers, which happen after acquisition and therefore do not impact the publisher's bottom line, serve only to frustrate the user and need to be removed from academic library e-book models.

USE DATA AND USER NEEDS

One thing that e-books offer is the potential for better understanding of how library users interact with monographs. In the print world, circulation data could tell whether a book was checked out (but not whether or how that book was used while checked out), and sometimes reshelving data could be used to indicate that someone had looked at that title in the library. In theory, librarians can learn much more from studying e-book use than was ever possible when studying print book use, and those lessons can help to understand print collections better. In reality, librarians have done a poor job studying e-book use so far, partly because the reporting tools do not give a nuanced enough view of use. COUNTER book use reports, for instance, tell only how many section views took place, but often do not clearly define whether a section is a page or a chapter or something else ("The COUNTER code of practice for e-resources," 2012, p. 16–17). Some vendor platforms, such as EBL's LibCentral, provide more meaningful measures of use, such as the length of time in the book, number of pages viewed, and whether a download occurred. More vendors and publishers should follow EBL's lead in this regard.

Nardini's (2016) chapter, "Platform Diving: A Day in the Life of an Academic E-Book Aggregator," provides an example of another interesting way of looking at use. As he points out, so often quantitative views of use, made possible by the reporting tools described above, omit more subtle but telling observations, such as the times of day when e-books are accessed and the degree to which there are clusters of subject overlap. As e-books come to represent larger portions of library monograph collections, it is crucial to gain a deeper understanding of use patterns.

Although the ability to measure use has not significantly changed librarians' understanding of user behavior, it has fundamentally shifted how they build collections. Most significantly, it has allowed the development of DDA, which has benefited libraries by allowing them to present their users with a much larger pool of content from which to choose than was possible under traditional prospective purchasing models. But as the recent adjustments by publishers to STL pricing have shown, an unintended consequence of this new model is a decrease in predictable revenue for publishers and the potential for a decrease in their ability to publish some monographs. Gaining a better understanding of use may help publishers make better predictions about what to publish, and may push some monographs into other publication streams. Academic librarians must work with publishers to figure out how their choices will impact publication decisions, and in some cases may need to compromise their values around pricing and DRM in order to get potentially low-use monographs published.

CONCLUSION

From their first experiences with e-books, academic librarians have been excited about the possibilities they could offer in terms of greater use and better searchability. And equally, they have been frustrated because e-books do not ever quite reach their potential. Almost two decades after the first e-books appeared in academic libraries, it is clear that e-books are here to stay, but it is equally clear that problems remain. Librarians still want e-books to behave both more and less like print books (and should be able to have it both ways). They want better and more predictable access models. They want better platforms and easier access to e-readers. But there are some enormous opportunities. The ability to understand use can help shape access models, build better collections, and better serve users. The chapters in this volume express many of these frustrations, but also offer suggestions about how librarians, publishers, and vendors can provide a better e-book experience to end users.

REFERENCES

Abdullah, N., & Gibb, F. (2008). Students' attitudes towards e-books in a Scottish higher education institute: Part 1. *Library Review, 57*(8), 593–605. http://dx.doi.org/10.1108/00242530810899577

Amazon Kindle. (n.d.). In *Wikipedia*. Retrieved from http://en.wikipedia.org/wiki/Amazon_Kindle

Costanzo, P. (2014, May 23). The real reason enhanced ebooks haven't taken off (or, Evan Schittmann was right . . . for the most part). Retrieved from http://www.digitalbookworld.com/2014/the-real-reason-enhanced-ebooks-havent-taken-off-or-evan-schnittman-was-right-for-the-most-part/

The COUNTER code of practice for e-resources: Release 4. (2012, April). Retrieved from http://www.projectcounter.org/r4/COPR4.pdf

ebrary. (n.d.). Company. Retrieved from http://www.ebrary.com/corp/company.jsp

Horava, T. (2007). The renaissance of the ebook: Transformations and question marks. *Against the Grain, 19*(2), 1, 16.

Levine-Clark, M. (2007). Electronic books and the approval plan: Can they work together? *Against the Grain, 19*(2), 18, 20, 22.

Levine-Clark, M. (2011). Whither ILL? Wither ILL? The changing nature of resource sharing for e-books. *Collaborative Librarianship, 3*(2), 71–72.

Litsey, R., Ketner, K., Blake, J., & McKee, A. (2016). The simplest explanation: Occam's Reader and the future of interlibrary loan and e-books. In S. M. Ward, R. S. Freeman, & J. M. Nixon (Eds.), *Academic e-books: Publishers, librarians, and users* (pp. 159–170). West Lafayette, IN: Purdue University Press.

Machovec, G. (2003). NetLibrary revisited. *The Charleston Advisor, 4*(4), 21–26.

Nardini, B. (2016). Platform diving: A day in the life of an academic e-book aggregator. In S. M. Ward, R. S. Freeman, & J. M. Nixon (Eds.), *Academic e-books: Publishers, librarians, and users* (pp. 77–90). West Lafayette, IN: Purdue University Press.

Paulson, K. (2011). The story of patron-driven acquisition. In D. A. Swords (Ed.), *Patron-driven acquisitions: History and best practices* (pp. 63–78). New York, NY: DeGruyter. http://dx.doi.org/10.1515/9783110253030.63

Slater, R. (2010). Why aren't e-books gaining more ground in academic libraries? E-book use and perceptions: A review of published literature and research. *Journal of Web Librarianship, 4*(4), 305–331. http://dx.doi.org/10.1080/19322909.2010.525419

Thomas, J., & Chilton, G. (2016). Library e-book platforms are broken: Let's fix them. In S. M. Ward, R. S. Freeman, & J. M. Nixon (Eds.), *Academic e-books: Publishers, librarians, and users* (pp. 249–262). West Lafayette, IN: Purdue University Press.

Vassallo, N. (2016). An industry perspective: Publishing in the digital age. In S. M. Ward, R. S. Freeman, & J. M. Nixon (Eds.), *Academic e-books: Publishers, librarians, and users* (pp. 19–34). West Lafayette, IN: Purdue University Press.

Zhang, T., & Niu, X. (2016). The user experience of e-books in academic libraries: Perception, discovery, and use. In S. M. Ward, R. S. Freeman, & J. M. Nixon (Eds.), *Academic e-books: Publishers, librarians, and users* (pp. 207–222). West Lafayette, IN: Purdue University Press.

Contributors

Joni Blake, Executive Director, Greater Western Library Alliance, Prairie Village, KS.

Christine B. Charlip, Director, ASM Press, American Society for Microbiology, Washington, DC.

Aiping Chen-Gaffey, Bibliographic Services Librarian, Slippery Rock University of Pennsylvania, Slippery Rock, PA.

Galadriel Chilton, Head of Electronic Resource Services, University of Connecticut, Storrs, CT.

Josephine Choi, Electronic Resources/Serials/Acquisitions Library Technician, Ryerson University, Toronto, Canada.

Ann Marie Clark, Associate Professor of Political Science, Purdue University, West Lafayette, IN.

Ravit H. David, Digital Content and Metadata Librarian, Scholars Portal, University of Toronto, Canada.

Jim Dooley, Head, Collection Services, University of California-Merced, Merced, CA.

Naomi Eichenlaub, Catalogue Librarian, Ryerson University, Toronto, Canada.

Laureen Esser, Electronic Collections Librarian and E-Resources Coordinator for the Humanities, Information, and Technical Services, Harvard University, Cambridge, MA.

Karen S. Fischer, Collections Analysis Librarian, University of Iowa, Iowa City, IA.

Kathleen Carlisle Fountain, Collection Services Program Manager, Orbis Cascade Alliance, Eugene, OR.

Robert S. Freeman, Reference, Languages and Literatures Librarian, Purdue University, West Lafayette, IN.

Rhonda Herman, President, McFarland and Company, Publishers, Jefferson, NC.

Dracine Hodges, Head, Acquisitions Department, The Ohio State University, Columbus, OH.

Kenny Ketner, Software Development Manager, Texas Tech University, Lubbock, TX.

Vincci Kwong, Head of Library Web Services, Indiana University South Bend, South Bend, IN.

Michael Levine-Clark, Associate Dean for Scholarly Communication and Collections Services, University of Denver, Denver, CO.

Ryan Litsey, Document Delivery/Interlibrary Loan Assistant Librarian, Texas Tech, Lubbock, TX.

Stephen Maher, Assistant Director for Content Management and Scholarly Communication, Health Sciences Library, New York University, New York, NY.

Anne McKee, Senior Communications Officer, Greater Western Library Alliance, Prairie Village, KS.

Bob Nardini, Vice President, Library Services, ProQuest Books, La Vergne, TN.

Judith M. Nixon, Education Librarian, Purdue University, West Lafayette, IN.

Xi Niu, Assistant Professor, Department of Software and Information Systems, University of North Carolina at Charlotte, Charlotte, NC.

Rebecca A. Richardson, Electronic Resources Librarian, Purdue University, West Lafayette, IN.

Neil Romanosky, Assistant Director for Operations and Department Administrator, Health Sciences Library, New York University, New York, NY.

Tony Sanfilippo, Director, Ohio State University Press, The Ohio State University, Columbus, OH.

E. Stewart Saunders, Social Science and Humanities Collections Librarian (Emeritus), Purdue University, West Lafayette, IN.

Roger Schonfeld, Program Director for Libraries, Users, and Scholarly Practices, Ithaka S+R, New York, NY.

Matthew Connor Sullivan, Library Assistant, Information and Technical Services, Harvard University, Cambridge, MA.

Joelle Thomas, User Experience and Media Technologies Librarian, University of Connecticut, Storrs, CT.

Susan Thomas, Director of Collection Services, Indiana University South Bend, South Bend, IN.

Lidia Uziel, Head of Western Languages Division and Bibliographer for Western Europe, Harvard University, Cambridge, MA.

Nadine Vassallo, Project Manager of Research and Information, Book Industry Study Group, New York, NY.

Suzanne M. Ward, Head, Collection Management, Purdue University, West Lafayette, IN.

Tao Zhang, Digital User Experience Specialist, Purdue University, West Lafayette, IN.

Index